T0301623

JEWISH SOCIALISTS IN THE UNITED STATES
The Cahan Debate 1925–1926

Jewish Socialists
in the United States
The Cahan Debate 1925–1926

Yaacov N. Goldstein

sussex
ACADEMIC
PRESS

2 4 6 8 10 9 7 5 3 1

First published 1998 in Great Britain by
SUSSEX ACADEMIC PRESS
Box 2950
Brighton BN2 5SP

and in the United States of America by
SUSSEX ACADEMIC PRESS
c/o International Specialized Book Services, Inc.
5804 N.E. Hassalo St.
Portland, Oregon 97213-3644

British Library Cataloguing in Publication Data
A CIP catalogue record for this book is available from the British Library.

Library of Congress Cataloging-in-Publication Data
Jewish socialists in the United States : the Cahan debate, 1925–1926 /
[edited by] Yaacov Goldstein.
p. cm.
Includes, in English translation, the relevant telegrams and articles by Abraham Cahan which appeared in *Forward*, as well as those by other participants in the debate.
Includes bibliographical references and index.
ISBN 1–898723–98–2 (alk. paper)
1. Jews—United States—Politics and government. 2. Jewish socialists—United States.
3. Cahan, Abraham, 1860–1951—Journeys—Palestine. 4. Zionism—United States—History.
I. Goldstein, Jacob. II. Cahan, Abraham, 1860–1951.
E184.J5J585 1998
973´04924´009042—dc21 97–49483
CIP

Printed by Biddles Ltd, Guildford and King's Lynn
This book is printed on acid-free paper

Contents

Preface

Some years ago I began a research project on the development of relations between the Histadrut, namely the General Workers' Federation, as an organizational framework of the labor movement in Palestine (the official name of the territory west of the Jordan during the British Mandate in the years 1920–48), and the workers' movement in North America. I saw then, and still see now, great importance in this subject, for through the Histadrut Zionism captured a very large body of workers of considerable importance and influence who until then were in the best case indifferent to Zionism but generally hostile to it. Our interest is in the overall community of workers, but principally in the Jewish workers. The State of Israel enjoys the fruit of this achievement to this very day.

For the purpose of the study I examined not only Palestinian sources but also those located on the American side, including the Yiddish press published in New York. My main source was *Forward*, the most important newspaper of the Jewish workers' body, which usually adopted anti-Zionist attitudes, and also *Die Zeit*, the journal of Poaley Zion in the United States. Thus I came upon the visit by Abraham (Abe) Cahan, the omnipotent editor of *Forward* and a figure of immense importance in the Jewish and general workers' movement in America, to Palestine in 1925. Following his study tour, as he defined it, Cahan published a series of telegrams and articles in his paper which described, sympathetically, the national endeavor in Palestine in those days, the time of the Fourth Aliya. This led to the development of a wide-ranging debate, initiated by Cahan, which persisted from late 1925 to mid-1926. Its participants were an entire echelon of high-ranking personalities in the Jewish workers' movement in America. Essentially the debate centered on the position of Jewish socialists in America toward Zionism and Palestine, in light of the tragic circumstances of the Jews of eastern Europe and the closure of the gates of America to immigration.

This debate is of major importance for research into the attitude of a community numbering hundreds of thousands to Zionism and Palestine in the years under review. It reflects the traditionally hostile Bundist positions, but also the notable difference between them and the veteran Jewish socialists who immigrated to America in the pre-Bund years. The debate highlights the uncertainties and the ideological crucible through which a segment of the Jewish socialists passed due to the volatile conditions endured by the Jewish people in those years – uncertainties which ultimately caused some modification in their ideological, but chiefly practical position, and their adoption of a more positive approach to Zionism and Palestine. In this sense the debate constitutes a turning point, a shift toward affirmation of the national enterprise in Palestine by Cahan, the journal *Forward* and the group of leaders associated with it, but also by a group of activists among the leaders of the Jewish trade unions.

In the Introduction I describe the background and the general and Jewish range of issues in which the debate is anchored. Next I resolve to place before the English-speaking reader the source itself, namely the main parts of the debate translated from Yiddish. Sadly, the generation able to use sources written in Yiddish is dwindling, so I see great importance in these sources being made accessible to the interested reader through their translation into English. The translation is not entirely literary, but is meant to serve the historical purpose. I allowed myself some freedom in the translation, but took pains to express the writer's intention. Responsibility for any errors is mine alone.

The sources presented in the book are, as stated, mainly translated from Yiddish, but some were written originally in English. All the material was published in *Forward*, including its publications in English. I was also helped in the translations from Yiddish by Cahan's book, which contains his articles and telegrams written in Palestine in 1925 and 1929. The book was published by *Forward* in 1934 in New York (Ab. Cahan, *Palestine: A Bezukh in Yohr 1925 um in 1929*. New York, *Forward* 1934). This book does not contain his lengthy telegrams, which best set forth his views, or his articles in English printed in the supplements to his newspaper. After the Introduction the sources are divided into three parts: Part One contains Cahan's publications, Part Two reproduces articles by the participants in the debate, and Part Three presents Cahan's concluding reply.

Acknowledgments

———

I would like to acknowledge my grateful thanks to the following institutions for their generous support, which has assisted in the publication of this book:

The Faculty of Humanities, University of Haifa; The Sub-Department for the Studies of the Israel Labour Movement, University of Haifa; *and* The Bund Institute, University of Haifa.

The group picture on the back of the jacket was probably taken by Katzisna, a Polish photographer who accompanied Cahan on his trips to Israel. From left to right, bottom row: Berl Katznelson, David Zakai, Abraham Harzfeld, Joseph Ahronovitz, Zalman Shazar, David Ben-Gurion.

Introduction

A Different Reality: New Problems, 1918–1924

The historiography of the Jewish community in the United States generally puts the number of Jews residing in the thirteen colonies at the time
of the American Revolution at about 2,000. In 1825 their number still did
not exceed 6,000; in 1840 it was about 40,000. Yet by 1861 the figure had
leapt to 150,000, among other things due to emigration from the Central
European countries in the wake of the "Nations' Spring." The great
Jewish migration to the United States, mainly from Tsarist Russia, was
sparked by the pogroms unleashed in 1881–2 following the assassination
of Tsar Alexander II. Jews of other countries of eastern Europe, such as
Galicia, Romania, and more, also embarked on their westward flow. This
mighty influx brought about one million Jews to the United States by
1900. Jewish migration to North America rose steeply after 1903 as a
result of fresh pogroms in Russia, the most fearsome being in Kishinev,
the impoverishment of the eastern European Jewish communities, and
comprehensive and entrenched anti-Semitism in all its manifestations.
Consequently, in 1915 the Jewish community in the United States
numbered three million, and by 1925, had enlarged to 4.5 million, or 4
percent of the total population. By that year the Jewish community had
multiplied 300-fold while the population as a whole had multiplied only
tenfold.[1] From the early 1920s the trend reversed toward decline and stag-
nation owing to changes introduced into the immigration laws of the
United States.

Already, toward the end of the nineteenth century, voices were heard
in that country calling for restrictions on immigration from eastern and
southern European countries, consisting mainly of Catholics and Jews.
The rationale given was the need to safeguard the old character of the
United States against a deluge of unwanted religions and nationalities.
Many arguments were directed specifically against the Jews. As a result
of this mood, in 1898 the immigration authorities began to register the

race (Hebrew race) of each immigrant in addition to the country of origin.

After World War I the trend toward limiting immigration intensified, evincing renewed manifestations of anti-Semitism.[2] The amended legislation struck hard at Jewish immigration. In the early 1920s immigration legislation was based on the quota rule, seemingly objective but in fact biased in favor of immigrants belonging to the "Nordic race" and drastically curtailing Jewish entry to the United States. The law enacted in 1921 limited the annual entrants of any nationality to 3 percent of the number of that nationality present in the United States in 1910. The 1924 law, the Quota Act, struck even harder at the Jews, cutting down the annual number of entrants to 2 percent of the number of their nationality present in the country in 1890. The effect on Jewish migration to the United States in the 1920s was catastrophic. While in the prewar period there were years when 100,000–150,000 Jews immigrated, after the legislation the figure plummeted to 11,000 annually. At the end of the 1920s, "the United States ceased to serve as the main country of absorption for Jewish migrants."[3]

American Jewry consisted largely of immigrants from eastern Europe, and from the last third of the nineteenth century this fact shaped its character. It also created the great Jewish workers' movement. The migrants from eastern Europe, Russia in particular, included those with a radical world outlook influenced by the Russian pre-Marxist revolutionary movement. From the start of the twentieth century, especially in the aftermath of the pogroms of 1903 and later, many former Bund[4] activists migrated, still adhering to their universalist Marxist–socialist outlook. It was these former Bundists who left the deepest mark on the form and quality of the Jewish workers' movement. While the older generation of American-Jewish socialists were not acquainted with Zionism, the veterans of the Bund carried with them their party's worldview of the future of the Jews and their burning hatred of Zionism. They succeeded in instilling this hostility into the American-Jewish workers' movement.

It is noteworthy that even after having adopted its formula demanding national and cultural autonomy, the Bund utterly negated the Zionist perception of the oneness of the Jewish people as a world nation with a common fate and a single solution for all its problems. The Bund recognized the existence of Jewish communities across the globe, but claimed that each was subject to a set of different and special problems; therefore, the method of solving the difficulties of the diverse Jewish groups (as well as the solutions themselves), had to suit the particular circumstances and conditions of each individually. Moreover, while Zionism, namely the national movement of the Jewish people, was founded on the continued existence of Jewish national identity, the chief purpose of the Bund was to advance the economic welfare of the Jewish masses and improve the conditions of their life, not to ensure the continued existence of the Jewish people.

The Bund rejected the comprehensiveness in the Zionist ideology and the Zionist solution. In the bitter days of struggle prior to World War I it spurned the Zionist way even as partial relief for the distress of the Jewish people. It regarded the Zionist attitude as deflecting the masses from dealing with the present and struggling for betterment of their life in the Diaspora.

The Bund regarded the idea of rejection of the Diaspora as vain and dangerously utopian, and saw the future of the Jewish masses in the countries of their dispersal. In its view, every community bore responsibility for undertaking its own battle to improve its life conditions on the basis of civic and political equality and of national and cultural autonomy. The cornerstone for this autonomy was deemed to be Yiddish language and culture. The Bund considered Hebrew the dead tongue of the Scriptures, the religious functionaries, and a handful of people within the Jewish bourgeoisie. The Bund likewise dismissed the concept of territorial concentration in Palestine and the establishment there of a Jewish state.

The Zionist issue first came up for discussion at the fourth conference of the Bund (May 1901) and the party formulated an official position on it. The conference clearly resolved that the Bund was opposed to Zionism and prohibited the acceptance of Zionist workers into its economic or political organizations. A complete ban was imposed on Zionism, as emerges from the resolution of the conference:

> The Conference regards Zionism as a reaction on the part of the bourgeois classes to anti-Semitism and to the abnormal legal position of the Jewish people. The Conference regards the final goal of political Zionism, the acquisition of a country for the Jewish people – if only a small part of the Jewish people is to be settled in that country – as a matter devoid of major importance and one that does not put an end to the "Jewish Question." Insofar as Zionism means to settle the entire Jewish people, or a large section of it, in that country, the Conference sees it as a hopeless dream, a utopia. The Conference maintains that the Zionists' propaganda fans nationalist sentiment in the people and it is liable to impede the development of its class consciousness. The Conference deems the cultural activity of a few groups of Zionists to be like any other legal activity. In its debate on Zionism, the Conference resolved that the Zionists are in no way to be allowed a foothold in the economic and political organizations.[5]

As stated, laden with the ideological luggage described above, the people of the Bund migrated, or fled, to the United States, where they continued their relentless war against Zionism in every framework in which they operated. Moreover, the reality that arose there in consequence of the waves of migration – burgeoning Yiddish language and culture, the appearance of dozens of journals in Yiddish with a readership of hundreds of thousands, the publication of Yiddish books, Yiddish theater, a Yiddish educational system on various levels – all these fortified their consciousness of the rightness of their ideological and political course, and their belief in the possibility of continued national Jewish existence in the Diaspora on the basis of national-cultural autonomy, or cultural pluralism.

However, the Jewish situation worldwide, and in the United States in particular, was not static. The Great War of 1914–18, which caused immense suffering to the Jewish communities of eastern Europe, aroused deep feelings of solidarity in American Jews and positive national sentiments. The Balfour Declaration in 1917 and the recognition of Zionism by the nations of the world, including the government of the United States, enhanced Zionism in the eyes of American Jewry, including the Jewish working class, which, as stated, had until then been subject to powerful anti-Zionist Bundist influence.

In the postwar years Bundist orthodoxy in the United States became caught in a highly discomfiting situation regarding its positions on Zionism and Palestine. The Balfour Declaration, as noted, had gained the recognition of most international actors, including the United States. Furthermore, the League of Nations and world socialism also recognized Zionism as the legitimate national movement of the Jewish people. The General Federation of Labor in Palestine (the Histadrut) was a member of the Socialist International, which supported the enterprise in Palestine. The American Socialist Party (SP), which joined the Socialist International in 1923, gave its blessing to the work in Palestine and supported Histadrut fund-raising in the United States.[6] It was therefore strange that the Jewish Socialist Federation (JSF), and later the *Farband*, which were the autonomous Jewish wing of the SP, should oppose the Balfour Declaration and the Zionist enterprise in Palestine.

These new circumstances, as well as other processes affecting the American-Jewish community, including its workers, which cooled universalist-socialist ardor and strengthened Jewish national feeling, led to a kind of re-thinking. Its outcome was a change of heart in a section of the workers' leadership, principally the members of the older, pre-Bund generation, on the question of Palestine and support for the Zionist effort there. Their attitude increasingly showed a distinction, evident in other sectors of American Jewry too, between continued reservations about Zionist ideology and support for the building of the Jewish settlement in Palestine; they approved of the latter, and were willing to harness themselves in its support.

The former Bundists and their supporters, by contrast, steadfastly clung to their radical universalist-socialist world view and to all-out hostility both to the Zionist movement and the Zionist enterprise in Palestine. The difference of positions that came about in the American-Jewish workers' movement found clear expression in the dispute that developed over the serious crisis that befell Polish Jewry in the 1920s, and the traditional solution through absorption of Jewish immigration in the United States was blocked by the imposition of the stringent immigration laws.

The leadership of the Jewish workers' movement was in a dilemma: the Jews of Poland were pressing to emigrate owing to their suffering, and the gates of the United States were sealed before them. The only alternative that appeared was emigration to Palestine. The American-Jewish workers' movement was called on to declare its position and its support for this emigration and for the Zionist enterprise in Palestine. The discord reached its peak with the visit of Abe (Abraham) Cahan, the powerful editor of the widely distributed Yiddish paper *Forward*, to Palestine in 1925.

The Condition of Polish Jewry

The new Poland was created after World War I out of a combination of territories that previously had been under the rule of Russia, Germany and Austria, the states that had carved up the old Poland among themselves in the second half of the eighteenth century. The territories restored from Russia were those of central Poland, and also Ukrainian and Byelorussian lands in the east; the territories restored from Germany were those of Upper Silesia, the Poznan region and Pomerania; Galicia was restored from Austria. The territories on the eastern border were annexed to Poland only after its war against Communist Russia, which ended with the peace agreement signed in Riga in March 1921, which determined Poland's eastern border. In the eastern regions, then annexed to Poland, the Polish population accounted for only a quarter of the total. This fact added to the problem of the national–religious minorities in the new Poland.[7]

The area of the new Poland that took shape after 1921 was 389,000 square kilometers, this being only one-sixth less than the area of Germany. In 1921 Poland's population was 27 million, and in the second census of 1931 the figure was 32 million. Although large in area, in population Poland was a medium-sized country, despite the fact that its soil was fertile and its natural increase the highest in Europe. Poland also enjoyed many natural resources: oil, coal, iron and other metals, salt, countless forests for the timber industry, and so on. Despite this natural wealth Poland was stricken by economic problems and poverty, and clearly belonged to the agrarian economic type. According to the first census in 1921 (which was incomplete as it did not yet include Upper Silesia, the city of Vilna and other nearby districts), 75 percent of Poland's population inhabited villages and only 25 percent dwelt in cities and towns. In the second (complete) census of 1931, the share of urban population rose by a mere 2 percent, making a total of 27 percent. Urbanization in Poland proceeded at a very slow rate.

The principal reason for Poland's backwardness was perhaps the severe agrarian circumstances that prevailed, which were marked by their polarity. On the one hand, there were the great landed estates which were concentrated in the hands of a small stratum of aristocrats and magnates, and on the other there, was ever-increasing parcelling of the small area of land owned by the peasants, which constituted the great majority of the people. This parcelling was the result of the laws and customs of inheritance. Thus arose the characteristic feature of Polish agriculture, namely small farms that could not provide their owners with a living. In addition, 15 percent of the rural population were landless, and a further 14.5 percent were hired farm laborers. On 28 December 1925 the Polish Sejm (parliament) did indeed decide on an agrarian reform intended to meet this problem, but in fact it was hardly implemented. The crying poverty of the village greatly limited the internal market and added to the factors that held up the development of industry. In parallel, the sluggish development of industry delayed urbanization and did nothing to solve the problem of unemployment in the towns. In turn, surplus workforce caused a fall in wages and lack of social stability, and reduced the purchasing power of the city.

The government of Poland wished to change its economic character by rapid and comprehensive industrialization which would bring about accelerated urbanization. In this way, they hoped, the village-to-town

Table 1 Population statistics

Census year	Total population	Jews	% of total population
1921 (excluding Upper Silesia, Vilna and adjacent districts	27,176,717	2,855,318	10.5
1931	31,915,779	31,113–933	9.8

Table 2 Demographic distribution of the overall and Jewish population in Poland in percentages

Region	1921		1931	
	Jews	Total population	Jews	Total population
Central districts	41.5	56.6	42.0	56.8
Southern districts	28.0	25.8	26.5	25.4
Eastern districts	15.5	15.9	17.4	16.6
Western districts	1.1	15.1	1.0	14.0

Table 3 Number out of every 100 Jews living in a town and a village[8]

Year	Town	Village
1921	75.0	25.0
1931	76.4	23.6

ratio would change, as would the socio-economic structure of the Polish population. To realize these goals the state needed large capital investments and initiatives of great vigor and capacity. These hopes and desires did not materialize. Against this background the state constantly intensified its massive intervention in the economy, and a situation of economic statism arose, making itself felt in most branches. The state owned a range of monopolies: industry and trade in alcohol; the tobacco, matches, and salt industries; and more. To varying degrees the state controlled the different transport branches, the timber industry and vast tracts of forest. Economic statism became so widespread that most of the banking even came into the state's hands. In 1938 the state controlled 77 percent of all banking. It concentrated enormous economic power, with the result that it was the governments of Poland that determined the economic conditions and the living of the Polish population, for good or ill.[9]

The Jews of Poland constituted the largest community in Europe and the second largest in the world. On the eve of World War II it numbered 3.5 million, equal to the population of Denmark or that of Lithuania and Estonia combined. The Jews of Poland also formed the biggest Jewish minority and accounted for about 10 percent of the total population and one-third of the urban population of Poland. The great demographic weight and the economic role of the Jews arose from special historical processes and conditions.

It is true that already from the end of the nineteenth century, as a result of the advance of capitalism in the areas mentioned, the economic role of the Jews in Poland began to lessen somewhat. But this process greatly accelerated as a result of the deliberate economic policy of the Polish governments, the purpose of which was to drive the Jews out of various economic areas to the benefit of the Poles. Their aim was Polonization of most of the population. Furthermore,

> the more reaction intensified in all areas, the more the authorities saw the need to portray the Jews as the chief obstacle before the socio-economic progress of the state. Thus occurred the ever-steeper decline in the condition of the Jews in Poland over a period of twenty years, and, at the end of that period, on the eve of World War II, the descent into catastrophe, with no way out.[10]

From the data of the second census in 1931 two facts become clear: first, natural increase of the Jewish population was lower than that of the general population, which stood at nine percent annually. Secondly, the position of the Jews in the urban population was marked by a decline in light of the growth, albeit slow, of the city owing to the movement there of the rural Polish population.[11] These statistics contradict the feeling and the propaganda of the Poles, who claimed that Jewish natural increase generally, and in the city especially, was high in absolute and relative terms. Despite the processes noted, there were still cities with a massive Jewish presence, or a majority, hence their Jewish character.

The overall approach adopted in the economy of the new Poland led from economic liberalism to economic and cooperative statism of a distinct Polish-nationalist hue, namely with a distinct and unequivocal preference for the Polish element. This was the decisive factor forcing Jews out of entire economic branches and reducing their share even in the areas of commerce and small manufacture. The credit policy adopted by the state and the factors dependent on it was also formulated out of national-religious rather than economic considerations. This general policy caused a drastic reduction in the livelihood of the Jews and their tight concentration in medium and small trading and in small manufacture, a fact which exacerbated their vulnerability. The following table highlights this unhealthy state of affairs.

Table 4 Jewish population in the big cities from the two censuses (1921 and 1931) in round numbers[12]

| City | 1921 | | 1931 | |
	Number	% of total population	Number	% of total population
Warsaw	310,300	33.1	352,700	30.1
Lodz	156,200	34.5	202,500	33.5
Lwow	76,800	35.0	99,600	31.9
Krakow	45,200	24.6	56,500	25.8
Vilna	46,600	36.1	55,000	28.2
Bialystok	39,600	51.6	39,100	43.0
Lublin	37,300	39.5	38,900	34.7
Czestochowa	22,600	28.2	25,600	21.9
Radom	24,400	39.7	25,200	32.3
Stanislaw	15,900	56.2	24,800	41.4
Rovno	21,700	71.2	22,700	56.0
Bendin	17,300	62.1	21,600	45.4
Brisk	15,600	52.9	21,500	44.3
Horodno	18,700	53.9	21,200	42.6
Sosnowica	13,600	15.8	20,800	19.1
Pinsk	17,500	74.6	20,200	63.4
Kalisz	15,600	34.9	19,300	35.0
Tarnow	15,600	44.2	19,300	43.0
Kielce	15,500	37.6	18,100	31.0
Luck	14,900	70.2	17,300	34.0
Przemysl	18,400	38.3	17,300	34.0
Poznan	2,100	1.2	2,000	0.8
Katowice			5,700	4.5

In greater detail it is seen that Jews were excluded from commerce in agricultural produce, in which they had been a significant element for centuries, by the network of cooperatives established at the initiative of the government, which concentrated about 80 percent of this trade in its own hands. The Jews were excluded from foreign trade, in which they had predominated for many generations. All ministries and government agencies concerned with the manufacturing, services, commerce, transportation and education branches were closed to Jews by deliberate policy. Not surprisingly, the impoverishment of Polish Jewry grew steadily worse, encompassing ever wider strata. In 1938 there were 300,000 Jews without work and sustenance. With their families the number reached one million, meaning that a third of the Jewish population of Poland required public assistance.[13] As a result of these economic processes most of the Jews were confined to the petit bourgeoisie. Only a small part managed to enter large-scale industry and commerce. Proletarianization was limited by the policy of discrimination pursued by the Polish government, so Jewish workers were not to be found in the service branches or in large- and medium-scale industry. Even Jewish employers occasionally refused to take on Jewish workers owing to the problem of Saturday Sabbath observance.[14]

Table 5 Ratio of Jews in branches of the Polish economy according to 1931 census (in percentages)[15]

Community	Agriculture	Industry	Trade	Transport	Other
Roman Catholic	63	71	37	83	77
Greek Catholic	15	3	1	3	5
Russian Orthodox	18	2	1	1	3
Evangelists	3	3	2	1	3
Jews	1	21	59	12	12

The picture in the free professions was equally grim. In addition to all the areas closed to the Jews, the government allowed them no foothold in such professions as veterinary medicine, agronomy, engineering and architecture. To engage in pharmacy, a license was needed and to obtain one was impossibly difficult. The Jews had little choice, therefore, but to concentrate on law and medicine, which were relatively independent of the government or non-Jewish employers. The Polish authorities devised a systematic means of squeezing the Jews out of the free professions. First, there was constant pressure for special legislation to close various professions to the Jews. As stated, in practice this occurred even without legislation. Second, the Jews were expelled from professional associations. Third, from 1923 an unofficial *numerus clausus* was instituted in respect of the number of Jewish students at higher learning institutions. It began in the faculties of medicine and spread thence to dentistry, pharmacology, veterinary medicine, chemistry, etc. The percentage of Jewish students declined continuously. In 1921–2 they accounted for 24.6 percent of the entire student population; in 1938 the figure was 8.2 percent, namely less than the percentage of Jews in the population as a whole.[16] Raphael Mahler's conclusion seems to me most appropriate to describe the condition of Polish Jewry:

> Even without the explicit policy of national discrimination, the economic policy of the Polish authorities was enough to limit the sphere of Jewish commerce. The monopoly on the production of tobacco, alcoholic drinks and salt resulted in these branches not remaining in Jewish hands except for the retail trade. These were also the results of the increasing activity of the state and municipal authorities in setting up industrial and commercial enterprises of their own, such as export of timber and agricultural produce. Another aspect of this statism was the credit policy of the state

banks, which exercised bias against commerce in other economic branches. Bias against commerce was also the guideline of taxation policy, which imposed taxes on merchants out of all proportion to earnings in this branch as compared with industry and agriculture. In the field of commerce itself preferential treatment was accorded to cooperative trading companies over private commerce.

In addition to the statist tendency in economic policy, already in that period the policy of discrimination against Jewish commerce was evident. The law of absolute compulsory rest on Sundays, which was enacted against the urgent protests of the Jewish delegates in the Polish Sejm in November 1919, struck especially at the commerce of the Jewish minority in the small towns. The peasants were indeed in the habit of doing their shopping on Sundays after church . . . Even worse for Jewish trade was the fact that the duty of implementing the laws was given to a bureaucratic machinery whose clerks were for the most part unfriendly toward the Jews, some of them downright hostile. The system of discrimination in practice by imposing taxes often caused the entire depletion of Jewish merchants ("Grabski's wagon"). The police also hit Jewish shopkeepers with fines for even the slightest infringements of sanitation laws and the like.[17]

The economic anti-Semitism was combined with popular and state-instigated political anti-Semitism. This was so despite the fact that at the Versailles Conference, where the peace treaties constituting the basic document of the new Polish state were signed, an agreement was concluded with Poland on the protection of minorities. According to the agreement, Poland undertook to grant the national, linguistic, racial and religious minorities absolute freedom and civic and political rights. Similarly, the new state promised to allow the minorities to establish, at their own expense, religious, educational and social institutions, and also the right to speak their own language. The Jews were likewise assured that they would not be compelled to perform acts involving desecration of the Sabbath on Saturdays. The League of Nations was charged with overseeing the fulfillment of the agreement. For this reason Poland gave the Jews, according to the Constitution of March 1921, complete equality of civic and political rights. These regulations were also included in the Constitution of April 1935.

But all of it remained on paper. In practice the governments of Poland, as described above, behaved quite differently. The regulations of the constitutions of March 1921 and April 1935, in all matters concerning the Jews, were not implemented. "And in any case the courts and government ministries acted not according to the Constitution but according to the regulations of the Tsarist regime, which were utterly contrary to its principles."[18]

In summer 1922 the constitutive Polish Sejm dispersed; its attitude to the Jews, despite the grant of equality in the March 1921 Constitution, created an inimical foundation and largely determined the future. This Sejm fixed Sunday as the weekly day of compulsory rest. From the viewpoint of the Jews, this meant the loss of another day's earnings, because henceforth they could not trade on two days in the week. The law was directed exclusively against the Jews. This Sejm also rejected a bill intending to cancel restrictions imposed on Jews from the Tsarist period.

The elections to the second Sejm, actually the first to be held, took place in fall 1922. This Sejm was active for five years. The Jews were highly successful, returning 35 delegates to the Sejm and twelve to the Senate. Despite the strength of the Jewish representatives, they were unable to alter the basic hostile and discriminatory policy directed against their constituency. Moreover, a bill to impose a *numerus clausus* on Jews in higher educational institutions was rejected only through the personal intervention of Poincaré, the President of France.[19]

In mid-December 1923, the right-wing coalition government headed by Witos reached the end of its course. This government had been in conflict with the minorities in the Sejm and also caused a rift with Marshall Pilsudski, who resigned in protest from all his state posts, returning to them only after the "May Revolution" of 1926. Wladyslaw Grabski[20] served as Minister of Finance in Witos' government but because of his colleagues in the administration, who frustrated his efforts to increase taxation of the well-to-do classes, he resigned before the fall of the government. After the failure of efforts to establish a government resting on a parliamentary majority, in 1924 a government was formed that lacked such a majority, and the President appointed Wladyslaw Grabski as Premier. Grabski held office in 1924 and 1925, and he saw his chief task as the stabilization of Poland's shaky economy.

By maneuvering among the parliamentary factions, Grabski succeeded in obtaining far-reaching powers on a range of fiscal laws, the chief of which was the establishment of a state bank and the issuing of the new currency of the zloty. Grabski held down the cost of living and inflation, thereby gaining relative social stability. The taxpaying public expanded, but most taxation fell on spheres of commerce, thus striking particularly hard at the Jewish population.[21] The new tax laws became a lethal weapon for stripping the Jews of their remaining economic positions, among other ways by imaginary assessments of their taxable income. One story concerns a Jewish woman who owned a lemonade stand on a street in the city of Radom whose income was so assessed that to earn it she would have had to sell lemonade 24 hours a day for a hundred years. The taxes imposed on the Jews were far higher than those on the Poles. This was deliberate policy, and its disastrous effects were not unknown to Grabski; moreover, Jewish elements made strenuous efforts to present the facts of the destruction of the economic existence of the Jewish masses, but to no avail. In winter 1925–6, 83 percent of all Jewish workers in Warsaw and 59 percent in the country as a whole were out of work. The crisis struck the textile industry particularly hard. "In one way or another, the status of wide strata of the well-off in the Jewish population had collapsed. Fearing bankruptcy and lacking any other course, the Jews gathered together what remained of their property and left the country."[22]

One outcome of this catastrophic state of affairs was the onset of migration, which owing to the barred gates of the United States turned to Palestine. This was the "Polish Aliya," the "Grabski Aliya," or the Fourth Aliya (*aliyah* is Hebrew for immigration to the Land of Israel) in the historical list of migrations to Palestine; it acted as a pivotal factor in the intensification of the debate in the American-Jewish workers' movement on its positions regarding Zionism and Palestine.

Background to Abraham Cahan's Journey to Palestine

The policy that led to the drastic limitation of certain classes of migrants entering the United States has been mentioned. The general American workers' movement supported the policy of the Administration and of Congress unreservedly owing to the economic recession that began in the United States in the 1920s. This, among other things, caused a massive desertion of members from the American trade unions, which were unable to sustain their membership.[23] At the 42nd conference of the AFL, the unions' roof organization, held in Cincinnati in 1922, it was resolved to support the policy of closing the gates despite the opposition of the Jewish unions.[24] In subsequent years too the AFL persisted in this stance, under the leadership of Gompers and his successor, Green. In 1924, even with the serious crisis of Polish Jewry and its pressing need to emigrate, Gompers called on the biggest Jewish trade union, the ILGWU, an important organization in the AFL and one which dared to voice disapproval of official policy, to submit to the majority resolutions on the Administration's immigration policy.[25] The AFL did not move from this position even later, and reaffirmed its resolutions at the Detroit conference in 1926, when once again it rejected the reservations of the Jewish trade unions by a large majority.[26]

The American-Jewish workers' movement in its entirety[27] was placed in a very difficult situation. From the standpoint of all-American interests, including those of the American workers' movement, it would seem that support had to be given to the policy of closing the gates, which sounded the death-knell for Jewish immigration; but from the standpoint of the Jewish interest it was necessary to fight this policy. The position of the American-Jewish workers' movement was clearly one that might, and indeed did, generate the accusation of disloyalty on the part of the Jewish workers to the general American interest in favor of the particular Jewish interest. From this to the charge of dual allegiance – and even betrayal of the Jews' new homeland – was but a short step.

In these circumstances great courage was required to oppose the policy of the Administration in general and of the AFL in particular. The Jewish unions in the AFL framework attempted to remain aloof to the latter's position on the question. The UHT, the roof organization of the Jewish unions, and the *Farband*, the autonomous Jewish faction in the all-American Socialist Party, attempted to protest against the immigration policy, which so severely harmed the Jews. But the impression is of a weak, wavering tone and bloodless action, either due to lack of inner conviction as to the justice of their cause or to lack of civic courage, or both.[28] Against this background it is easier to understand the genuine concern, combined with remorse and guilt feelings, over the crisis of Polish Jewry which was left with only one escape route – to Palestine.

News of the serious crisis that had erupted in Poland began to reach the United States in 1924. In *Forward* of 18 June 1924 an item appeared on "*Der shreklishe krizis in Lodz*" (the terrible crisis in Lodz), which had caused extremely widespread unemployment among the Jewish workers in the city, many of whom were going hungry. In summer 1924, Baruch Charney-Vladek, a leader of the American-Jewish workers' movement and a director of *Forward*, and Vasafski, the director of HIAS, left for a tour of eastern Europe, Poland in particular. On their return they both presented a harrowing report on what they had witnessed, and also on the necessity for migration by the Jews. They also told of 6,000 Jews who were roaming around various parts of Europe with the aim of reaching the United States, but they had no chance of entering the country. The Forward correspondent in Warsaw supplied his readers with information on what was taking place in Poland, and wrote that as a result of the crisis, "*di wichtigste passierung in Polin iz yetz der gelaf von Yiden nach Palestine*" (the most important event at the moment in Poland is the Jewish surge to Palestine). Although the writer did not believe in the ability of Palestine to satisfy the needs of the Jewish migration, he admitted that the monthly absorption in Palestine of about 2,000 immigrants greatly relieved the Jews' distress.[29]

Another correspondent wrote that Grabski's fiscal and economic policy which was ruining the Jews had by then been in operation for about two years. The closure of the gates of America made the Jews try their luck in other countries of the world, but what they heard from those places about absorption was not good. This was the cause of large-scale emigration to Palestine. True, in Palestine too, absorption was difficult, but the widespread feeling was that if one had to suffer then let it be among Jews. The immigrants to Palestine were not idealistic Zionists but people who had chosen that country for lack of alternative, to find a new basis for existence there. In his accounts the journalist mentioned the term "*Grabskis zionisten*," a close enough rendering of the term that became current at the time, "the Grabski Aliya." The correspondent was also filled with wonder at the immigration and agricultural settlement of a group of Hassidim, led by their rabbis, in the Haifa region.[30]

Reports on the harsh conditions of the Jews of Poland arrived with increasing frequency. Much detailed information was also obtained as a result of visits by leading American Jews there. Such visitors included Judge Jacob (Yaacov) Panken, a leader of the socialist movement and of the *Farband*, whose impressions were published extensively in the pages of *Forward*. Panken reported to his readers that almost a million Jews in Poland lived in absolute penury and were on the verge of destitution. The Bundist orthodoxy, which found itself in extreme discomfort because of the information flowing in from eastern Europe generally and Poland especially, which upset its ideology on the future of the Jews in the Diaspora, censured the gloomy accounts of their comrade Panken, finding them "*abissel tzu pessimistish*" (rather too pessimistic). For the Bundist orthodoxy, the situation in Poland was indeed difficult, but they were convinced that the dark colors being presented were exaggerated.[31]

David Bergelson, who covered the Zionist Congress in Vienna in 1925, was forced to admit that if until then Zionism had been like a dream, now it was experiencing a miracle because in eastern Europe there were two million Jews ready with their bags packed. "They are being forced to emigrate in circumstances in which the gates of America and other countries are closed to them. Only the gates of Palestine are open." For that reason about four or five thousand Jews were arriving in that country each month. Bergelson too stressed that a non-Zionist, even anti-Zionist population was streaming into Palestine, having no other alternative.[32]

There is no doubt that from 1924, and especially 1925, the Jewish workers' movement aligned itself with the general American-Jewish community, aware, concerned, and helpless before the ruination of eastern Europe Jewry. The Jews of Poland, crushed under the press of Grabski's taxation policy, and their desperate need to leave, formed a special case.[33] This is the setting in which Abe Cahan's journey to Palestine should be seen.

Abe (Abraham) Cahan (Cohen) was born on 6 July 1860 in the township of Podvizhia in White Russia, the only son of a Hebrew teacher. He acquired a Jewish education, including a year at a yeshiva at the age of 13–14, and he also knew Hebrew to the level of reading the books of Yehuda Leib Gordon and Avraham Mapu. He also learned and knew Russian.[34] In 1878 he entered the Jewish Teachers College at Vilna, where he studied for four years.[35] As a student during his Vilna years he was influenced by socialist circles, in which he became involved. In 1881, he graduated, and began to teach in the Vitebsk region. That year he apparently met Yisrael Belkind in Mogilev, and in conversations between the two he informed Belkind that he was not enamored with the idea of Palestine because he was a socialist. In these discussions with Belkind the idea took shape within him to emigrate to the United States.[36] It seems that the police had his name owing to his activity in socialist circles in Vilna, and this factor ultimately obliged him to flee Russia, with the aim of reaching America.[37] In his flight he reached Berdichev, and there he made the acquaintance of a group of people of Am Olam, whom he joined; with them he crossed the frontier into Austria, reaching the town of Brody in the spring of 1882. He moved on with this group, and with them sailed for Philadelphia, where he arrived on 6 June 1882. In the United States he parted company from the Am Olam group over his reservations about the idea of farming and cooperative villages as a way also supposedly leading to the realization of socialism. Cahan preferred the city to the country. From Philadelphia he moved to New York, which he regarded as his home for the rest of his life.[38] The new immigrant established himself and became bound up in the life of his new country and city. Beyond public life he desired to make his name as a writer. But in that sphere he left no mark, although he published a series of literary works, the best known being *The Rise of David Levinsky*, which appeared in 1917.

Cahan's contribution derived chiefly from what he was: a public figure, an American socialist leader, one of the heads of the American-Jewish workers' movement, and the powerful editor of *Forward*. He had been a founder of the paper in 1897 and its first editor. Subsequently, after a break of several years, he became its editor-in-chief and the almost exclusive ruler of the paper and of its Corporation without interruption from 1907 until the day he died in 1951 at the age of 91.[39] It should be recalled that *Forward* was not only a successful newspaper with a readership numbering hundreds of thousands, but also, under Cahan's direction, a successful economic corporation that controlled a range of areas which underlay its economic power. Owing to its manifold economic activities and achievements the *Forward* Corporation provided a living of thousands, as well as being a highly important supporter and financial backer of the all-American socialist movement and the American-Jewish workers' movement.[40] From this Abe Cahan derived his high stature and power in the Jewish community and in the American-Jewish workers' movement.

Cahan's strength did not lie in the domain of abstract ideology. He spurned doctrinaire approaches and affirmed a pragmatist-realist grasp of life. Intuitively he felt and understood the leanings and desires of the Jewish masses, whose attitudes and tastes his paper in no small way determined. His socialist views were fairly loose, and generally he may be deemed to belong to the social-democrat current. Cahan belonged to the first generation of pre-Marxist Jewish socialist immigrants, who were not in fact partners to the formation of the Bund and were not among its members, with all that this implies. He was a sworn enemy of communism and of Soviet Russia.[41]

Prior to Cahan's visit to Palestine, *Forward* was hostile to Zionism, or in the best case indifferent. The newspaper did indeed cover, here and there, issues of Zionism and Palestine, but its focus and chief interest were economic and Jewish life in America, and in second place the life of the Jews in Europe. Cahan's great ambition was to turn his paper into an all-American organ, not just American-Jewish.

As noted, his journey to Palestine was the outcome of three main factors: (1) the serious and ongoing crisis of Polish Jewry, principally from 1924; (2) the closure of the gates of the United States to Jews and their consequent migration to Palestine; (3) as a realist unimpeded by doctrine, and with a feel for the undercurrents and moods coursing through the Jewish masses, including the workers, he sensed and understood the shift that was taking place from universalist socialist radicalism of the Bundist type toward national Jewish solidarity.

One of his biographers, Melech Epstein, gives the actual reason for his visit:

> sensing the growing nationalist mood among his readers here, Cahan was ready to open the columns of his paper to a favorable voice on Palestine and to publish Liessin's nationalist poems.[42]

Abraham Cahan's Journey and the Formulation of His Positions on Zionism and Palestine

On 1 July 1925 an announcement appeared in *Forward* that Cahan was about to depart on a trip to Europe and Palestine. Two days later the 65-year-old Cahan and his wife left for Europe.[43] There Cahan was to participate as the SP delegate at the Congress of the Socialist International to be held in August in Marseilles.[44]

Cahan reached Palestine on 26 September 1925, and apparently left on 21 October – a visit of less than a month. In this time he intensively toured the entire country, and met people of various circles including the British administration and Arabs. In all he was abroad for about five months. He returned to New York on 1 December.[45] During his stay in Palestine he was accompanied, apart from his wife, by his secretary and a photographer who captured his travels for posterity.

Cahan's visit to Palestine took place as the peak of the Fourth Aliya was passing and before the great drop in immigration to Palestine which set the Yishuv on a headlong spiral downward into economic crisis, and into the great social and ideological crisis of 1926–9 that ensued.

In 1925 the population of Palestine (excluding nomads) was 757,000, including 122,000 Jews, namely 16 percent of the whole population. In 1924, the first year of the "Polish Aliya," 12,856 people immigrated to the country and 2,037 emigrated; the population in that year increased by 10,819. In 1925, the peak of this migration, 33,801 people immigrated and 2,151 emigrated – an addition to the Yishuv of 31,650 people.

In terms of numbers, the "Grabski Aliya" may be divided into two completely opposite sub-periods. The first was characterized by mass immigration, lasting from June 1924 to June 1926. In these two years about 55,000 people entered Palestine while only 5,000 left. The monthly average number of immigrants in this period was about 2,000. The peak of the wave was in June 1925, when 3,700 people arrived. This was the first mass immigration and therefore its effect was enormous. Dan Giladi, author of a comprehensive monograph on the Fourth Aliya, writes that

> in that year there were many who envisaged the Jewish people flowing in an unending stream into Palestine. This sense grew stronger following the shock caused to Jews throughout the world by the closure of the gates of the United States to mass immigration . . . The composition of the Aliya also, which included many ordinary people, created the feeling that at least the Jewish people, just as it was, was coming to Palestine. Moreover, the rate of construction and development in the country in the aftermath of this mass immigration was unprecedented and inspired the feeling that the Zionist vision was materializing and turning into a living reality.[46]

The second sub-period was marked by a decline and fall, which lasted from mid-1926 to the end of this migration wave in 1929. In those years there was a drastic decrease in the rate of immigrants, to less than 4,000 a year. From July 1926 to the end of 1928 the balance of migration in Palestine was negative: 8,000 arrived and 12,000 left. Recovery began only in 1929.

In contrast to the commonly accepted idea, over 50 percent of the "Polish Aliya" were in the category of "workers," not in that of "capitalists" (according to the Mandatory government's classification). The latter and their families accounted for only 25 percent of all the immigrants, while the remainder were classified as family members of veteran residents and others. In absolute numbers, more organized workers and pioneers arrived than in the Third Aliya, yet the latter has been awarded the distinction of a pioneering and constructive immigration, while the Fourth Aliya bears the stigma of being "bourgeois" and parasitic. This image should apparently be put down to the first wave of this migration in 1924–6: of this wave 40 percent were indeed in the "capitalist" category, while from 1926 onward their share in the total fell to only 12 percent. In absolute terms, compared with the past in a brief time span many "capitalists" entered Palestine, and, significantly, they possessed "capitalist" consciousness and ideologies.[47]

Not all the immigrants in this period came from Poland, those who did accounted for only about 50 percent. The remainder were from other eastern European countries and elsewhere in the world: 20 percent immigrated from the Soviet Union, 5 percent each from Romania and Lithuania, about 12 percent from Asia (chiefly Yemen) and Iraq, and 2.8 percent from America.

The Fourth Aliya lifted the Yishuv out of the economic and socio-ideological crisis that had gripped it in 1922–3. This fact, together with the upsurge in immigration in 1924–6, brought about spiritual uplift and great optimism over the future building of the land and the possibility of realizing the Zionist vision. For the first time Palestine gave support to Zionist ideology, being the chief factor taking in the ruined and disintegrating Jewish masses. Abe Cahan's visit to the country occurred at the high point of this national euphoria.[48]

The Palestinian press, not only that of the workers, generally welcomed Cahan's visit, at the same time highlighting disagreement with his views. Cahan was at pains to ensure a fitting reception, and accomplished this by declarations and interviews published before his arrival in Palestine.[49] Moreover, it seems that Max Pine, who until 1925 was the chairman of the UHT and also the leading personality and chairman of the Histadrut fund-raising campaign (or as it was known in Yiddish, the *geverkshaften kampayn*) was involved in the preparations for Cahan's visit:

> To overcome the strong Socialist opposition to his campaign he planned to win the sympathy of Abraham Cahan, the leading Jewish Socialist. He made arrangements for Cahan to visit Palestine and see with his own eyes the miracle that was being performed by the Histadrut.

Pine himself said the following to several of his colleagues at some point:

> I wrote to the Jewish leaders there [in Palestine] to give him a hearty welcome, as if he were a friend, and to show him the great achievements of the chalutzim, and the important work of the Jewish idealists in Palestine.[50]

Cahan's visit appears to have been prepared not only by Cahan himself but also by people associated with the Histadrut who had an interest in affecting, through his visit, a change in the attitude to the Palestine enterprise and to the labor movement there. Such a change, they hoped – and their hope was vindicated – would ease their work for the Histadrut in the United States.

As early as 13 September 1925, *Davar* cited *Forward* on Cahan's planned visit to Europe and Palestine. In Palestine he was due to be joined by the famous European photographer Alter Kachizna who would shoot typical pictures of life in the country for *Forward*'s art supplement. In the *Davar* issue of the following day, Z. David (David Zakai) wrote in the "Brief Notices" section about Cahan's forthcoming visit with trepidation and with hope. The trepidation was because "the lion [was coming] out of his lair, the king of *Forward* himself," and therefore "the heart does not fear but throbs excessively." Zakai ascribed great importance to the visit because of the visitor's enormous influence on public opinion in the United States. "At his whim he will present her [Palestine-Y.G.] live to *Forward*, and at his whim he will turn his hand down and drown her in the ocean . . . When he praises, millions will praise after him; and when he scorns those millions will scorn still more than they have until now." Further on Zakai urged that the visitor be given a warm reception, writing in his high-flown language: "but this time, take note of my request to you [again, personification of Palestine – Y.G.]: Be wise and welcome him, be joyful and radiant, for 'the time of love' has come, for you will be spoken of in fine words, for Uncle has come from across the sea." (The original Hebrew plays on the word for love, *dodim*, and the word for Uncle, *dod*.)

An item appeared in *Davar* of 21 September stating that Cahan's secretary, M. Vinograd, himself a young writer in New York who knew Hebrew, had arrived in Palestine directly from America and was awaiting the arrival of his superior. The same issue published a long interview with Cahan by Mark Yarblum, a leader of the World Federation of Poaley Zion, held in Marseilles when both were present at the congress of the Socialist International. In the interview Cahan analyzed the processes at work on the American-Jewish workers' movement, which organized about 300,000 people. The interviewee indicated the process that in the future would cause the movement to endure a single generation only. He likewise pointed to the abandonment of Yiddish culture and the shift to English language and culture as inevitable and irreversible. Regarding his forthcoming visit to Palestine he stated that "I treat Zionism in an entirely non-partisan way. I do not believe in it, but there is no hatred for it in my heart." Later he added, "I believe [this should evidently be 'I do not believe' – Y.G.] in Zionism, but I can appreciate the idealism of many Zionists, who interest me individually. But Zionism is one thing and migration to Palestine is something else; the migration is an undeniable fact."

The day following Cahan's arrival he was warmly welcomed in a column in *Davar*. The article hoped that the visitor would report to his readers on the Jewish settlement honestly and genuinely, even though "we are not unaware that we are divided by profound conflict of opinion: on the future of the Jewish people, on the role of the Jewish worker in the nation, on the purpose of Palestine in the life of our people. Nor have we any wish to blur these disagreements."[51] The writer asked that Cahan be shown respect as a man with many achievements in the American-Jewish workers' movement. There was discord, but the connecting element had to be kept in view. The writer went on to bestow warm words on the visitor: "We see him as our brother, our comrade, a bone of our bones, flesh of our flesh." Thereafter *Davar* covered Cahan's tours, activities and statements, including his articles in *Forward* and the responses to them.

On 24 September, a discussion took place in the Histadrut Executive in which David Remez reported his meeting with Cahan. Remez had the impression that "we can influence him." He suggested that Cahan be assisted in setting up his base in Tel Aviv and that an escort be attached to him. Similarly, "it would be desirable to hold a discussion with him in a limited forum, to introduce him to our comrades in the settlements, and then to hold a meeting." The subject of the visit was also raised at another meeting of the Executive on 12 October.[52]

Ha'aretz published a detailed article on Cahan's arrival on 21 September. The newspaper stated that "until today he has conducted an endless war against Zionism and its supporters." There followed an extensive survey of Cahan's statements and life history, ending on an upbeat note regarding the likelihood that the visit would bring about a change in the visitor's hostile attitudes.[53] On 13 October, the paper reported Cahan's trip to the settlements of the northern valleys, accompanied by A. Hartzfeld and D. Hacohen. The writer formed the impression from the visitor's speech to the members of Ein Harod that "clearly he wished to make amends for his negative position until then on the workers' movement in the land and that he was beginning to adopt a positive view of all the enterprises of the workers' movement in Palestine that he had seen during his visit."[54]

Do'ar Hayom of 9 September also welcomed the visitor from America with warmth and hopefulness.[55] In its 12 October issue the paper quoted the visitor's speech at a reception for him given by the Histadrut; his words justified the paper's optimism.[56]

The most reserved attitude to Cahan was evinced by the newspaper *Hapo'el Hatza'ir*, which moreover did not trouble to cover the visit. Only on the day of Cahan's departure from Palestine did Yitzhak Lufban mention it, claiming that it was important to open Cahan's eyes to the Palestinian reality, but this had to be without flattery and servility, especially as the visitor continued to criticize Zionism and the Palestine endeavor. Lufban totally rejected a statement that he attributed to Cahan: "It is true that in your Palestine there are many nice things that have made a strong impression on me, but still, this Zionism . . . is no big deal; if you said 'Palestine' just like that, you might be able to get a few dollars out of us, but if you say 'Keren Hayesod,' that's official Zionism already." Lufban was unwilling to allow such words to pass without comment, and he also harshly chastised the visitor's ignorance of anything concerning Palestine, and above all the impression made by the visitor that he was proud of it.[57]

During this and after his visit, Cahan's telegrams and articles (about 23 in number) in Yiddish and English were published in *Forward*. These sparked a lively debate conducted in the pages of the newspaper. From the articles and the debate, as well as from Cahan's statements and speeches, it is possible to learn his views on Zionism and Palestine as they took shape and were set forth in light of his study tour of the country.

The decision that the powerful editor of *Forward* and the renowned socialist leader should depart for a study tour of Palestine was the subject of a political controversy among members of the paper's editorial board. The opponents regarded the planned visit not as a personal act by the journalist, Abe Cahan, but recognition, in practice, of a change regarding the status of Palestine, perhaps even of Zionism, on the part of the Jewish socialist movement in the United States. Three positions developed in the editorial board by virtue of the debate: three members adopted an orthodox Bundist view, and entirely opposed the journey. "They feared that my journey would be interpreted as acquiescence to the Zionists." Against them Cahan argued that "if you are genuine socialists, why are you afraid Zionism?" Three others favored the trip, two of them wholly and one half-heartedly. The two "talked like full-fledged Zionists. One of them – Iskolsky – admitted that for forty years he had been a Zionist at heart." The pragmatists, "among them myself, spoke as thoroughly practical men, and expressed the view that it was ridiculous to object to the journey" because of anxiety about how it would be understood.[58] The dissenters seem to have been correct in seeing Cahan's journey as a public act, with all that this signified, and not the private affair of some journalist, as Cahan liked to present it.[59]

The rationale behind the journey has already been noted. Evidence for it is found in Cahan's speeches in Palestine and in the many publications he issued in consequence of it. In Palestine, the visitor claimed that "the interest of the Jewish masses in America has increased by a hundred percent in the last year, on account of the great immigration that reached Palestine from Poland. That is why I decided to come here." Elsewhere he stated that "because the gates of America have been closed to the immigrants, and because the Jews from Poland are forced to leave, they have nowhere to escape to."[60] In the same spirit he wrote to his paper from Paris and stressed the great popularity that Palestine was currently enjoying everywhere: "Where formerly its appeal was to Zionists alone it is now almost universal." Cahan reported to his readers on the gathering waves of anti-Semitism in Europe, which strengthened national feelings, and on the wide-ranging sympathy, interest and great hopes of the Jewish masses in Europe regarding Palestine. When one heard of one corner of the world where Jews could make their home, "one's heart warms to the prospect." What had taken place in Palestine itself in recent years created the impression that "nothing succeeds like success, and Palestine was beginning to look like a successful realization of nationalistic dreams." Furthermore, echoes of the idealism of the pioneers and the positive attitude of the Zionist movement to the working settlement greatly strengthened the status of the Zionist movement not only among the Jewish masses but also among the non-Jewish "left" socialists, and these evinced great sympathy for Palestine.[61]

On his arrival in Palestine Cahan declared on various occasions that he had no preconceptions, and his visit would proceed with maximal objectivity with the aim of reporting only the truth to the Jewish and working community in the United States. Furthermore, Cahan stated that in the past he had not been among the haters of Zionism and had never fought against it. He explained to his hosts that he had migrated to America before the Bund was founded, so he had played no part in its battles against Zionism, and the hatred by Bund members for Zionism was strange to him, and was certainly not relevant to the American reality.[62] These statements, which also had political purposes, namely to break down barriers and to find a common language with his hosts in Palestine, contained some truth, although one cannot ignore that fact that prior to his journey Cahan had been in no small way under universalist Bundist-socialist influences, and *Forward* had displayed an attitude varying from indifference to hostility toward Zionism. Before his listeners Cahan confessed to his own ignorance, and to that of the public in the United States, about Palestine in general and the Palestine labor movement in particular. It was quite obvious that events and personalities that had by then become sterling assets in the heritage of Jewish settlement and the labor movement in Palestine, such as the events of Tel Hai and the Trumpeldor saga, the work and death of Brenner, and the like, were completely unknown to him.[63]

The study tour was marked by Cahan's emotion and amazement at almost everything he witnessed. The visitor did not lose his keen powers of observation nor was he dazzled, but even so his great sense of moral elevation, the enthusiasm that gripped him and the deep appreciation he evinced for everything he saw in the country were evident. Jewish Tel

Aviv, Jerusalem the eternal city, the Western Wall, a relic of the Temple
– all these spoke to his heart and his inner being. It was as if a dam within
him had burst, and all the Jewish content stored deep in his heart gushed
out. Above all, he was captivated by the Palestine workers' movement and
the agricultural settlement with its moshavim and kibbutzim, which he
considered the crown of the unique creation taking place in the country
and a positive symbol of idealism and sacrifice for the sake of social and
national ideals. He ceaselessly reiterated this admiration in his speeches
and articles. The title of one is characteristic: "Abe Cahan Is Filled with
Spiritual Joy at the Pioneers Building Palestine. The 'pioneers' – students
with university diplomas – haul bricks and hew rocks. They are workers
imbued with the socialist spirit and they speak of the new Palestine as the
cradle of freedom, brotherhood and the ideals of happiness." In the article
he notes that he found that the work of construction of the land was done,
especially by the youth, with contagious enthusiasm and idealism. Most
of the agricultural workers he met burned with the fire of self-sacrifice,
excitement and idealism. The people he encountered were of the finest
quality and they were convinced that the national home they were
building would stand on socialist foundations. This youth belonged to the
Palestine labor movement, and this "occupies a most important place in
the present reality." Cahan repeated these words of praise in passages of
his articles in English:

> There are lots of beautiful things in Palestine . . . There are many things
> that arouse one's sympathy and admiration . . . but I don't want the reader
> to imagine for a moment that the local socialist or communist farmer, or
> anarchist farmer (you find some of the latter too), do not pour out their full
> hearts upon their idealism. You see here among them masses of people of
> wonderful character and wonderful enthusiasm. They sacrifice a lot and
> they are prepared to sacrifice more and more for their ideals. These are not
> merely words.

Cahan explained for his readers the ideology and special structure of
the Palestinian labor movement and the Histadrut, and the complete
difference between these and their counterparts in the United States. He
pointedly stressed that there could be no doubt about the "purity, the
devotion of motives and behavior. The movement was built on a foundation of the most lofty ideals. The leaders too possessed the highest moral
motives." The labor movement was constructed in a centralist manner
and it constituted a "tremendous power" in Palestine, its strength
increasing from month to month. The labor movement embraced the

national and the socialist ideology together, but the national element predominated. Cahan noted this distinction on several occasions: "Palestinian socialism actually is a part of this sacred mission. But this is a part of secondary significance." In the English version he wrote the following about the supremacy of the national aspect among the Histadrut leaders:

> Of these two aims [the socialist and the national -Y.G.] the latter is thus far the most important . . . Zionism is their first objective, and socialism the second. They should like to achieve both ideals, at once.[64]

It has already been mentioned that his heart went out to the members of the moshavim and kibbutzim ("*mayn hertz geyt mir ois tzu dize menshen . . .*"), whom he met and whose settlements he toured. At Ein Harod a reception was held for him, at which he said: "I'll tell you the truth. This evening is one of the happiest evenings I have spent in all my 65 years. For this alone my journey would have been worthwhile. You are bringing true the best of my dreams and the dreams of my friends of forty years ago. I feel that I am surrounded by saints and pure people. I respect you. I embrace and kiss each one of you, with all my heart I am with you."[65] In his response to well-wishers at a mass meeting held in mid-December 1925 at the Opera House in Manhattan to mark his return, Cahan one again turned to the subject of the kibbutzim: "To be at the commune, observing their hardships; to see their great self-sacrifice like the purest ideologists; to see their lives and not to be uplifted by it – for this a man would have the mind of a *misnogid* pedant."[66]

Analysis of Cahan's Articles, Lectures and Speeches

From analysis of Cahan's articles, lectures and speeches the positions that he formulated as a result of his long tour of Europe and Palestine emerge as follows.

A. Non-communist nature of the Palestine labor movement
There was no connection between the Palestine labor movement and the working settlement on the land on the one hand, and communism on the other, regardless of the communal life in the kibbutzim.[67] This fact was very important considering Cahan's fierce hatred of communism and Soviet Russia. Moreover, the great significance of this issue becomes clear

in the setting of the hard and ongoing struggle in the 1920s in the Jewish unions between the proponents and opponents of communism. *Forward* and its editor put their entire weight and resources behind the opponents of communism. The depth and fierceness of the struggle, especially in the trade unions, may be gathered from the fact that it lasted many years and almost broke up several of the unions. In addition, Cahan's visit to Palestine took place only a few years after the split in the Jewish Socialist Federation, the autonomous independent Jewish framework within the SP, when the anti-communist minority was forced to leave the Federation; they founded the anti-communist social-democratic Jewish Socialist *Farband*. Among the pro-communists were several members of *Forward*'s editorial board, such as Zivion (Dr Ben-Zion Hoffman), who just a few years later reversed their course. It is clear from this how vital, turbulent and painful the communist issue was. For this reason the unequivocal statement by Cahan that the Palestinian labor movement was not communist, but even anti-communist, was of utmost importance.

B.   Palestine probably not a major center
Cahan harbored many doubts as to the chances of Palestine becoming a major center that would relieve, at least partially, the sufferings of the Jewish people.[68] For all his ardor about the settlement of the land, he was convinced that the future of Palestine should not be built on agriculture if the country was to absorb the masses. The only future possibility for taking in large numbers of Jews was by intense urbanization based on the development of centers of commerce and industry. If this indeed occurred, which he greatly doubted, the centers of commerce should not be geared to serve the market at home but those in the countries of the Middle East and even further away. Only such an economy would permit the absorption of the masses, and in that way Palestine might play its part in alleviating the distress of the Jewish people. Cahan was firm in his opinion that the future of Palestine lay, if anywhere, in the commercial, industrial city and not in agriculture.

From the viewpoint of the Zionist vision too, which desired the creation of a Jewish majority in Palestine, Cahan believed that urbanization based on commerce and industry was vital, because only by such a process could this goal be attained. The natural increase of the Jews could not measure up to the Arab majority and Arab natural increase; therefore, only massive immigration that could be absorbed by the industrial and commercial city could achieve the aim of a Jewish majority:

For the immigration to be absorbed, infrastructures have to be established that are free of the effects of recession, for example, a short-term boom of commerce in real estate . . . . For Palestine to become a Jewish homeland of significance, it is impossible to achieve the goals of Zionism except on the basis of large-scale industrialization in the country in fields of commerce and industry, suited to the opportunities existing there.[69]

Furthermore, the conversion of Palestine into a commercial-industrial center, which would serve the backward countries of the Middle East, might foster good relations with the Arabs of the region.

Despite his doubts as to the likelihood of his ideas being realized, Cahan did not discard them, but maintained the hope that with Jewish genius, ingenuity and vigor it might indeed be possible to build the Land of Israel along the economic lines – vital in his view – which he had drawn. Without such development he looked on the future pessimistically:

Without industry there will not be a large Jewish population. There will be no possibility for large immigration to Palestine in order to turn it into the homeland of the Jews. As the Zionists understand it, it is necessary to achieve a Jewish majority over the Arabs.[70]

On innumerable occasions Cahan repeated his assumption (or determination) that the future of Jewish Palestine did not lie in agriculture. This was a small country, and even if the Jews turned the land bought from the Arabs into a flowering garden, it would still be impossible to absorb a large Jewish population on the basis of agriculture. And again, if there was any chance of absorbing a million and a half Jews in Palestine, it could be accomplished solely

through the rapid growth of the Jewish cities . . . The loyal and tireless work of enthusiastic farmers will not, alas, be able to build Eretz Israel. The building up of Palestine cannot depend upon its agriculture. . . . Neither is it to be found in the building fever of Tel Aviv. He who wishes to look upon its economic possibilities must see whether there is a possibility of the development of industries or trade centers that will draw their existence not only from themselves but also and chiefly from other countries, from those that surround it and perhaps from more distant ones.[71]

He wrote in a similar vein in his summary of the debate conducted on the pages of *Forward* in consequence of his articles. Again, despite his doubts and reservations regarding the future of Palestine, he did not abandon his belief in the Jewish genius, through which "a great commercial center will arise in Palestine in the fullness of time." The country might in the future become a link and a bridge between Europe and the entire East, and then centers of commerce and industry would arise in it, and these would boost the development of the land.[72]

These views of Cahan the socialist were amazingly close to those of Zeev Jabotinsky and his Revisionist party, which was founded in the same year, and seemed to run counter to the ideology then dominant in the Zionist movement under the leadership of Weizmann, and certainly to that of the Palestinian labor movement. Not by chance did the Fourth Aliya instigate a debate in the Zionist movement on the directions of development and investment policy, to match the distribution of the meager Zionist budget. The discussion appeared to concern the preference for rural settlement or urbanization, agriculture or trade and industry. In retrospect it seems that both general demographic spread, which came about through the back-to-the-land movement, and urbanization were essential for the realization of Zionism.

C. Importance of Palestine for the Jewish masses

Cahan believed that even if his misgivings about the economic and demographic future of Palestine proved true and the country did not become a haven for mass Jewish immigration with all its implications, it would still occupy an extremely important place in the heart of the Jewish masses. Therefore, it was essential to treat everything done there favorably. For him too, "Palestine is a part of the heart, a part of the emotions." And for the masses of Jews, "Jerusalem is situated . . . at the center of the world." Other nations had possessed countries that they had lost and forgotten; not so the Jews, who did not forget their ancient homeland and continued to pray for it:[73]

> It seems to be clear that Palestine as a Jewish center will at any rate not disappear altogether. It may remain small, but in view of the present world situation Palestine will always play some role in Jewish life . . . As for the idealists who sacrifice themselves for the upbuilding of Eretz Israel and the colonies – those of our comrades who lead the real life of martyrs in the communes – they deserve, in any event, the warmest feelings and the best wishes of every Socialist.[74]

Elsewhere, writing for the huge numbers of Yiddish-speaking Jews, Cahan stated the following:

> I would wish that Eretz Israel will be the greatest homeland for the Jews. Unfortunately, I must doubt this, although I am not convinced that there

30
Introduction

is no hope at all that it will come to pass . . . But even if many or few Jews live there, as a Jewish center in Palestine I love the villages, the cities, the towns and the neighborhoods. The most important thing to me seems to be this fact: hundreds of thousands, even millions, of Jews love what there is in Palestine. They have a special attitude and special feeling for what is going on there: there, in Eretz Israel, where once was the home of the Jewish people, there is steadily being built a Jewish center, with a city like Tel Aviv where the Jews rule themselves, where they feel at home, where they are free of the sense of being a stepson, as is their lot everywhere else in the world . . . Still, for those hundreds of thousands of Jews who have such warm feelings for Eretz Israel, the country does not appear to be one that will solve the problem of the Jewish people, or will become the home of the Jewish masses. For them Eretz Israel is a part of the heart beating with Jewish feelings.[75]

In sum, Cahan believed, even if Palestine did not contribute to the solution of the problems of the Jewish people owing to its inability to absorb mass immigration, it was still necessary to hold a positive attitude to the country, if only on account of three factors. First, the historical, religious and emotional ties of the people to its ancient homeland would continue to maintain Palestine as a highly significant element among the Jewish masses. Second, anti-Semitism was forcing many to adopt the idea of Palestine as their future home. Third, the magnificent pioneering spirit inherent in the building of the Jewish settlement deserved the support of every Jew, including Jewish socialists.

D. *The Arab problem*
Cahan was apparently influenced by and accepted the "Effendist" outlook that prevailed in the 1920s in the Palestinian labor movement, whose essentials were: (1) the advantage of the Jewish enterprise for the Arab population, which benefited from it; (2) reduction of the danger posed by the Arabs to the Jewish settlement; (3) negation of the Palestinian Arab national movement.[76]

E. *The political dimension*
Cahan was convinced that the Jews brought only blessing to Palestine. They were turning the desolate land into a flourishing garden. The Jews were taking civilization to that corner of the world. These facts gave them the right to a national home in Palestine, in addition to the historic tie, despite the arguments of the Arabs. Cahan also believed that the principle of the Jewish national home in Palestine had the support of the masses of

Jews in the world, and he identified with that position. In his travels in different countries in Europe he had met many Jews, and everywhere found great sympathy and support for the national home. Cahan described for his readers how unwilling many were to hear any criticism or doubts about the future of the national home. The idea that somewhere, in one corner of the world, they had such a home was precious to them all, especially in light of the grave conditions in many countries: "They grasp at the straw of a homeland in Palestine." Cahan insisted that his readers must not ignore the fact that just as a religious Jew poured out his heart's bitterness in the synagogue, so did the secular Jew now display the same emotions by expressing faith in and enthusiasm for the national home.[77]

F. Cahan and the Bund

On several occasions, especially during his tour of Palestine, Cahan emphasized that he had not been among the founders of the Bund and that he had never been a member of that movement: he belonged to the generation that predated its establishment. This biographical detail, which Cahan was at pains to stress more than once, is noteworthy, as it was of great ideological, psychological and political significance. Russian socialism at the end of the 1870s and beginning of the 1880s, which was the inheritance of Cahan's generation, was still Narodnik in hue, and was not identified with Marxism with its doctrinaire concepts that informed the outlook of the Bundists, who belonged to a younger generation. Although undoubtedly influenced by Marxism and by Bundism, Cahan had not been a member of the Bund nor had he undergone its socialization. This largely freed him from emotional and psychological sentiments and certainly from the anti-Zionist political tradition inherent in the former Bundists of Russia and Poland.

His argument against the latter was that the sources of their hatred of Zionism lay in eastern Europe and were entirely irrelevant to the circumstances of the United States. They were anachronistic and misplaced, and in determining their positions they ignored concrete reality:[78]

> Still, for us in the United States to be guided by a sentiment which has nothing to do with our own political life would be absurd. We can afford to be unbiased and sober minded, and we must be.

For Cahan, even the struggle being fought in Poland between the Bund and Zionism, which also inflamed the hatred of Bund members in the

United States for Zionism and Palestine, should not determine the position of the Jewish socialist movement in America, which was entirely
unaffected by these matters:

> The Palestine situation is something which we cannot afford to treat in the
> light of those conflicts in Poland . . . Maybe the present enthusiasm for
> Palestine is only a temporary wave of exaltation, but even so it is a fact full
> of heart-warming elements which entitle it to our friendly interest. To be
> sure, one should tell the whole unvarnished truth, even about Palestine;
> but the tone makes the music, as the French say. Whatever criticism we
> have to offer should be expressed in the language of a friend and brother,
> and as remote as possible from a spirit of enmity.[79]

As noted, from the time of his study tour in Palestine, Cahan began
point up the difference between himself and the Bundists: "*Kayn 'soneh
tziyon' bin ich kaynmal nit geveyn. Mir, amerikanishe sotzialisten, hoben mit
di tzionisten nit gehat di politishe kampayn, was di bundisten hoben gehat in
Russland un in Polen.*" For that reason he was able to treat the concrete
present objectively and without prejudice.[80]

G. Socialism and Zionism

In absolute opposition to the stance of his Bundist colleagues, Cahan
believed that coexistence between the two was possible. He pointed out
that, over time, concepts and outlooks had changed in Jewish socialism:
"There were times when it was believed that a Jewish socialist had to
speak out against the Jews, otherwise what kind of a socialist was he? I
myself never was such a socialist. When they beat Jews, it hurt me as a
Jew."[81] In the not too distant past it had been thought that socialism could
not abide together with religion, and therefore a true socialist could not
be religious. Cahan attested to himself as one who sharply censured those
who held that in order to emphasize their socialism they desecrated the
sanctity of Yom Kippur, causing outrage; his view favored religious tolerance. On this account he had been condemned as a poor socialist. Now
everyone identified with his attitude, and the principle of tolerance
toward religion and religious people was accepted throughout the socialist
movement.[82]

Cahan's conclusion was that the reality of Jewish life was highly
dynamic, and different from what had characterized it in the past. These
changes called for a necessary and essential adjustment in the stance of
Jewish socialism on the concrete problems of the present: "The condition
of the Jewish masses in most European countries is such that they clutch

at Palestine as a drowning man clutches at a straw. Therefore, the attitude of socialists toward Palestine must change, and that's a fact."

Furthermore, Cahan stated unequivocally that Zionism was not an anti-socialist ideology, so coexistence between it and socialism was certainly possible. This was the mood he had found at the congress of the Socialist International at Marseilles which he had attended. Cahan indicated a similar position on the part of many leading figures in international socialism, such as Ramsay MacDonald, Wedgewood, Philip Snowden, Léon Blum, Edouard Bernstein and others, who evinced great appreciation of Zionism, and this did not diminish their commitment to and belief in socialism: "Zionism concerns the Jewish sphere while socialism concerns the international sphere, so there is no conflict between Zionism and socialism."[83] In light of these facts too a change was needed in the attitude to Palestine. As far as Cahan was concerned, the Jewish workers in Palestine were no less socialists than the Jewish workers in the United States. In addition, the workers of Palestine were remarkable for their idealism and self-sacrifice, and they were of the same flesh as the workers in America. Cahan's conclusion, therefore, was clear: "Let us not let them go hungry! We cannot finance their entire existence, but let us do everything in our power for them."[84] Cahan believed that aid and support for Palestine did not contradict socialist ideology. The common claim of the Bundists that extending help to the kibbutzim in Palestine might harm socialism in the United States seemed to him senseless. He regarded those who argued in that way as extremist fanatics.[85]

H. Zionism and Palestinism

Cahan's declarations that he was not a Zionist and that his journey to Palestine had not made him one, reflected his feelings and his views.[86] He was in no way affected by pure Zionist ideology, with its monolithic character. The change that took place in Cahan, due to the tragic existential reality of the Jewish people and his visit to Palestine, found expression in his abandonment of indifference (even hostility) toward Zionism, and his adoption of a position sympathizing with the Palestinian endeavor. In this way he in fact assumed the stance of such people as Louis Marshall, who in those years favored extending aid to the Jewish settlement in Palestine without this committing them to becoming Zionists. This distinction between Zionism and Palestinism is most important, and may be understood in light of the processes at work in the 1920s and 1930s in American Jewry, including the Jewish socialist workers' movement.

The characteristic feature of the Jewish community in the United

States was its socio-economic advancement, which found expression, among other things, in the transition from the working class to the middle class, especially among second-generation immigrants. In this sense, the Jewish workers' movement in America was of a single generation. Social mobility brought about a gradual abandonment of universalist-socialist worldviews, and increasing identification with specific Jewish interests. This process was enhanced by the impressive involvement of the Jewish trade unions in the all-American labor movement (American Federation of Labor – AFL), which was a pragmatic trade-unionist movement, remote from the cosmopolitan, socialist fervor of the Bundist veterans and their successors.

The outcome of these processes was to generate in American Jews, including the workers, feelings of all-Jewish solidarity, producing a sympathetic attitude toward Zionism, especially its enterprise in Palestine. Moreover, in the 1920s a highly significant shift took place in the nature and activity of the Zionist movement. The usual Zionist ideology gave way to a Palestinian ideology (Palestinism). To very many it seemed that support for a national movement with a world organizational framework, like Zionism, might expose them to anti-Semitic attacks and to the charge of dual loyalty. By contrast, support for Palestine seemed a positive thing, channeling the sense of solidarity and Jewish identity into a project that had won legitimacy from American society. Such support did not create a problem of dual identity or loyalty, and matched the accepted norms in American society, in which the various immigrant groups supported their countries of origin.

The processes outlined here created a common denominator for the diverse camps in American Jewry, by which non-Zionists, such as Louis Marshall and his colleagues, could join the "enlarged" Jewish Agency.[87]

Against this background it is possible to understand the change that occurred in Cahan, who stepped onto the path already paved, ideologically and politically, by non-Zionist elements of the Jewish community. Furthermore, within the Jewish workers' movement itself, in those very years, a current was forming that identified with the ideology of Palestinism even though its adherents did not identify themselves as Zionists. These set up the *Geverkschaften* project, namely the "Histadrut Appeal." Cahan identified with the activists of this fund-raising campaign, and began to support them. By this support, albeit with a delay of several years, Cahan strengthened the current, and helped to change it from a marginal element in the workers' movement to a significant and recognized factor in Jewish socialism.[88]

I. Attitude to the Palestinian labor movement

In this area the greatest change of all occurred in Cahan. It was reflected in the transition from an indifferent, reserved and even unsympathetic attitude, to unconditional support and enormous esteem. It found immediate expression in the change in *Forward*'s general position, and also in the unrestrained and active support that the paper extended thereafter to the Histadrut Appeal. Cahan admitted that the Palestine labor movement was unique in nature; he gave absolute legitimation to its socialist essence and was filled with admiration for the Histadrut enterprises, in the first place the working agricultural settlement.[89]

In sum, Cahan's study tour of Palestine was of marked significance in terms of the Palestine endeavor. The surrounding reality and the visit caused a qualitatively positive change in his attitude to the building of the land and likewise to the Zionist movement, which thenceforward he recognized as an important and powerful factor in the life of the people and in plotting its future – although he did not become a Zionist. Cahan greatly contributed to the elimination of the taboo which until then had existed in the American-Jewish workers' movement against the settlement being built in Palestine. An outcome of this was a powerful and significant boost to the process of legitimization of support by Jewish socialists for Palestine in general and for its labor movement and its enterprises in particular.[90]

The Position of the Bundist Socialists on Zionism and Palestine

The general situation of eastern European Jewry, the closing of the gates of the United States, and finally Cahan's articles in *Forward* in September–December 1925, together with his lectures and speeches, caused great turmoil in American-Jewish socialism. The leaders of the movement reacted to the circumstances that had arisen. This awakening boiled over into a stormy public debate, conducted mainly on the pages of *Forward* during the months December 1925 to May 1926. The articles were in part commissioned by Cahan, who was anxious for a thorough airing of the question, which would serve his purposes and those of his paper, as well as the cause of Palestine. The debate in *Forward* in the mid-1920s was one of the major events in Jewish public life generally, and especially in the Jewish socialist workers' movement. The discussion highlighted the various positions in American-Jewish socialism on

Zionism and Palestine. Many of the leading Jewish socialist figures of time participated in the polemics such as Baruch Charney-Vladek, Zivion (Dr Ben-Zion Hoffman), Morris Hillquit, Abraham Litvak, Jacob Lestchinsky, David Einhorn, Judge Jacob Panken, Max Pine, Hillel Rogoff, Alexander Kahn, and more.

The harshest and most extreme opponents of Zionism and Palestine were the former Bundists, who in the United States continued to maintain strong ties with their party in eastern Europe, especially Poland. Here the party had inherited the Russian Bund after its liquidation in Soviet Russia. Their opposition to Zionists drew not only on the spiritual ties with their party and the organic and personal attachment to the Polish Bund, but they continued to adhere fervently to the ideology of their movement as it had crystallized in eastern Europe at the beginning of the twentieth century,[91] regardless of the major changes in the political and economic circumstances of the Jews and all over the world after World War I. Their opposition to Zionism and Palestine was not merely theoretical, it was laced with hostility and hatred. Their ideological negation of Zionism focused principally on the following matters.

A. Rejection of Zionist ideology
Baruch Charney-Vladek, the revered leader of the former Bundists in the United States, acknowledged the positive contribution of Zionism, which had awakened Jewish national consciousness in certain strata: "What the Bund succeeded in doing among the Jewish workers by arousing in them the awareness of their Jewishness is what Zionism has done among the Jewish middle class and intelligentsia." Still, he proposed treating Zionism as a political and ideological movement offering a certain path to the solution of the nation's problems. Vladek equated Zionism with communism, regarding both movements as fanatical and "monotheistic," totally excluding any other course. He regarded this as a disqualification of Zionism.[92]

His like-minded colleagues also evinced fierce opposition and absolute negation, because of the all-encompassing and exclusive nature of Zionist ideology expressed in rejection of the Diaspora and territorial concentration of the nation in Palestine. This was not, according to the Zionists, just another country where Jews might migrate and settle, but the *only* country that could provide an absolute and exclusive solution to the affliction and deep-rooted distress of the people, in particular to the problem of preservation of national identity. This outlook appeared to the opponents to be radically wrong, and unacceptable to any thinking person who observed reality and analyzed it rationally.[93]

The Bundists and their supporters were not indifferent to the continued existence of the Jewish people; but they believed in the eternity of Israel in the Diaspora, at least in the foreseeable future. To ensure this, their ambition was to realize, even in the United States, their ideological and political platform, meaning national and cultural autonomy whose main instruments would be Yiddish language and culture.[94] The Bund and Zionism had different aims. While political Zionism ultimately focused on the goal of preserving Jewish identity and national existence, the essential thing for the Bund was concern for Jewish masses wherever they were. Here lay the difference in attitude to the Diaspora and to Yiddish and its culture:

> The development of Yiddish language and culture does not aim to ensure the national existence of the Jewish people and of Jewish nationalism, but only to help the cultural development of the Jewish masses imbued with Yiddish culture and language. In truth, the outcome is the same: anyone working for the development of Yiddish culture and language is in any case working for Jewish national existence. Nevertheless, there is a great difference regarding which target is set up. If the target is to preserve Jewish nationalism, then there is room for Zionism, if only it would adopt Yiddish. But if the target is the cultural development of the Jewish masses of the people, this has no connection with Zionism, because this is not its goal. Zionism does not believe in the possibility of existence and development of Jewish culture without a homeland, so it cannot be harnessed to the development of Yiddish culture in the Diaspora . . . When the issue is protecting national Jewish existence, then Zionism is supreme, because Zionism sets this as its goal.[95]

The fundamental divergence of purpose, the monolithic nature of Zionism, the exclusive affirmation of Palestine as against the absolute rejection of the Diaspora, for which Zionism prophesied destruction – these aroused the enmity of the Bundists and their supporters to Zionism and their utter rejection of it. Their opposition was also on the grounds that they regarded it, just as the fanatical religious orthodoxy did, as false Messianism and a vain dream. As such it was likely to cause, among other things, an attenuation of consciousness and steadfastness of the Jewish masses to fight for the improvement of their condition in the countries of the Diaspora; and when the vain dream exploded it would create an acute psychological crisis in the Jewish masses, who would then have to contend with bitter reality.[96]

B. The preference in principle for the Diaspora over Palestine
According to Zivion, a leader of the *Farband* and the Arbeiter Ring
(Workmen's Circle), and one of the great publicists of *Forward* (with a
regular column entitled Yiddishe interessen which he signed with the
pen-name "Baruch Razman" or "Zivion") the Diaspora was not just a fact
of life for the Jewish people. Zivion waxed lyrical in an idealization of the
Diaspora, which he saw as preferable to Palestine as a framework for the
existence of the Jewish people. In his view the greatest Jewish creative
works, the Bible and the Talmud, were composed in exile. The Jews had
actually become prominent and excelled in the Diaspora, while during
their historical existence in Palestine they had been obliged to invest all
their energies and ingenuity in securing a livelihood and in defending
themselves.

All Jewish figures of renown, Zivion wrote, had appeared in the
Diaspora, and he ascribed this fact to the interaction between Jewish
culture and the cultures of other nations. Jews were no abler than others,
but the conditions of their existence in the Diaspora, and in particular
their being an urban element, nurtured the abundance of famous men
among them. If the Jews returned to Palestine they would undergo a
serious decline as a result of their living in a poor and wretched land in a
backward and depressed region – in contrast to the European culture in
which they were currently immersed.[97]

C. The right of self-determination and a Jewish state
"The Jews are entitled to a country of their own and a state of their own,
just like other nations. But the question is if they can accomplish this."[98]
Such was the accepted position of the American Bundist. However,
among the Bundists there were those who in addition to their pragmatic
denial of the possibility of the establishment of a Jewish state in Palestine
negated such a state even if it was realizable. This perception was evident
in Baruch Charney-Vladek: "Not only do I not believe in the possibility
of the realization of Zionism, I believe that even if it were possible to
realize Zionism it would be a disaster." Vladek based his view on the difficult situation that had arisen in eastern Europe through the creation of
new states there, and also on complete pessimism as to the capacity of
Jewish politicians to manage a state dependent on British bayonets and
surrounded by Arabs.[99]

D. The impossibility of coexistence between socialism and Zionism
Bundist orthodoxy utterly rejected any possibility of coexistence between
socialism and Zionism, and held that a Zionist could not be a socialist, and

vice versa. Zivion wished to present the problem in the form of a rhetorical question: "Is it logical for a socialist to believe in Zionism?" His answer, of course, was negative. For him, a socialist dealt solely with real things, and his approach to problems of society and nation was based on rational economic analysis alone. Zivion stated that in these respects Zionism was a dream and a dangerous illusion because it was built only on sentiment and not on pragmatic realistic foundations. Therefore, again, a socialist could not be a Zionist. Nor did Zionism solve the immediate concrete problems of the people, but being entirely an ideology drawing on the past and based on the past, it also pulled the people to the past – to romance and nostalgia. These did not contribute to the solution of the people's problems in the present:

> Zionism is a nationalism that hauls us backwards. Zionism draws all its vitality from the Jewish past, and therefore it also pulls us back to the past . . . Zionism cannot exist together with socialism; in places where such coexistence was tried Zionism swallowed up socialism.[100]

E. Eretz Israel and Palestine

The Hebrew name for the Land of Israel, *eretz yisra'el*, evoked many emotional and historical associations in every Jew. By contrast, the name "Palestine" was devoid of any associative emotional charge and therefore could be treated in an objective manner. Palestine was a small and poor country ruled by the British and inhabited by a primitive Asiatic people. Where Eretz Israel was poetry, Palestine was prose. Regarding Eretz Israel, all fantasies and dreams were possible, but "Palestine has to be approached with cold calculation, and right from the start with the question as to whether it is possible."

Eretz Israel was woven into the Jewish religion, a holy place connected with the World to Come, whereas Palestine was linked to this world: "Palestine is for the body, and Eretz Israel is for the soul." As an example vindicating this distinction, the Bundists pointed to the ultra-orthodox Jews, who, on the one hand, greatly loved Eretz Israel, but on the other, were opposed to Zionism.[101]

F. Negation of Palestine in economic terms

Zivion compared Palestine to Switzerland in terms of size, but unlike Switzerland it could not support even the existing population of 800,000 people (in 1925). If it developed like Switzerland it might reach a maximal population of about two million, most of whom, according to the existing situation, would be Arabs. Yet he did not believe that the country would develop like Switzerland for the following reasons: From the viewpoint of agriculture, the climate of Palestine was harsh and its land was meager and unsuited to an agriculture that would produce a reasonable living. Furthermore, most of the land was Arab property. From the viewpoint of industrialization, the country had no raw materials, and therefore it was impossible to develop profitable industry in it. If an attempt was made to base industry on imported raw materials, the products would be very expensive and could not compete on the world market. In addition, Zivion drew attention to British colonial policy, which tended not to allow the countries it ruled to develop industry but used them as markets for its own industrial goods. In such economic conditions he saw no likelihood that Palestine would develop a notable and healthy economy, which could absorb even a small portion of the Jewish immigration. Even if a few thousands entered the country, this still would not ease even a fraction of the distress of the Jewish people because of natural increase.[102] Zivion followed Dubnow and Ahad Ha'am in his reference to natural increase, and believed that the great majority of the people would remain in the Diaspora in the future.

It should be emphasized that Zivion and his like-minded comrades did not object to Jewish agricultural settlement in Palestine: they just did not believe it could succeed. Moreover, Zivion opposed Jews working the land, which he regarded as wearying labor that did not provide a decent living for those who engaged in it. It is true that he supported the Jewish settlement in the Crimea, but that was due to lack of an alternative for Jewish existence in Communist Russia. Also, in a survey he conducted he found that the settlement in Russia had many economic advantages as compared with that in Palestine. He likewise favored the settlement in Mexico, Brazil, Cuba and Argentina. And again, Zivion repeatedly stressed his lack of credence in the success of the agricultural settlement in Palestine, even if it were done on the basis of a communal form of living. He likened the kibbutzim and the moshavim to colored soap bubbles, meaning that they attracted attention and evoked wonder because of the pioneering, the self-sacrifice and the socialist way of life, but in the long run this form of settlement too would not have an economic existence.[103]

> The entire foundation of Zionism, as far as I see, and the Zionists them-
> selves agree with this, stands on emotion. The appeal of Zionism is to
> emotion . . . But a people has never been built on the basis of the emotional
> element. Peoples become settled and grow strong only in places where
> economic conditions allow it.

Again, the Bundists argued that everyone agreed that Palestine was not a fertile land. From the Jewish perspective, only one percent of the entire Jewish people lived there, compared with 60 percent who lived in eastern Europe. They claimed that in the best case only 6–7 percent of the Jewish people could settle in Palestine. It was thus not possible, on the basis of these facts, to state that Palestine would allay the hardship of the people.[104]

G. *Immigration and absorption*

Here too the chief spokesman was Zivion. He was aware of the grave situation of the Jews of eastern Europe generally and of Poland in particular, although he thought that the pessimistic reports were exaggerated. Despite this, and despite the closure of the gates of America, he did not see Palestine as an alternative, not even partial, for the absorption of Jewish migration: "As for Palestine, it is impossible today to consider it as a target country for Jewish migration. The Zionists know this better than anyone."[105]

Zivion accused the Zionists of hypocrisy, because they made the pretence of being opponents of the mandatory government's policy limiting immigration, although in reality they were pleased with it. The Zionists feared that if the restrictions were lifted immigration would increase, and an economic crisis would erupt in the Yishuv that would bring about its collapse. It seemed to Zivion that only two kinds of migrants could go to Palestine: those with wealth and people who were willing to suffer there, namely pioneering youth.[106] Therefore, Palestine would perhaps help a few thousand Jews, but it would certainly not resolve the hardship of the many. In various formulations Zivion voiced his opinion that "Zionism in Palestine is incapable of contending with the problem of Jewish immigration. Palestine does not provide and cannot provide any answer to the real needs of the Jews."[107] Even in the best circumstances it could not effect a change in the economic, political, and cultural life of the Jewish masses in the Diaspora, and so influence their destiny. The inevitable conclusion, he felt, was that people had to break free of the Zionist dream. The Jews must understand that they were likely to remain in their countries of origin, and there they would have to fight for their rights.[108]

Many Bundists were of the opinion that the flaws of Zionism on the pragmatic side were no less great than those on the ideological side. Once more, their oft-repeated claim was that Palestine was incapable of resolving the problems and the distress of the Jewish people in the Diaspora. The proof for this, among other things, they believed, lay in the fact that Zionism, which had been active now for decades, had not succeeded in building an impressive structure in Palestine. Moreover, in several countries more Jews had been absorbed than in Palestine, and this contradicted all the hopes pinned on that land. Many Bundists also stressed incessantly the poverty of the country, which lacked water, raw materials, industry and other economic elements.[109] The long-held and consistent position of the Bundists was that "Zionism is incapable of solving the problem of the Jews in Palestine or of helping Jewish migration."[110]

H. The Arab problem
Those who rejected Zionism and Eretz Israel belittled the importance of the Balfour Declaration and stressed that the latter did not make Palestine Jewish, but a British mandate. Above all, they argued, it had to be realized that the territory in question had an overwhelming Arab majority. For every Jew there were six Arabs, so clearly Palestine was an Arab land which did not have then, nor would it have in the future, any chance of becoming a country with a Jewish hue. In fact, they said, Zionism served the interests of Britain, but it could not be built on this basis because of the decisive Arab majority in the country, with the all-round support they received from tens of millions of Arabs and Muslims, which would destroy the goals of Zionism.[111]

I. Negation of the Palestinian labor movement
In this matter the hostility of Bundist orthodoxy was most striking, being unwilling to distinguish in its attitude among Zionism, Palestine and the Palestinian labor movement, including the working settlement which Cahan and other socialists saw as a paragon of national and socialist self-sacrifice. The Bundists regarded them all as a single whole, which was unacceptable and had to be fought with full force and without compromise. Furthermore, Bundist criticism denied the socialist essence of the Palestinian labor movement, and accused it of cooperating with the Zionist bourgeoisie, from which it received benefits. Only by virtue of Weizmann, the servant of the British, had the Histadrut accomplished any achievements. Idealism and pioneering in Palestine were a shocking waste, because Palestine, they believed, in any case, would not contribute to solving the problem of the masses of the people. Bundist orthodoxy believed that the Palestinian labor movement, including its communal section, not only was not socialist but bore a clearly national chauvinist character. Its chauvinism became evident, the Bundists said, also in the

principle of "conquest of labor" the significance of which was none other than the rough ejection of the Arab worker from his place of work. If the Jews had done anything similar in the Diaspora voices would have been raised in protest at the scandalous deed. In the last analysis, the Bundists claimed, the Palestinian labor movement was an integral part of Zionism, so it could not possess a socialist outlook. This was based on the position that socialism could not coexist with Zionism and therefore anyone who was a Zionist could not be a socialist.

From this attitude stemmed absolute rejection of the Histadrut Appeal run by the UHT. The Bundists expressed outrage at those members of the *Farband* who supported the fund-raising campaign, and even called for their expulsion from the movement.

Zivion attacked kibbutz members frontally, and took an implacable stand against their supporters who were members of the Jewish socialist movement: "I entirely do not understand how it is possible to call these fanatic chauvinists by the name of socialists." He was particularly enraged by the workers in Palestine, who, in his opinion, were the fighting avant-garde against Yiddish: "These are the Zionist workers in Palestine who imposed a ban on the Yiddish language there, and forbade its use in public." Here too arose Zivion's and his comrades' fierce opposition to any special support for the Histadrut through the Histadrut Appeal.

To summarize, Bundist orthodoxy rejected the distinction common at the time in the Jewish community between Zionism and "Palestinism." On the basis of the latter, non-Zionist Jews, including socialists, could support the Jewish settlement in Palestine. For the Bundists such a distinction was wholly unacceptable. Because they did not believe in any possible coexistence between socialism and Zionism they dismissed the Palestine labor movement, which they considered to be the avant-garde of the Zionist movement bearing a nationalist stamp; for this reason it merited no special treatment or assistance. Through cool rational, economic analysis the Bundists rejected Palestine as a solution for the suffering of the people by means of absorption of massive Jewish immigration.

For all that, the Bundists did not deny the giving of aid to the Jewish settlement in Palestine or to the workers there. Their demand was that such aid only be given in equal measure to that given to Jews or workers elsewhere in the world. The issue here was defined by Baruch Charney-Vladek in Yiddish: "*Palastine auch, tzi Palastine nur*" (Palestine also or Palestine alone). While he accepted the first part of the formula, he completely rejected the second, which he saw as the essence of Zionist ideology.[112] In light of these views it is not surprising that the *Farband*, which was under the exclusive influence of the Bundists, would oppose the Histadrut fund-raising campaign conducted from 1924 by Max Pine and his supporters.

At the fourth conference of the *Farband* on 8 January 1926, under Bundist pressure resolutions were again passed against Zionism and Palestine. The conference likewise reaffirmed a resolution opposing the Histadrut Appeal, although the resolution did pay lip service to the idealism and self-sacrifice of the workers of Palestine. The resolution was as follows:

> The Fourth Conference of the Jewish Socialist *Farband* reaffirms its view that Palestine cannot solve the Jewish problem, and as a country for migration it is incapable of absorbing large groups of Jews. Zionist ideology can only weaken in the Jewish masses the faith in their ability to struggle for their freedom and equality in the countries where they live.
>
> As for the Jewish workers in Palestine, the Conference indeed sympathizes with their idealism and devotion, yet it does not believe that these are the chosen ones and the only builders of the Jewish future. Therefore, they deserve our attention and our assistance, but at the same rate as, and proportionate to, that given to needy Jews in other lands.
>
> Therefore the workers of America must ensure that the Jewish workers in Palestine will receive their fair share out of all the general fund-raising campaigns organized here.
>
> Members of the Jewish Socialist *Farband* are not obliged to participate in any special fund-raising campaign organized for the benefit of the Jewish workers in Palestine. If however a special campaign is required for Palestine, as for other countries, due to special circumstances, the Executive will decide on our position.[113]

There was special significance in the fact that Morris Hillquit, a prominent leader of the all-American Socialist Party (SP), joined in the public debate. Except for his early years in the United States, Hillquit never participated in Jewish life or in Jewish activity, and did not even identify himself as a Jew.[114] In terms of religion he declared himself agnostic, and rejected any form of religion, including Judaism.

Hillquit opposed the insertion of specific Jewish issues into the socialist movement, and therefore also opposed the grant, in 1912, of independent status to the Jewish "Federation" in the SP framework. He also objected to the fact that the SP identified with specific Jewish matters in its policy in the American arena. Paradoxically, Hillquit, the universalist and all-

American, had to depend almost throughout his public career on Jewish support.

In 1926, Hillquit entered the debate at the explicit request of Abraham Cahan. He could not refuse because *Forward* bore most of the financial burden of the SP. Still, he asked Cahan to state in the paper that he was joining the public debate at Cahan's request. For his part, Cahan was most anxious that a figure such as Hillquit, with authority in the SP should join the discussion, both to add to its importance and in the belief that Hillquit's identification with Cahan's own views would be beneficial for his position.[115]

In his election campaign for Congress in 1918 and 1920 Hillquit, the politician, supported independence for Ireland but opposed Zionism. He explained his position by distinguishing between the national movement of oppressed peoples, such as the Irish, and Zionism, which he regarded as a movement attempting to establish a Jewish state in Palestine at the expense of the Arabs and by denying them their right to self-determination.[116] In later years Hillquit was called on to make statements on the Zionist question, and on the rare occasions when he did so his statements were of a very general nature.[117]

As noted, in April 1926 Hillquit was asked to formulate his position on Zionism and Palestine. An article he published contained a number of statements favoring Jewish nationalism. The "composition" produced by Hillquit's pen is an example of the art of making generalizations that can be interpreted in any direction – apparently the author's intention:

> There is no inherent antagonism or even incompatibility between Socialism and Zionism. Zionism is a nationalistic movement, Socialism is essentially internationalistic. But a sane internationalism does not exclude the recognition of legitimate national aspirations.[118]

Up to this point, he aligned himself with Cahan's views, two of which he accepted: he recognized Zionism as a legitimate national movement; and he recognized that in this there was no clash between socialism and Zionism.

Next Hillquit argued that socialism recognized the existence of nations. It desired only to remove the tensions and enmity among them. Socialism wished all nations, large and small, to obtain the right and the possibility to develop unhindered so that they might be able to realize all the qualities within them, "and to live their lives free from outside interference and oppression." Hillquit noted that the immediate reason for the

founding of the First International in 1863 had been a workers' demonstration on behalf of the Polish insurgents who rose that year against the
Russians. From then on socialism, in the author's view, held a consistent
line of support for oppressed nations striving for self-determination.
After these clarifications he directly addressed the question at issue:

> Whether the Jews, homeless, scattered, may be considered as a nationality
> . . . and whether the reestablishment of a Jewish political State or even a
> center of specifically Jewish culture is feasible or desirable is a question of
> individual judgment or sentiment, not one of principle . . . Personally I am
> not a Zionist. I doubt the possibility of recreating a Jewish State in Palestine
> and am not convinced that the Jews as an organized nationality can make
> a distinct and valuable contribution to the world's culture . . . But I am not
> an anti-Zionist. While I cannot accept the principal program of Zionism in
> any formulation, I have learned to realize that the value of social move-
> ments may not always be measured by their concrete achievements or the
> feasibility of their aims.

Hillquit went on to note that there could be utopian movements from
the viewpoint of real political achievements, at the same time possessing
great moral influence and indirectly also influencing the progress of
human society:

> Zionism makes a strong sentimental appeal to me, chiefly as a manifesta-
> tion of awakening national self-respect of the Jewish people. I prefer to see
> the Jew proclaiming his equality with the other races and nations of the
> world, rather than seeking to deny his race in implied admission of national
> inferiority.

Hillquit argued for a clearcut division between legitimate national goals
and chauvinism:

> Zionism, like the other national movements, must guard itself against the
> danger of degenerating into jingoism. If it ever develops in that direction
> it will forfeit all claims to Socialist sympathy.[119]

If Cahan had hoped for an unequivocal, affirmative declaration from
Hillquit, he was disappointed. Yet within the debate conducted here there
was support, and not inconsiderable, from an angle different from that
expressed by Bundist orthodoxy.

The Position of Socialists Who Supported Palestine

These constituted an ideologically widely varied group with the following features: its members were not associated with the Bund, so they had not experienced the socialization and ideological internalization of that movement before their immigration to the United States. Some of them had in fact immigrated in the period prior to the establishment of the Bund; some of them were connected with the *Forward* Corporation and the UHT. During the years under review the latter became a major factor supporting the Histadrut in Palestine and it carried the main burden of the Histadrut Appeal in the United States; some were close, indeed very close, to Zionism, although they did not accept all its tenets. The leading personalities of this kind were Max Pine, Alexander Kahn, Hillel Rogoff, Isser Ginsburg and others, among them some who were leading activists in the Jewish unions in the garment industry such as Joseph Schlossberg and Max Zaritzky. Their positions may be outlined as follows.

A. Socialism and Zionism
In contrast to the Bundists they held that there was no conflict between socialism and Zionism, and the two could exist together. Therefore, a socialist could be a Zionist and the reverse. Moreover, the combination of socialism and nationalism was to be found in other nations and there was no reason for it not to be possible among the Jews.[120] This stance was well expressed in the opening speech of the first Histadrut fund-raising campaign in 1924, delivered by Max Pine: "There are among us those who fear that our struggle will encourage the Zionists. They are still afraid that the Jews are making a bad 'deal' with Zion. So I ask: 'Why should I be afraid of them more than Ramsay MacDonald, Snowden, Wedgewood and others? If they are not afraid, why should I be?'"[121]

The socialist supporters of Palestine utterly rejected the position of the orthodox Bundists, who based their hatred for Zionism and Palestine on socialist ideology. Against them the pro-Zionists argued that there were no grounds in socialist ideology supporting their approach or forbidding a socialist to be a Zionist: they went still further, stating that "all will agree that there is no set socialist code whereby one must pass judgment that Zionism is unrealizable."

Alexander Kahn, a leader of Jewish socialism, reinforced his stance in the debate by citing the position of Baruch Charney-Vladek; the latter believed that Zionism made a positive historic contribution in that it aroused independent national awareness in the Jewish middle class and intelligentsia. Kahn extended Vladek's argument, pointing out that the socio-economic process in the United States showed that the Jewish working class was in constant transition to those classes, and therein lay the great importance of the latter. In addition, Kahn indicated that world socialism was investing great efforts to draw the middle class and intelligentsia into its ranks, or at least to gain their support for its positions. Finally, on the basis of the arguments he raised, Kahn called on his opponents to reconsider positively their attitude to Zionism and Palestine.[122]

Max Pine arrived at the most extreme formulation of the issue. On the one hand, he said of himself and of his comrades that "We are not Zionists," but on the other, he clearly stated the superiority of the national element in the Jewish socialist:

> The old refrain that we are not Jews but Yiddish-speaking socialists – this refrain has long ago passed from the world, together with all the propaganda preaching assimilation of the Jews. The position that we are only internationalists and have nothing to do with the fate of the Jewish people has gone with the wind.

And

> We are not Zionists . . . but we are Jews and as such the condition of the Jews will always be of interest to us. That is why we have so much to discuss on the subject of Palestine even if we are not Zionists.

Pine went on to argue that in the concrete circumstances of the Jewish people many socialists were devoting themselves to giving succor to the people crying out in their anguish, and their activity in no way weakened their socialist awareness and their class struggle. Their enthusiasm for what they were doing for their people showed that "the Jewish socialists possess Jewish national consciousness." In the past there had indeed been many who denied their nationality but this was no longer so. Every nation, including its socialists, was first and foremost close to itself. Pine was in no doubt that, for the Jewish socialist, the interest of his people was nearer to him than the interests of other nations. Hence his conclusion was clear: "It is impossible to deny national feeling, so it is not a sin if a Jewish socialist is greatly concerned to help his people in every sphere."[123]

It transpires that the socialist supporters of Palestinism deemed it most important to establish an ideological basis for their position: this was that no conflict existed between socialism and Zionism, and therefore their support for Palestine, which the Bundist socialists regarded as support for Zionism, was legitimate.

B. *Pragmatism and sentiment*

It has been mentioned that the orthodox Bundists constantly argued that their position on Palestine derived not only from their ideology but also from their rational, pragmatic and economic outlook, according to which Palestine had no chance of developing the capacity to absorb the Jewish masses, and so become an important world Jewish center. The Bundists accused their opponents of a sentimental utopianist approach that was detached from reality and incapable of giving birth to anything.

The socialist supporters of Palestine placed the debate on the level of a discussion in principle on the preservation of national Jewish identity in the problematic and complicated conditions of modern times, which jeopardized the continued existence of the people. For this essential issue, they claimed, Bundist socialism and Zionism proposed entirely different solutions. In light of the great hardship suffered by the Jewish masses in eastern Europe, especially Poland, and in light of the assimilation processes in the United States, it seemed to many of this trend that, in fact, Bundist-socialist ideology was pure utopia and the alternative Zionist ideology was not. The conclusion thus followed that "we see a greater chance and a wider basis for preserving the existence of the Jewish people in the Palestinian homeland."[124]

Furthermore, to construct a great enterprise, like the salvation of a people, the members of the group argued, auxiliary pragmatic, economic factors were inadequate. Realization of a multi-faceted national goal, like that of the Jewish people, demanded idealism, devotion, and self-sacrifice – namely spiritual elements by which means alone it was possible to bear the material and spiritual burden involved in these mighty endeavors. The socialist supporters of Palestinism pointed to the lesson to be learned from Jewish settlement projects in various countries of the world: the attempts at Jewish settlement in Cuba and Mexico had failed; in Brazil and Argentina, Jewish settlement had cost enormous sums, and still, despite the massive investment, it had failed, "because to build something great financial factors are not enough; it has to be accompanied by vision and grandeur of spirit, and these exist in Palestine." Therefore it was essential to recognize that only the combination between the historic spiritual connection of the Jewish people to Eretz Israel and the "vision of the national home is the driving force that prevails over the youth and others to labor in unbearable conditions, but with great faith that they are building a center for their downtrodden people. They are building a land in which the Jews will be able to display their ability, a land in which they will again restore to themselves their self-respect."

These views on the issue in question evince absolute rejection of the orthodox Marxist-Bundist outlook, which took into consideration only material factors but disregarded emotional and spiritual elements of great force that operated and still operate in individuals and peoples.[125]

C. *Support for Palestine*

This was given by these socialists unreservedly as a combination of sentiment and evaluation of the actual and potential contribution of Palestine to answering the needs of immigration and absorption of the Jewish masses. A factor that intensified and strengthened this tendency of these socialists in the mid-1920s was the crisis of Polish Jewry and their absorption as the Fourth Aliya from 1924 on. Support for Palestine, they believed, did not require the supporter to be a Zionist, "but when the Zionists are making real progress and are concerned with building a home of thousands of Jews who have to be rescued from starvation and suffering, then I must support them."[126] Max Pine reinforced this concept when he wrote: "I speak in my own name and in the name of many comrades who think as I do. We are very concerned to know what influence the presence of a considerable Jewish population in Palestine will have on the improvement of the condition of Jews in other countries."

These socialists also did not believe that Palestine was able to solve the entire Jewish problem. It was clear to them that such a small country could not absorb 14 million people. Nor did they hold that this was the task of Palestine or the mission imposed on it. They based their view on the belief that even the Zionists did not think that it was indeed possible. From their viewpoint, just as not all the Greeks lived in Greece, so was it not essential that all the Jews converge on Palestine.

Once again, the harsh reality in which the Jews were trapped enhanced the importance of Palestine: the pogroms in Ukraine were unleashed with the assent of Petlura, who was considered a social democrat; Russia closed its gates and became a vast jail; the new countries of eastern Europe celebrated their Independence Days by savaging Jews in pogroms. The United States itself closed its doors.

So, against the background of this horror, "there is in the Near East a land, albeit small, but in a process of development, a place where Jews have fought for years against the attacks of the Arabs. There is a place where Jewish heroes fell, weapon in hand; they fought there for a long time, and absorbed new immigrants until they achieved a situation in which they no longer feared attack. There in that land a wonderful workers' movement has arisen . . . "[127]

Nor did the socialists of Pine's caliber accept all the pragmatic, economic calculations of their opponents. The latter sought to demonstrate the paucity of the country's resources, which would necessarily leave it in poverty with no capacity to develop any agriculture, commerce and industry worthy of the name. By contrast, these socialists believed in the country's inherent economic possibilities, and with the help of Jewish ingenuity, "Palestine will become a great Jewish center of enormous political and economic importance for the Jews."[128]

The Jews lived in the world in two kinds of states: those that persecuted them, where the Jews suffered in terms of their physical existence but their national and religious Jewish identity were strong; and those in which the Jews enjoyed freedom and a decent economic existence, but where there was serious danger of assimilation. "Only in Palestine is it possible for Jews to develop in a healthy way both the material side and the spiritual side. Only in Palestine can a Jew maintain his Judaism in its entirety and not be deprived in the domain of human rights or in economic opportunities."

Furthermore, some exponents of this view argued that Bundist ideology, with its belief in the possibility of the preservation of Jewish existence in the Diaspora on the basis of national and cultural autonomy, was a delusion. They did not believe that it was possible to develop a whole and healthy Jewish life in the Diaspora even though they assumed that the majority of Jews would continue to live in it. They pointed out that even in the United States there was a process of assimilation and that Jewish life was declining: "In the Diaspora there is a process of bodily dwindling and in America the process of decline is spiritual. Only the Jewish homeland can ensure the preservation of Jewish identity, and whoever is not an assimilationist must admit this." These words of Hillel Rogoff, a member of the *Forward* editorial board, could undoubtedly be endorsed by Zionists too. Rogoff was also an optimist regarding the economic potential of Palestine.[129] His colleague on the editorial board, Dr Isser Ginsburg, highlighted the special attitude shown by all strata of the people toward Palestine. The spiritual uplift, faith, hope and love revealed in such people could be manifested only to that country. The special feelings for the Jews of Palestine was not due to their being better or nobler, "but because in the Jews of Palestine the people see the builders of their future." In his view, Jewish culture was being created in Eretz Israel, not in the Diaspora.[130]

D. *The Palestinian labor movement*

In the view of the socialist supporters of Palestine, the Palestinian labor movement, with its range of Histadrut enterprises and the working agricultural settlement, was the leaven and absolute legitimation of their stance and their actions. They were in no doubt whatsoever as to the movement's socialist essence: "The labor in Palestine that we wish to support . . . is socialist labor. In the debate we are not discussing just any Zionist enterprise, but specific projects in Palestine: the communes, the cooperatives and the trade unions."

Max Pine and his comrades were filled with admiration for the Palestinian labor movement, and Pine was also the major figure in the Histadrut Appeal. For him the labor movement in Palestine was "an example for the world. In Palestine has arisen the most moral workers' movement, creating models of socialist life."[131]

The Position of Abraham Liessin on Zionism and Palestine

Abraham Liessin enjoyed special status in the American-Jewish socialist movement. This was by virtue of his past in the Russian Bund, his renown and eminence as poet, writer and publicist, and his stature as editor of the monthly *Zukunft*, which beginning from 1913 he turned into the leading journal in literary cultural Jewish life in the United States. Precisely against the background of his achievements and his Bundist past and socialist present, Liessin's nationalist views stood out and marked him off from his comrades and their positions on Zionism and Palestine. Liessin was imbued with Jewish culture and possessed the most profound Jewish historical awareness. These foundations determined his views, as a socialist, on Zionism and Palestine. It may be said that Liessin was a socialist and a nationalist, who gave clear priority to the nationalist element. As early as 1918, after the publication of the Balfour Declaration, the Jewish Socialist Federation in the United States, in which Liessin was active, was invited to a special conference to determine its position on (a) the war that still raged in Europe, and (b) Palestine and Jewish nationalism in light of the Balfour Declaration. On the second subject three principal positions took shape at the conference. The first, represented by Liessin, called for recognition of the rights of the Jews to self-determination and to a state of their own, just as these rights were recognized in other peoples in keeping with Wilsonian principles. Liessin insisted that Jewish socialists should not let the national question become the monopoly of the Zionists, and argued that they, the socialists, had to join in the call for a Jewish state in Palestine. His proposal was not accepted by the conference.[132]

Liessin persisted in his views and indeed reinforced them in the 1920s. He warned his readers and listeners that the Balfour Declaration might become a mere piece of paper if the Jews stood idly by and did not fill it with real content. Liessin analyzed the situation particularly gravely because he believed that as long as Palestine, throughout the centuries of Turkish rule, had remained desolate, the Jews still had the possibility of returning there. Owing to the mandate that handed rule over Palestine to Britain, the country was likely to develop. If in the new circumstances Zionism were to fail, Liessin argued, the hope of revival of the people in its land would die, this time with no chance of resurrection.

As noted, Liessin had a Bundist and socialist past, but for him the idea that a danger existed of losing the country for which there had been so much weeping and so much yearning for millennia was unbearable: "This dreadful thought causes shudders of fear, and a sharp pain rends my heart." Liessin argued that in the Diaspora the Jewish people had never determined their fate, but the Balfour Declaration and the national home offered a chance that the Jews could take their destiny in their hands. If the Jews did not exploit the opportunity "this will be our fault and our crime. The greatest national crime that has occurred in our history. This must not happen and it will not happen."

In Liessin's view the Bund's demand for national, cultural autonomy in the Diaspora was a minimum national plan, while he considered the idea of creating a Jewish state in Palestine a maximum plan. He countered his various kinds of opponents by stating that there was no law on earth forcing the Jews to remain a wandering people, "the only people in the world that is forbidden to have a homeland of its own, that must be the eternal wanderer among the nations." Liessin, it is true, favored the continuation of national, cultural activity in the Diaspora, but in parallel he called for the building of Palestine. As a socialist he believed that only the Jewish workers were capable of accomplishing this because, for the wealthy, the concept of "Zion" was identified as the place where they made their money.

Liessin was not a Zionist in the sense that he did not believe that

Palestine would solve all the problems of the Diaspora, although he deemed it a very important solution. Above all, Palestine, he believed, "could solve the problem of the continued existence of Jewish national identity and of national existence. Every new Jewish immigrant in America is a candidate for assimilation, while every new immigrant to Palestine does not doubt that he will continue to be a Jew."[133] In these positions Liessin anticipated by many years the majority of socialists, who during the 1920s became adherents of support for Palestine. Liessin was also the outstanding and leading figure in respect of support for Palestine and of sympathy, as a socialist, for the Zionist movement. Liessen gave public expression to his views: "In Zionism I see splendor, great splendor, unequalled in human history." He was filled with gratitude for the miracle that was unfolding with the return of the Jews to Palestine, and full of wonder and admiration for the enterprise of revival being accomplished in Palestine, which he called *"Am yisrael hay!"* (the people of Israel lives).

Liessin entirely rejected the views of his former comrades from the Bund and the socialist movement who reviled Palestine and belittled its value and importance both in the present and in the future on economic, rationalist grounds. He believed that Zionism had already left the point of failure behind, and was to become a popular movement which even the anti-Zionist orthodox left would join. Again, prophesying in Ahad Ha'amist language: "I do not believe that Zionism will solve the Jewish question to a considerable degree, but I do believe that it will solve, to a considerable degree, the Judaism question."

Liessin admitted that from childhood he had had a deep connection to Palestine in parallel with his being a socialist. He had held that socialism addressed the Jewish present, and therefore he could not allow himself, unlike the Jewish bourgeoisie, to be misled by dreams, namely Zionism. He himself had worked hard for the Bund in Russia and in America, and he greatly admired the contribution of this movement to the Jewish issue. Liessin confessed that two loves existed in him at the same time: for Palestine and for the Bund. It was, he felt, the rise of Zionism that had sparked the Bund's positive attitude and deep involvement in the Jewish national question, although it took its "authorization" for this from the doctrine of Austrian social democracy.

On repeated occasions Liessin stated unequivocally that in no socialist code was it written that the Jews were forbidden to have a country of their own. He ascribed the Bund's hatred for Zionism and Palestine to the historic friction in Russia between the two movements and also to the present conflict between the movements in eastern Europe, especially Poland. Furthermore:

> It is beyond my capacity to understand the bitterness of the Bundists in Warsaw toward the socialists in New York because they, the socialists in New York, refuse to engage in conflict with the Zionists in New York. The Zionists in New York are a faction for Palestine alone, and the socialists in New York do not wish to extend Bundist bitterness at the Zionists in Warsaw to the pioneers of the Jewish workers in Palestine.

In Liessin's view the Jewish worker was not only a part of the world proletariat, he was also an organic part of the Jewish nation, and therefore Liessin could not remain aloof from and indifferent to "the fine and wonderful effort that Zionism is making now, after eighteen and a half centuries, in Eretz Israel." Moreover, in Palestine, uniquely socialist ways of life were developing. He regarded the pioneers in Palestine as "the best and the most-loved among us." The love, admiration and hopes that Liessin hung on Palestine were intermixed with his extremely high regard for the Diaspora and Jewish creativity that had evolved there over centuries. Liessin also believed in the continued existence of the Diaspora, and so called for a synthesis between Palestine and the Diaspora:

> Little Eretz Israel, even if built upon her hill, even if redeemed and delivered, without the great Diaspora behind her, without the influence and without the enthusiasm of the great Diaspora behind her, is liable to become orientalized, to shrivel, and to lose her natural vigor. But the great Diaspora – what would it be worth but for the light of this miracle of little Eretz Israel? For would we not be like Gypsies then, in national terms, without our yesterday and without our tomorrow?[134]

To Conclude

Certain processes resulted in the generation of attitudes in American-Jewish socialism that gradually began to undermine the walls of indifference and hostility to Zionism and to Palestine, the fruit of the Bundist tradition. These processes were the legitimation won by Zionism and Palestine following the Balfour Declaration from the countries of the world, the United States, the League of Nations, the Socialist

International and the American Socialist Party; social and economic processes within American Jewry, including the workers, which led them to greater Jewish awareness and national solidarity; the collapse of Jewish existence in eastern Europe, mainly Poland, owing to popular and state anti-Semitism; and the closure of the gates of the United States before Jewish immigration. The harnessing of the Jewish workers in America to support for Palestine started in the early 1920s, grew stronger in the middle of the decade, and received an impetus at the start of the 1930s with the rise of Nazism. This development was furthered by the distinction between Zionism and Palestinism, which in fact was made by all Jewish factors in the United States, including the Zionist movement itself, which committed itself to aiding the Jewish settlement in Palestine. Adopting a position on the basis of Palestinism, without accepting Zionist ideology, made it possible to respond to the national Jewish conscience while not infringing the norms that were acceptable in American society generally.

Notes to the Introduction

Abbreviations

UHT	United Hebrew Trades
ILGWU	International Ladies Garment Workers Union
ACWA	Amalgamated Clothing Workers of America
AR	*Arbeiter Ring* (Workmen's Circle)
AFL	American Federation of Labor
PRC	People's Relief Committee
JSF	Jewish Socialist Federation
JSF	Jewish Socialist *Farband*
SP	Socialist Party
SLP	Socialist Labor Party
JDC	Jewish Distribution Committee (Joint)

1   Arye (Lloyd) Gartner, The formation of American Jewry (1840–1925), *Issues in Jewish History*, no. 5, Jerusalem 1977, p. 9. See also Hersh Libman, Jewish immigration into the United States 1899–1925: Demographic analysis, ibid., pp. 26–9.
2   Shmuel Ettinger, *History of the Jews in Modern Times*, Dvir, Tel Aviv 1969, pp. 263–5 (Hebrew). Note should be made of the publication of the *Protocols of the Elders of Zion* in the United States in those years under the title *The Jewish Peril*; it was widely distributed. Henry Ford was especially active in this. In 1922 the president of Harvard University proposed instituting a *numerus clausus* for Jewish students.
3   Ibid., p. 266.
4   The General Covenant of Jewish Workers in Lithuania, Poland and Russia, or *Der Bund* for short, was founded 25–27 September 1897 in Vilna.
5   Shmuel Eisenstadt, *Chapters in the History of the Jewish Workers' Movement*, I–II, Hakkibutz Ha'artzi, Merhavia (n.d.), II, p. 16 (Hebrew).
6   In *Forward* of 2 July 1923 an item appeared on the joining by the American SP, together with the British Labour Party, of the Socialist International, which was established after the war in Hamburg.
7   Raphael Mahler, *The Jews of Poland between the Two World Wars*, Dvir, Tel

Aviv 1968, p. 9 (Hebrew).

8   Ibid., pp. 18–28.
9   Ibid., pp. 11–16.
10 Ibid., pp. 7–8.
11 Yisrael Halperin (ed.), *Jewry in Poland I*, Department for Youth Affairs of the Zionist Federation, Jerusalem 1948 (Hebrew); L. Berger, *Socio-economic Structure of Polish Jewry (1918–1939)*, p. 203 (Hebrew).
12 Ibid., p. 204.
15 Ibid., pp. 206–14.
13 Natan-Michal Gelber, *History of the Jews in Poland from the Beginning of Its Partition to the Second World War*, pp. 126–7 (Hebrew). (See note 11).
14 Mahler, pp. 56–89.
16 Ibid., pp. 161–73.
17 Ibid., pp. 130–1.
18 See note 11; Gelber, p. 126; A. Hartglass, *The Struggles of the Jews of Poland for Civil and National Rights*, pp. 135–7 (Hebrew). Hartglass states that due to anti-Semitism the Poles published the agreement on minorities only in 1920, after external pressure was brought to bear on the country, while the Versailles agreements had been published earlier. In his view, the formulation of the agreement on minorities, which was concluded with several states, not only Poland, was extremely flawed: there was no guiding line, the clauses were disordered, there was inconsistent use of terms and definitions, the definitions themselves were incomplete and incomprehensible, and the English and French versions differed, which left room for diverse interpretations and violations.
19 Hartglass, pp. 140–1.
20 Grabski had a brother called Stanyslaw who was a prominent leader of the right and served as Minister of Education in the government of his brother Wladyslaw.
21 Moshe Landa, *A Fighting Jewish Minority: The Struggle of the Jews of Poland 1918–1928*, Zalman Shazar Center, Jerusalem 1986, pp. 193–4 (Hebrew).
22 Yisrael Halperin (ed.), *Jewry in Poland* I (see note 11); Hartglass, p. 142.
23 *Forward*, 11 June 1922. Harry Lang's article on the forthcoming 42nd congress of the AFL in Cincinatti. The writer, basing himself on the report of the organization in preparation for the congress, points out that in comparison with 1920 about one million members had left.
24 *Forward*, 20 June 1922, leading news item in the paper.
25 *Forward*, 29 March 1924.
26 *Forward*, 13 October 1926, p. 10. The paper reported on the resolution of the AFL Congress in Detroit against free immigration into the United States. The reason for this policy, given by Matthew Wall, the AFL vice-president, was that if the gates of the United States were opened the country would be swamped with masses of immigrants who would lower the wage level.

27 Usually the term "American-Jewish workers' movement" is deemed to contain four components: (1) the so-called "Jewish" trade unions in the garment industry such as the ILGWU and the ACWA, etc.; (2) the AR (*Arbeiter Ring* or Workmen's Circle); (3) the Jewish Socialist Federation and later the *Farband*, namely the Jewish autonomous framework within the all-American Socialist Party, the SP; and (4) the *Forward* Corporation, with all its economic branches.

28 *Forward*, 13 October 1926. At the Detroit congress, the ILGWU, and also the unions of the hat and cap makers and the millinery workers, submitted draft resolutions demanding that the congress support an easing of the immigration laws; *Forward* of 17 January 1924, p. 1, published that the UHT was calling for a mass protest against the immigration decrees. On 4 January 1923 the paper reported that the *Farband* was calling for a conference of all factions of Jewish labor to decide together on counter-measures to the immigration decrees and to the difficulties that were about to be introduced into the naturalization process. Invitations to the conference were sent out by Kanin, the secretary of the *Farband*, and among the invitees mentioned were the big Jewish unions of the garment industry: ILGWU, ACWA, furriers, hatmakers, etc.; *Forward*, 9 May 1925, reported on p. 1 that at the *Arbeiter Ring* conference, criticism was leveled at the immigration decrees. The conference also allotted $50,000 to support charitable institutions in the United States and Europe; in *Forward* of 17 January 1925 in his regular column *Yiddishe interessen*, B. Razman (Dr Ben-Zion Hoffman – or as he was known by his pen-name Zivion) bitterly attacked the "quota laws."

29 *Forward*, 21 May 1925, p. 5. The information was submitted by the reporter Yosef Perl.

30 *Forward*, 29 May 1925, p. 5. The article was written by S. Galut (perhaps a pseudonym), *Forward*'s special correspondent who visited and toured Palestine. The title of the article is interesting: "*Poylishe rabeim un zaynere chassidim arbayten als farmers in Palastine*" (Polish rabbis and their followers work as farmers in Palestine).

31 *Forward*, 4 August 1925, on the first page, owing to Panken's respected status. See also the response of B. Razman (Ben-Zion Hoffman – Zivion) in the paper's issue of 8 August 1925, p. 3, in the regular feature *Yiddishe interessen*.

32 *Forward*, 8 September 1925, p. 4. David Bergelson, "*Bilder, stzenes, bagegnishen oyf dem tziyonistishen kongres in Vien.*"

33 *Forward*, 9 January 1926, p. 1. An item appeared stating that thousands of unemployed Jews in Warsaw surrounded community institutions and demanded bread; *Forward*, 25 April 1926: on p. 1 an appeal was published to the Jews of New York to send immediate aid to the Jews of Eastern Europe. Among other things, it stated that out of 2,700,000 Jews of Poland, 900,000 were starving to death. The appeal was published to instigate a

fund-raising campaign, which was conducted, for this purpose, by the JDC.

34 *The Education of Abraham Cahan*, a translation by Leon Stein, Abraham P. Conan and Lynn Davison of Cahan's Yiddish autobiography *Bleter fun Mein Leben*, the Jewish Publication Society of America, Philadelphia 1969, pp. 34–77.

35 Melech Epstein, *Profiles of Eleven*, Wayne University Press, Detroit 1965, pp. 54–5.

36 *The Education of Abraham Cahan*, pp. 158–84.

37 Ibid., pp. 58–60.

38 Ibid., p. 60; see also note 34, pp. 198–200.

39 Ibid.

40 On the Jewish workers' movement in the United States and its components, see Will Herberg, The Jewish labor movement in the United States from its first years to the First World War, *Issues in Jewish History*, no. 5, Jerusalem 1977, pp. 125ff (Hebrew). See also Will Herberg, The Jewish labor movement in the United States, *The American Jewish Year Book*, vol. 53, 1952, pp. 3–74; Robert Asher, Jewish unions and the American Federation of Labor power structure 1903–1935, *American Jewish Historical Quarterly*, vol. 66, nos 1–4, September 1975 to June 1976, pp. 215–28.

41 *The Education of Abraham Cahan*, pp. 205–7. Also, Albert Waldinger, Abraham Cahan and Palestine, Jewish Social Studies, vol. 39, 1977, pp. 75–93.

42 Waldinger; also Epstein, *Profiles of Eleven*, pp. 96–104.

43 *Forward*, on dates given.

44 *Forward*, 2 December 1925.

45 Waldinger, p. 75; *Forward*, 1 December 1925; *Davar*, 21 October 1925, p. 1, reports on a departure celebration held on 20 October 1925 for Cahan by the Executive Committee of the Histadrut.

46 Dan Giladi, The *Yishuv at the Time of the Fourth Aliya*, Sifriya Universitayit-Am Oved, Tarbut Vehinukh, Tel Aviv 1973, pp. 36–9, 41–5 (Hebrew).

47 Ibid., pp. 39–41.

48 Ibid., pp. 41–5.

49 Waldinger, p. 75.

50 Hyman J. Fliegel, *The Life and Times of Max Pine*, Hyman J. Fliegel, New York 1959, pp. 33–4.

51 *Davar*, 27 September 1925; *Do'ar Hayom*, under the headline "The Arrival of Abe Cahan." The short item also reported that the previous morning, 26 September, Abe Cahan and his wife had arrived from Egypt. At the Lydda railway station they were met by Avraham Hartzfeld and Sofia Yudin. Cahan arrived on Saturday and was scheduled to remain for a month. On Wednesday [30 September] the Histadrut Executive was due to hold a special session in honor of the visitor.

52 *Minutes of Meetings of the Histadrut Executive*, vol. 6, 1925: 24 September,

section 2, pp. 232–3; and 12 October 1925, section 4, p. 246 (Hebrew).

53 *Ha'aretz*, 21 September 1925, p. 9, article headed "Abe Cahan." See also *Ha'aretz*, 4 (5) October 1925, p. 4, article headed "In Jaffa and in Tel Aviv" and the front page, article headed "Editor of the New York *Forward* at the Histadrut Executive."

54 *Ha'aretz*, 13 October 1925, p. 4, article headed "Visit of Abe Cahan to the Jordan Valley."

55 *Do'ar Hayom*, 29 September 1925, p. 2, article headed "Abe Cahan (on the Occasion of his Arrival in the Country)."

56 *Do'ar Hayom*, 12 October 1925, p. 4, article headed "Abe Cahan's Feast." The reference is to the reception arranged by the Histadrut for Cahan on Wednesday 30 September 1925, at the Bank Hapoalim building in Tel Aviv.

57 Y. S-R. (Yitzhak Soker – Yitzhak Lufban), *Hapo'el Hatza'ir*, 21 October 1925, no. 3–4, p. 16, "Notes," item 3, Abe Cahan.

58 *Forward*, 23 October 1925, p. 4; *Davar*, 1 October 1925, p. 1; in *Davar* the item is by a reporter and the quotations were apparently translated by him from Yiddish, in which Cahan delivered his speech, into Hebrew. Hence these are not first-hand citations; see also Waldinger, p. 87, noting that he takes the *Davar* report, which I cite, as his source.

59 Waldinger, Also in *Forward* and *Davar*.

60 Ibid., (both sources). This is not a direct quotation but is taken from the article by S. Galut, the *Forward* correspondent then in Palestine, who cited Cahan's words in the paper from a speech he made at a reception held in his honor by the Histadrut Executive (note 56 above), the first official meeting. See also *Forward*, 11 November 1925.

61 *Forward*, 25 November 1925. The articles are in Yiddish and also in the English supplement of the newspaper.

62 *Forward*, 4, 23 October 1925; *Davar*, 1 October 1925.

63 *Hapo'el Hatza'ir*, no. 3–4, 21 October 1925, p. 16, Y. S-R. (Yitzhak Soker – Yitzhak Lufban), "Notes," item 3, Abe Cahan; *Forward*, 23 October 1925.

64 *Forward*, 3, 4, 6, 8 October, 7 November, 19 December 1925; *Davar*, 1 October 1925.

65 *Davar*, 16 October 1925, p. 3.

66 *Forward*, 14 December 1925.

67 *Forward*, 13 October 1925, 2 December 1925. The communists were ejected from the Histadrut and were of no importance in Palestine.

68 *Forward*, 10 November, 20 November 1925, 2 December 1925.

69 *Forward*, 11 November 1925.

70 *Forward*, 14 December 1925.

71 *Forward*, 15 December 1925.

72 *Forward*, 7 May 1925, p. 4.

73 *Forward*, 14 December 1925.

74 *Forward*, 15 December 1925.

75 *Forward*, 16 December 1925; 6 May 1925, p. 4; 7 May 1925. Cahan sharply

admonished his Bundist colleagues, and unlike them he believed that one should not go to extremes in estimating the importance of economic factors in fashioning the life of the individual and society. For all the importance of these factors, there operated, in the individual and in society, additional powerfully influential elements. Cahan argued that this basic assumption was acceptable in society and in socialism: "*Di ekonomishe lehre iz richtig, ober zi iz nit altz. Der mensh beshtet nit in gantzen nor fun ekonomike.*"

76   *Forward*, 2, 15 December 1925. As stated, Cahan formed the impression that the Arabs did not pose any danger to the Yishuv. From afar the danger seemed greater than from nearby. The Arabs enjoyed a wealth of improvements that the Jews had brought; they understood this, and therefore displayed friendship to the Jews. He himself observed this manifestation at every turn. Even if riots broke out, the Jewish youth were ready for them, and presumably Britain would prevent such events.

77   *Forward*, 13, 26 November, 15 December 1925.

78   *Forward*, 23 October 1925; *Davar*, 1 October 1925.

79   *Forward*, 26 November 1925.

80   *Forward*, 6 May 1925, 2 December 1925, p. 4.

81   *Forward*, 3 December 1925.

82   *Forward*, 14 December 1925.

83   Ibid.

84   *Forward*, 6 May 1925.

85   *Forward*, 7 May 1925.

86   *Forward*, 2 December 1925; *Davar*, 21 September 1925.

87   Yonathan Shapiro, The deepening rootedness of the Jews of America: The transition from Zionism to Palestinism, *Issues in Jewish History*, no. 5, Jerusalem 1977, pp. 173ff (Hebrew). See also Yonathan Shapiro, *Leadership of the American Zionist Organization 1897–1930*, Chicago and London 1971, pp. 195–6. "Information and propaganda of the Zionist movement dealt only with the subject of Palestine, the extensive Zionist literature of the time, and also Palestinian journalism. Zionism and the settlement in Palestine became synonymous terms."

88   *Forward*, 11 November 1925, p. 7: "There are many who have no interest in Zionism, but they would be interested in Palestinism."

89   *Forward*, 8, 13 October, 7 November, 9 December 1925, 6, 10 May 1926.

90   Melech Epstein, *Jewish Labor in the USA 1914–1952*, Trade Union Sponsoring Committee, New York 1953, vol. 2, pp. 409–10. Also Melech Epstein, *Profiles of Eleven*, p. 106; Waldinger, pp. 75–7. Also *Forward*, 14 January 1926 reported on its front page the arrival of a Histadrut delegation consisting of Yitzhak Ben-Zvi, David Remez and Yosef Baratz (later Avraham Hartzfeld joined them). The delegation arrived on 13 January 1926, its purpose being to assist the Histadrut fund-raising campaign and to approximate the American labor movement to that in Palestine. The delegation visited Cahan at the *Forward* offices and Ben-Zvi reviewed before the

newspapermen events in Palestine. On that day, that is, 14 January 1926, the paper reported, there was to be an official reception for the delegation at the Cooper Union Hall, at which Wedgewood, Pine, Feinstone, Abramson, Max Zuckerman, Shiplacoff, Schlossberg, Baruch Zuckerman, etc., were to speak.

This was the first time that the paper gave such wide coverage, and on the front page, to the Histadrut fund-raising campaign and the Histadrut delegation. The issue of 15 January 1926 printed, again on the front page, another extensive report on the opening ceremony of the campaign at a large gathering at the Cooper Union Hall. It was reported that the campaign was opened by UHT chairman Abramson and that Pine chaired the meeting.

In its 1 March 1926 issue, *Forward* reported on the UHT meeting on 15 February 1926, at which Abramson reviewed the good progress of the Histadrut campaign. He said that in Chicago there appeared at the campaign meeting "both the secretary of the national Socialist Party Kirkpatrick and the party leader, Eugene V. Debs. Both gave their blessing to the campaign." The appearance itself of these two gave official recognition and support of the SP to the Histadrut campaign, that is, to the Palestine labor movement.

91 As is known, in May 1901 at the Fourth Congress in Bialystok, the Bund resolved to demand that Russia be turned into a "federation of nations, each one of which will have full national autonomy, independently, on the territory in which it dwells. The Congress recognizes that the term 'nation' also applies to the Jewish people." From the time this resolution was adopted, the Bund stood for national-cultural autonomy for the Jewish community in Russia, to be founded on Yiddish language and culture. See Shmuel Ettinger, *History of the Jewish People in Modern Times*, Tel Aviv 1969, pp. 195–7 (Hebrew).

92 B. Charney-Vladek, *Forward* 9 January 1926.

93 Zivion, *Forward*, 28–9 December 1925.

94 Idem, *Far Funftzik Yor Geklibene Shriften*, New York 1949, Introduction, p. xxxviii.

95 Ibid., p. xi; B. Charney-Vladek, *Forward*, 9 January 1926.

96 J. Panken, *Forward*, 6 February 1926, p. 6; J. Lestchinsky, *Forward*, 20 February 1926, p. 8; D. Einhorn, *Forward*, 8 March 1926, p. 8.

97 Zivion, *Forward*, 28–29 December 1925.

98 Ibid.

99 Ibid.; B. Charney-Vladek, *Forward*, 9 January 1926.

100 Zivion, *Forward*, 28–29 December 1925; S. Rabinowitz, *Forward*, 22 March 1926, p. 8; A. Litvak, *Forward*, 3 January 1926, and also 23 January 1926, pp. 7–8; D. Einhorn, *Forward*, 8 March 1926, p. 8.

101 Zivion, *Forward*,; Litvak, *Forward*, 23 January 1926, pp. 7–8.

102 Zivion, *Forward*, *Yiddishe interessen*, 19 June 1926.

103 Zivion, *Forward*, 28–29 December 1925; B. Charney-Vladek, *Forward*, 9

January 1926; A. Litvak, *Forward*, 3 Janaury 1926.

104 J. Panken, *Forward*, 6 February 1926, p. 6; J. Lestchinsky, *Forward*, 20 February 1926, p. 8.

105 Zivion, *Forward*, 8 August 1925.

106 *Forward, Yiddishe interessen*, 13 September 1924.

107 *Forward, Yiddishe interessen*, 21 February 1925, 20 June 1925, 3 July 1926.

108 *Forward*, 28–29 December 1925.

109 B. Charney-Vladek, *Forward*, 9 January 1926.

110 A. Litvak, *Forward*, 3 January 1926, his lecture before the *Farband* conference, entitled "Palestine and the Jewish settlement in Russia." Also 23 January 1926, pp. 7–8; J. Panken, *Forward*, 6 February 1926.

111 Zivion, *Forward*, 28–29 December 1925; J. Panken,*Forward*, 6 February 1926, p. 6; D. Einhorn,*Forward*, 8 March 1926, p. 8.

112 Zivion,*Forward*., 28–29 December 1925; A. Litvak, *Forward*, 23 January 1926; S. Rabinowitz, *Forward*, 22 March 1926, p. 8; Weinberg, *Forward*, 3 Janaury 1926; B. Charney-Vladek, *Forward*, 9 January 1926.

113 *Forward*, 3, 4 January 1926. The text of the resolution appeared in the issue of 8 January 1926, p. 8.

114 Melech Epstein, *Profiles of Eleven*, p. 222.

115 Irvin Yellowitz, Morris Hillquit: American socialism and Jewish concerns, *American Jewish History*, vol. 68, no. 2, 163–88, December 1978. An *American Jewish Historical Society Quarterly publication*.

116 Ibid.

117 *Forward*, 25 May 1924, p. 3: "I am quite in sympathy with those who stand for strengthening the sense of Jewish independence and of national dignity."

118 *Forward*, 18 April 1926 in the English supplement.

119 Ibid.

120 M. Pine, *Forward*, 2 January 1926; A. Kahn, *Forward*, 27 February 1926, p. 7.

121 Hayman I. Fliegel, *The Life and Times of Max Pine*, New York 1959, pp.25–31.

122 A. Kahn, *Forward*, 27 February 1926, p. 7.

123 M. Pine, *Forward*, 2 January 1926.

124 H. Rogoff, *Forward*, 30 January 1926, p. 8; Dr I. Ginsburg, *Forward*, 15 January 1926, p. 4; S. Broyland, *Forward*, 14 February 1926, p. 4. The last stressed the process of assimilation being experienced by the Jews of the United States and the abandonment of Yiddish. She was very pessimistic about the future of that language, but not about Hebrew. Broyland mentioned the debate that had taken place not long before on the future of the Yiddish schools of the AR in which all the debaters reached the conclusion that with the closure of the gates of the United States to Jewish immigration "the death sentence has been passed on Yiddish language and culture in the United States." The writer reached a clearcut conclusion: If

the Jewish people wanted to survive they, like every nation, needed a language and culture of their own, a farming class and a territorial base from which they could not be expelled. For her, this place was only Palestine despite its shortcomings.

125 M. Pine, *Forward*, 2 January 1926; A. Kahn, *Forward*, 27 February 1926, p. 7; Dr. C. Spivak, *Forward*, 13 March 1926, p. 7. The last believed that the love of the people of Israel for the Land of Israel, enduring for thousands of years, was a fact beyond all pragmatic considerations. If the Jews functioned solely through logic and considerations of practicality and efficiency they should long ago have assimilated and the people should have disappeared. In light of this he preferred "wisdom of the heart" to "wisdom of the mind."

126 A. Kahn, *Forward*, 27 February 1926, p. 7.

127 M. Pine, *Forward*, 2 January 1926.

128 Ibid.

129 H. Rogoff, *Forward*, 30 January 1926, p.7–8.

130 Dr I. Ginsburg, *Forward*, 15 January 1926, p. 4, and continuation on 16 January 1926, p. 8; M. Pine, *Forward*, 2 January 1926.

131 H. Rogoff, *Forward.*, 30 January 1926, pp. 7–8; S. Broyland, *Forward*, 14 February 1926, p. 4; M. Pine, *Forward*, 2 January 1926; A. Kahn, *Forward*, 27 February 1926.

132 *Forward*, 13 May 1918.

133 A. Liessin, *Der englisher mandat oyf Eretz-Yisroel* (The British Mandate over Palestine). In the monthly *Di Zukunft*, September 1922, ed. by A. Liessin, Publication of the *Forward* Corporation, New York.

134 A. Liessin, *Selected Writings*, Book I: *Remembrances and Experiences*. Am Oved, 1943, selected by Berl Katznelson and translated by A. Kariv (Hebrew). See there the article, Palestine and the Diaspora, July 1926, pp. 227–37.

Individuals and Institutions

Cahan, Abraham (1860–1951)   Born in White Russia, only son of a Hebrew teacher. From 1878 studied four years at teachers' training college in Vilna. During his studies became involved in revolutionary activity. On completing studies in 1881 worked as a teacher for some time. For fear of arrest fled Russia and migrated to US. En route became attached to the Am Olam group, but immediately on reaching US parted from them. Lived and was active in New York almost all his life. Married, no children. Active in the American Socialist Party in its various manifestations. Was a rebel against the leadership of Daniel De Leon and a founder of the new socialist party, SP, in 1901 under leadership of Eugene Debs. A founder of *Forward* in 1897. Omnipotent editor of the paper and head of its commercial corporation almost all his life, hence his great influence on Jewish life generally and American-Jewish socialism in particular. Had great ambitions in literary field and published many stories and books including autobiography.

Charney-Vladek, Baruch (1886–1939)   Born in a village in Minsk district of Russia. Orphaned at early age. Studied in *heder* and yeshiva, but was drawn to the secular world. In 1904 was arrested in Minsk, and in prison his socialist education matured; there too he formed connection with the Bund, which he joined. Was immediately conspicuous by political activity, many talents, and especially rhetorical power, therefore nicknamed "the young Lassalle." "Vladek" was his underground name but he became well known by it, and so he adopted it as his own. In 1907 was Bund delegate to Russian SD conference in London, and there supported Bolsheviks. Because of political activity was forced to flee Russia, and migrated to US, arriving December 1908. In 1911 married Clara Richmann, with whom he had 3 children. Directed *Forward* office in Philadelphia for several years, while also active in SP and studying at University of Pennsylvania. Acquired US citizenship in 1915. In 1916 moved to New York as city editor of the paper. In 1917 was elected to Williamsburg local council in Brooklyn. Won all-American status in American Socialist Party and in American trade unions. Was a fierce opponent of communism in 1920s. Was among the foremost activists of JDC and HIAS. Was involved in construction of workers' housing in Bronx and Manhattan. In 1934 New York mayor La Guardia appointed him director of urban housing. From 1932 was president of ORT. In

1934 tried to influence AFL to identify politically with those persecuted by fascism and Nazism. Was vital spirit in founding of Jewish Labor Committee in February 1934 as united front of workers for war against Nazism-fascism in Europe. In 1936 toured Europe and Palestine. In 1937 was elected to New York municipality.

Einhorn, David (b. 1886)   Poet, publicist and writer of children's stories. Born in White Russia. First wrote his poems in Hebrew, but influenced by socialist ideas he changed to Yiddish. Among the first rank of lyric poets who wrote in Yiddish. Published prolifically in Russia in journals of the Bund, of which he was a member. His first collections of poems were published in 1909 and 1912. Arrested in 1912 and imprisoned for six months for his clandestine political connections. Was obliged to leave Russia because of his political activities. Lived in Switzerland, then moved to Warsaw. In 1920 took up residence in Berlin, and some years later moved to Paris, where he lived until the Nazi invasion of France in 1940. Was writer for *Forward*. Fled from France to the US in 1940, and settled in New York, where he continued his literary publicist activity.

Pine, Max (1866–1928)   A Jewish socialist leader. Born in Lubavitch in White Russia. Orphaned at age three. From childhood worked as printer's apprentice. In 1886 migrated to US and after working at various jobs entered the garment industry where he became active in organizing trade unions. By mid-1890s Pine was a well-known figure in Jewish socialism. Was among those who rebelled against the leadership of Daniel De Leon in SLP. A founder of *Forward*. From 1906 onwards was several times Secretary of UHT. In World War I was active on People's Relief Committee (PRC), and its representative to the JDC. The first among the socialist leaders to become harnessed to supporting the Histadrut in Palestine. Organized and headed the Histadrut Appeal from 1923 until his death.

Forward   Jewish Yiddish daily, published in New York. Founded in 1897 by a group of Jewish socialists who split from Socialist Party (SLP) in defiance of leadership of Daniel De Leon. For many years the paper was edited and its course shaped by Abraham Cahan. Grew to mass circulation and was of rare influence in the Jewish community in presenting a moderate socialist line and in being the forum of masses of immigrants from eastern Europe. The paper also established a commercial company of much activity and many resources, which encompassed a large group of Jewish personalities of stature in socialism and Jewish trade unions. For many years *Forward* took indifferent or hostile position on Zionism. The *Forward* Corporation, centered on the paper, acquired great economic power and this gave it additional influence over Jewish socialist life and the Jewish street.

Ginsburg, Dr Isser (1872–1947)   Born in Kovno region in Lithuania to a poor family. Studied at Vilkomir and Vilna yeshivas. From an early age was drawn to

Haskalah literature. At 16 he turned to socialism, and was influenced by Bund founders and leaders (Arkady Kremer, Mendel Rosenbaum, and others). Taught Hebrew and Yiddish literature. In 1891 migrated to the US. In 1900 completed medical studies at Cornell University. From early age published in the newspaper *Hamelitz*. In US became a professional journalist and newspaper editor. Regular and leading contributor to *Forward*.

Hillquit, Morris (1869–1933)　Born in Riga, Latvia. Family name originally Hilcowitz. Mother tongue and education German. From secondary school level received Russian education. Grew up bilingual and had a cosmopolitan world outlook. In 1886, at age 17, migrated with his family to US. Began life there as worker in the garment industry. Was a founder of UHT in October 1888. Qualified as attorney in 1903. Was among the first and outstanding heads of the SP, in which he led the mainstream. Was candidate for various public offices on behalf of SP. Except for his early years did not participate in Jewish public life despite drawing most of his political strength from Jewish support.

Kahn, Alexander (1881–1962)　Jurist and socialist leader. Born in Smilansk. Arrived in US in 1893. A founder of *Forward* and its legal adviser. From 1939 was general manager of the paper. An activist in American Socialist Party and its candidate for various public positions. A founder of the Liberal Party of New York State and its vice-president. Very active in Jewish affairs. A founder of the JDC and vice-president of the organization.

Lestchinsky, Jacob (1876–1966)　A foremost scholar in sociology, economics and demography of the Jewish people. Born in Ukraine. In his youth was influenced by Ahad Ha'am and was a member of Beney Moshe. Studied at universities of Bern and Zurich. Was active in propagation of socialist-Zionist ideas. Delegate to Sixth Zionist Congress in Basel, where he became a territorialist. A founder of the territorialist Socialist Zionist Party (SS) in Russia. After 1906 concentrated principally on academic activity. Left Russia in 1921 to settle in Berlin, became correspondent of *Forward*, with which he remained connected until his death. Author of many works in his specialty. After rise of Nazis to power in 1933 was expelled by them from Germany. In 1934 settled in Warsaw but was deported from Poland in 1937 after publishing material on the hard circumstances of Polish Jewry. In 1938 migrated to US, settled in New York where he worked and published. In 1959 immigrated to Israel, and lived in Tel Aviv. In 1964 moved to Jerusalem, where he lived until his death.

Litvak, Abraham (Chayim Yankl Helfand) (1874–1932)　A leader of the Bund, educator and publicist. Born in Vilna. Poor working-class origins. Studied at *heder* and yeshiva. Active in the Bund from early age. Brought to his party work all the weight of his knowledge in Yiddish literature and culture. Belonged to nationalist wing of the Bund. Was more prominent in the Bund in educational, publicist sphere than in political sphere. Spent much time in prison in Russia because of his activity. Migrated to US in 1911. Was one of the few Jewish socialist intellectuals who returned to Russia after the 1917 revolution. Rejected Bolshevik doctrine so left Russia for Poland. There (together with Vladimir Medem) was in serious conflict with Polish Bund which negated his anti-communist stance. Again migrated to US in 1925. Was highly active in the Workmen's Circle (AR), and the Jewish socialist wing of SP, the *Farband*.

Panken, Jacob (1879–1968) Judge and socialist leader. Born in Ukraine. Arrived in US as a child. Worked in leather industry in New York and studied at night. In 1905 qualified as attorney. In 1917 was appointed judge in City Court of New York, and held this position until 1928. In 1934 was appointed judge at Court of Internal Affairs, a position he held for 20 years. From his youth was active in workers' movement. A founder of Ladies Garment Workers Union in 1900. Was shot by Mafia in 1904 and attacked again by it in 1906 because of his activity in organizing workers. Active in SP and in Jewish affairs. A founder of the PRC, and a founder of American ORT and its president for many years. President of *Forward* from 1917 to 1925.

Rogoff, Harry (Hillel) (1883–1971) Writer and publicist. Born in Minsk district in Russia. Reached US with parents in 1893. In 1906 began career as journalist, publicist and a leading member of *Forward* editorial board. Editor-in-chief of paper from Cahan's death in 1951 until retirement in 1962. Also published several books, including a history of the US in Yiddish.

Part One

The Telegrams and Articles of Abraham (Abe) Cahan Appearing in *Forward* in Order of Publicaton Date

New York, Sunday, 4 October 1925
1.   **Palestine: A Different World**
Tel Aviv, 2 October

Today is my eighth day in Palestine. I spent five days in Jerusalem and this is my third day in Tel Aviv. There are many things to hear and see here. Life is different from what I imagined and expected to find. Everything here is in a state of change. Every month, every week, brings about innovations not only regarding physical, external objects and colors, but also in the area of the facts and problems that arise concerning the near and distant future.

I have talked to many people, especially factory owners, businessmen and bankers, who understand the present economic situation, and are well acquainted with potential economic opportunities. Yesterday evening, for example, I spent five hours asking questions and hearing answers from one of the biggest silk industrialists in Tel Aviv, Mr Dalpiner, who came from Vienna and invested considerable sums in silk transactions. I also had a short talk, and then arranged to meet for a more thorough conversation, with Mr Halperin, the Director of the Anglo-Palestine Company, who impressed me as a man with broad horizons and good intentions. He understands the economic situation of Palestine very well, better than others. I also spoke with representatives of three more banks, many factory owners and people already in business and others planning to start.

In the economic domain the special status of the trade unions is remarkable. There is a system here by which the trade unions themselves are building contractors, so it turns out that they are the contractors and the building workers at one and the same time. Everything is done on a cooperative basis. The system is special and interesting, and important to observe and learn. Naturally, I met the trade union leaders, two of whom, who are very familiar with the situation, gave me two days of their time. With them I discussed the workers' situation and from this many things that are incomprehensible for an outsider became clear to me.

Generally it may be said that a quiet struggle is taking place here between two trends. One represents the finest idealism and the loftiest goals of the workers and of progressive nationalism. The other is material in nature. This is a conflict between the pragmatic-economic world on the one hand and numerous workers' and Zionist factors on the other, with a different approach. The idealistic-ideological aspirations have taken on the character of a sort of new Jewish religion.

The future of Palestine lies in industry, with attempts being made to establish it in Tel Aviv, and in the cooperative agricultural settlements, which, I was told, are developing extraordinarily in the Jezreel Valley and the Haifa area. Perhaps in the future a way will be found to merge the two tendencies mentioned above into a single firm trend. Various commentators hold that the basic question in Palestine is the quality of the life being built here, and what future development will be like. From my discussions and my studying the situation I reached the same conclusion.

It would not be proper for me to reach final conclusions already because I have only just begun to learn what is taking place here. However, I have planned my program and taken the first steps to carry it out.

Meanwhile I have seen many things of interest to our readers; for example, the city of Jerusalem, rich in colors, in scenes, and which provides enormous attraction for a journalist. Everything I saw in the Old City of Jerusalem touched my heart and moved me. I have described these in several articles that will appear later in *Forward* . . . that I sent by mail. Unfortunately, because of the mail they will reach New York later on and cannot appear before the end of the month; or Tel Aviv, a new city that grew up overnight, filled with color and scenes. It is a far different city from what I imagined till now. Everybody talks about it but few people really know it. Later on I will describe the city for readers in a number of articles, but before that I will do so in some telegrams.

The whole day was taken up by meetings. It is Friday today, and the mail and the telegram office will close soon because of Sabbath Eve. As I understand it, Friday night is entirely different from in New York, and even from what it used to be like in the townships in our countries of origin. Here everything is completely different from what we are accustomed to. I came to Palestine with a single-minded resolution to describe all the shades of life and each and every corner honestly. For this purpose

I must undertake hard work, many journeys, including some to remote settlements, and repeated visits to Jerusalem, Haifa, and Tel Aviv. Despite the great burden the task is incomparably enthralling. I wish to find out everything so as to get deep down into the problems and understand the situation correctly. All this is without preconceptions and standing firm against influences of any self-interested elements, groups and parties.

It has to be kept in mind that each of the interviewees answers the questions presented to him from a biased viewpoint. Therefore, caution is needed and I have to know whom I am talking to and what the person represents. It is necessary to rise above subjective positions in order to understand the real circumstances properly. As for me, I shall do everything in this direction.

New York, Tuesday, 6 October 1925
2. A Jewish Immigrant Ship from Russia
Tel Aviv, 5 October

Yesterday the ship *Lenin* arrived from Odessa carrying 371 immigrants from the cities and small towns of Russia. I received permission to go aboard, and I spent five hours on the ship. I sat at a table with the immigrants and the immigration officials as these examined the immigrants before allowing them to set foot on land. I heard and saw extremely important things concerning the very heart of the phenomenon of immigration to Palestine, including the current tragedy of the Jewish people. All these matters touch the heart and are also of great historical importance. For me this was a special opportunity to learn . . .

The scenes I witnessed on the immigrant ship that had arrived from Soviet Russia, and also at the Immigration Office, reminded me of similar scenes at Ellis Island in New York when the immigrants reach there. It also reminded me of the fact that America is closed to immigrants, and these unfortunates are like drowning people clutching at straws. They would escape to any place where they might find a glimmer of hope and a chance, even the tiniest, of finding a home where it would be possible for them to exist.

A considerable part of the immigrants were Zionists motivated by love and belief in Palestine. These, incidentally, spoke fluent Hebrew and answered in that language the questions they were asked by the immigration officials. Regarding the other immigrants, they obviously would have gone to America if its gates were not closed. It has to be stressed that many of those on board the *Lenin* came by virtue of a request by their sons, their daughters, or their relatives living here.

The desk for examining the immigrants stood on the top deck, and as the ship was anchored not far offshore, I could see the crowd of relatives and the Jews who had come to welcome their dear ones. A huge iron gate separates Jaffa port from the town itself. On that day only the officials were allowed to enter the port because it is small and if everyone were allowed in it would be impossible to go on with disembarkation. Therefore, the sons, the daughters, the brothers and the sisters waited outside the gate. A few of them climbed onto the roofs of the low office buildings while others jostled around the gate. Almost everyone was dressed in white, because it is still hot here, like New York in July, although the air is better and its is even quite cool in the shade. While I was sitting and listening to the replies of the immigrants who had arrived with the *Lenin*, and scanned their faces, I sometimes could not tear my eyes away from the throng of impatient relatives, wearing white, standing in the distance. They stood like that all day long and many of them did not eat a thing throughout that entire long day.

The sea was a lovely azure color, like the sky. Tel Aviv could be seen far off, with its low white buildings, and before it a strip of yellow ground separating it from the sea. The cluster of old grey houses on the seashore is Jaffa, which is, so to speak, the forepart of Tel Aviv. A great British warship stood in the port, and eight other ships were anchored alongside each other.

The harbor lighters, rowed by Arabs, plied incessantly between the ships and the shore. All this created a marvelous setting for what was going on at the tables where the immigrants were being examined by the British officials, and also by Yehoshua Gordon and his chief assistant, Mr Fineberg, in charge of the Immigration Office of the Zionist Administration. Some of the immigrants had embarked at Odessa as deportees, that is, they had been expelled by the Soviet authorities because of their activity in the Zionist movement. It was registered in their passports that they were forbidden to return to Russia. One man said that he was an employed carpenter but they had fired him from his job because they heard him speaking Hebrew. One old Jew was asked how he occupied himself and to this he answered with, nothing. When they kept on asking him what he had worked at in the past he answered in another way, and then they had taken everything from him. There were others who gave the immigration officials similar replies. One smiled, with tears in his eyes, when he related how everything had been taken away from him. A young man, when asked what was his profession in Russia, replied that he was an undesirable student, and when asked how he had got into that situation he answered that his father was registered with the authorities as a bourgeois.

A woman of about 40 had come from Russia to marry a man of 67 whom she had never seen. Her future husband lived in America and the connection between them had been established through correspondence; he had come to Tel Aviv, and the wedding was to be held at the office of the American Consul there, and then they would sail for America.

The case of the family that was held up from disembarking because the child had typhus was heartrending. Another family was also kept on board because it was not clear who would provide for an elderly father. In both these cases there was some hope that the families would eventually be allowed to land because the child was already in the final stages of recuperation, and there was hope of a solution for the old man. The Zionists spare no effort to help people in such circumstances.

A young man whom I met after he had gone ashore told me that almost every Jew would escape from Communist Russia if only there was somewhere to go. The youth spoke bitterly of the Communists in Russia, most of whom, he thought, were careerists who would have served the Tsar or any other regime. Of course, there were also idealists among them, but they were few. Corruption in the state was very widespread. In his view, everyone believed that Soviet Russia would turn into a state of peasants and a lower middle class.

Among the immigrants there were various types, and I also encountered touching situations that I will describe in a separate article. Many immigrants had the required sum of £500 ($2500), either in APC cheques or in other currency. One man even had £800. In many cases the money had apparently come from relatives who had deposited it for their kinsman. In other cases the money had been obtained through loans. The mandatory government believed that if the immigrants had £500 they could be relied upon to manage.

When asked about the occupations of their relatives in Tel Aviv, most of the immigrants replied that they were building workers. At the moment this is the most important branch in Tel Aviv. Some said that their relatives worked in factories, or in shops, or that they were teachers, musicians, and so on.

Tomorrow a Polish ship is due to arrive, and I shall go aboard her too. There the scenes and circumstances will probably be different. I took part in a large and interesting workers' meeting on the seashore. Many of the audience sat on the sand. I am also interviewing workers' leaders, representatives of various official bodies, bankers and factory owners: practical people and idealists of all varieties.

I met Ahad Ha'am, Bialik, Shemaryahu Levin, Colonel Kisch, and other prominent figures. Ahad Ha'am is old and sick. The street where he lives is closed to traffic to stop the noise. The man is elderly and kindly. Bialik looks younger than his years. A very interesting man. He has a magnetism that you sense at once.

The situation here is very interesting and full of extraordinary things. I have spoken to a lot of young people and I have witnessed many diverse circumstances. This week I am going to visit the agricultural settlements, where many matters have to be studied, which I will describe in telegrams and articles. The Palestine problem has two dimensions and each of these has many additional aspects and directions. First of all it is necessary to go deeply into all the issues in order to gain an understanding of them, and then it will be possible to take a position. Tomorrow I shall send a long telegram.

New York, Wednesday, 7 October 1925
3. The Situation of the Jews in Russia
Tel Aviv, 6 October

I meant to send a telegram to describe a certain aspect of Tel Aviv life, but before that I must spend time on another problem, referring to the dominant feelings at present in the Jews of Russia about the Jewish settlement in Crimea; I will write about Tel Aviv separately.

I spent three hours with the immigrants from Odessa who were held in detention for a day or two. I spoke with many of them. To tell the truth, they talked to me more than I talked to them because their heartache was overflowing. Some among them had a wide education, and the others too were very interesting. They longed to talk about the situation in Russia to ease the burden on their hearts. We spoke of many things, among them the subject of the Jewish settlement in Crimea.

From the conversations the predominant feelings among the Jews of Russia about this settlement became clear to me. Their position may be described as follows: they hope that the enterprise will have positive results and they bless the Jews of America who are providing assistance. One of the immigrants even knew that our comrades and *Forward* support the Jewish settlement project in Crimea, and he voiced his satisfaction with this. The Jews of Russia see the settlement project as a rescue operation from the dreadful conditions to which they are subject, from the impending catastrophe. Yet they have anxieties and fears about the future of the project.

"Let's hope," they say, "that our brothers will indeed be allowed to work the land and enjoy the fruits of their labor." They are concerned about the policy of the Soviet government, which may repossess the farms whenever it sees fit. In their opinion, the Jews of America are doing good work by raising funds to help the Jewish settlement in Crimea. Perhaps the Soviet government will not dare to cancel the project, but the heart is laden with anxiety. Apart from that, the immigrants said, it is impossible to know what the Russian peasants will do; there have been some bitter experiences with them.

Some immigrants interrupted each other, all of them wanting to tell their sad story. An immigrant from Zhitomir related that the Jews there had got some land, and on this basis they set up a cooperative. They gathered fodder but the peasants burned it and threatened the Jews with a pogrom. Generally, anti-Semitism among the peasants and among the Communists in the cities is very strong. "We are living on a volcano," the immigrants said; "at the same time, the settlement plan in Crimea is the best that can be done for our Jewish brothers who have nowhere to go. *Forward*, the Jewish socialists, and the trade unionists," they asserted, "deserve the highest praise for their support for the project."

They all were of the opinion that the present economic policy of the Russian government was more favorable for commerce. A considerable number of Jews had small shops, and they were trying to survive. But the great masses in the cities and towns were in a terrible situation, so the transition to farming in Crimea could be a blessing for them, if one could believe in the future of the enterprise.

In one group there was a young man who attacked the JDC because it raised millions for the Crimea settlement instead of Palestine, but the others silenced him.

On the subject of life in Russia a woman said that "apart from the oppression and despotism it is impossible to bear the constant fear of the Cheka. You're afraid of your own shadow and you can go mad with this endless terror."

New York, Thursday, 8 October 1925
4. The *Halutzim* (pioneers), Builders of Palestine. Problems of Yiddish and the Influence of the Religious People
Tel Aviv, 7 October

Speaking of Palestine, one must not confuse two things: on the one hand there are opportunities and changes of the future, and on the other is a lofty spirit regarding Palestine that prevails here in most people, but chiefly among the youth; these are two separate matters. What chance has the Jewish National Home in Palestine, and what is to be the character of this national home? This subject has to be studied and clarified well. I have immersed myself in this task, as far as my powers will allow, with love and vigor.

Meanwhile, I am not yet in a position to finalize my views. This, I hope, will happen later, when I have completed my work here. Everyone, regardless of outlook, must admit to the existence of the elevation of spirit. I have to confess that the enthusiasm present in most people far outstrips anything I read or imagined. The high morale is readily felt everywhere, and it is a particularly salient factor.

The masses of Jewish workers and farmers burn with the fire of excitement and high spirits. A large part of these young working men and women are highly educated, even with university degrees. They include about a thousand youngsters from Germany, *Yahudim*, university graduates, and here they work as unskilled laborers, porters, builders, stonemasons or carpenters. They work excellently, and with an inner ardor that burns inside them. I watch them at work through my window or as I walk down the street. Some of the heaviest and dirtiest work is done by educated young girls. You never hear complaints or grumbling from them. When they finish their day's work they gather in the cooperative canteen or in private rooms where they debate the events of the day or the trade union problems. After supper they stream into the street outside the cooperative kitchen and sing as if their hard labor, all the troubles and the suffering of the life of the *halutz* are the Song of Songs for them.

Most of the young people wear white cotton shirts belted at the waist, and white summer hats. The girls dress simply too.

I have talked to dozens of them, sometimes for two or three hours at a time. I tried to ask how long this state of enthusiasm could last; or if certain circumstances might not completely change the elevated mood. But those people created the feeling in me that to talk to them about the facts of life and about the prosaic nature of the human being was a form of sacrilege.

Not only the young men and women of 18 and 20 but even their leaders aged 35 to 40 are under the influence of a sort of intoxication and unlimited optimism. I have met people who talk seemingly logically, and who base their views on observation and sober understanding of reality in the country, and of human motivations and instincts that cannot be escaped. But this sobriety holds only up to a certain point, after which all rationality vanishes, and they suddenly become people whom dedication to ideals makes wholly oblivious to reality and the facts of life.

The organized labor movement to which these young men and women belong occupies, in the existing circumstances, a very important place here. All the people mentioned are convinced that the Jewish National Home will be built on the foundations of physical labor and in the spirit of socialism. They speak of Eretz Israel from two aspects: this is the ancient homeland of the Jews, but concerning the future, this homeland will be erected on new foundations of freedom, brotherhood, and the loftiest of new concepts that will lead to the happiness of humankind.

Their excitement draws on two sources, the first of these, I believe, being the stronger and more comprehensible: it is the national element. Eretz Israel is the Holy Land, but they are attracted to it out of national longings and desires. Their chief goal is to turn Palestine into our homeland and our country. Palestinian socialism for them is a part of a hallowed complex, but it is of secondary importance to nationalism. National ambitions are of primary significance. They will not admit this, and also become disconcerted when the point is put to them, but this is the impression one forms.

I can understand their mentality. I cannot help but marvel at the holy spirit that burns within them, especially when I think of the causes that led to it. These are the facts.

One may wonder about the kind of opinions and deep and hidden feelings embedded in the hearts of some of them at least – opinions and feelings that they themselves are perhaps not conscious of. Obviously, all that glistens is not gold. Human nature is also complex, and fashioned, usually, out of various motivations and conflicts, conscious and unconscious. But this is another matter.

I believe that I already have much material, although perhaps not enough. I must continue learning and understanding the situation, especially in the Jezreel Valley, where the finest things created out of devotion and self-sacrifice are to be found.

All in all, before I go on with my investigations, as a result of my conversations and my observations in Tel Aviv and elsewhere, I may say with certainty that Palestine is a honeymoon country and Tel Aviv is a honeymoon city. Some of the enthusiasts overdo it somewhat, and their frenzy borders on fanaticism, for example, an organization that is committed to propagating Hebrew, and demands the penetration of that language into daily life. This group has done some stupid and despicable things. They caught Ahad Ha'am and Bialik talking Russian, and made a great fuss about it. In several cases members of the organization acted by force, coercing people to speak Hebrew who still did not know a word of the language. At the same time, the leaders and great majority of Hebrew-speakers condemn these manifestations of fanatic outbursts. I happen to hear that Russian and Yiddish are spoken freely. Still, whoever lives in Tel Aviv and, in a shop or office, wants to speak a language other than Hebrew will find himself in a tight corner. I myself saw people who found it hard to explain to an old man, in Hebrew, what they wanted, yet did not dare to speak Yiddish to him out of fear of how the other people there would react.

The accepted view among the Zionists is generally that this is the desirable situation. Their argument is, it's not so bad, anyone who does not know Hebrew should make an effort and get a taste for learning a new language; also that it won't be too hard for long. In their view, Hebrew is our language, and anyone who wants to live here must learn it. Most of the young people speak only Hebrew in the street and in public places.

I have spoken about the fanaticism of the young people, but there is also another kind of fanaticism, that of the orthodox Jews in Tel Aviv. I will leave this for next time. Here I will say only this: the number of Jews of the old type who are seen in the streets, among them young hassidim, is small. Sometimes you come across a young man of twenty in a long kaftan and long sidecurls sticking out from under the traditional hat. Here, in the midst of the stream of modern men and women who fill the searing streets, he looks very strange. The religious people are trying to obtain control of Tel Aviv, without much success.

I saw a mezuzah on the door of the police headquarters and on doors of other government buildings. I was told that this is considered something traditional and not a national symbol. The borderline between nationalism and religion is at times not clearly and sharply defined, so it is not easy to distinguish them.

On Friday, when Sabbath Eve draws close, the shofar is sounded, as in the synagogue on Rosh Hashanah. At first I thought this was the work of the city council, but Mr Bloch – the present mayor of Tel Aviv – assured me that it was done by orthodox circles and the general public made fun of it. The municipal rabbi, I was told, is a man familiar with the ways of the world.

New York, Tuesday, 13 October 1925
5. The Socialist Settlements in Palestine
Tel Aviv, 12 October

I have just arrived back in Tel Aviv after a four-day journey through the Jewish settlements of the new kind. I visited the cooperative settlements. There I saw the people at work, I ate the evening and morning meal with them, I devoted many hours to observation, to reflection, to discussion and to debate. I visited five kibbutzim. I also visited the moshavim, where the private farm predominates, but there is cooperation in various spheres and hired labour is banned.

I spent some time with the renowned rebbe from Yablonka and his hassidim. I visited their moshava and I had an interested conversation with the rebbe. He is a young and impressive rabbi, and his hassidim are impressive too, filled with the enthusiasm they brought here with them to start a new life . . .

It is important to clarify to the American reader that when one speaks of the "communist settlements" these are not to be identified with Bolshevik Communists. In the towns of Palestine, a handful of Bolsheviks are to be found who also tried to split the Histadrut, but failed abysmally.

The collective settlements constitute a vital part of the organized working community in Palestine, which embraces both urban workers and agriculturalists. These undertake any kind of work that dignifies those who perform it without exploitation and without hired labor.

The Histadrut encompasses many institutions that are unknown and would not be possible in other countries. Even if various matters are not clear from a scientific viewpoint, there can be no doubt as to the purity of intentions and the administrative competence of these institutions. The Histadrut is based on the highest ideals and its leaders are characterized by the loftiest moral goals. The Histadrut is also remarkable for its distinctly centralist structure. All the idealistic settlements mentioned, the trade unions and collective bodies in the cities constitute sections or local workers' councils of this centralist organ.

Many new things have developed in the Histadrut in recent years. In general I do not believe that people in America understand its nature. The Histadrut is affiliated to the Amsterdam International of the trade unions.

The most powerful and influential body in it sends delegates to the congress of the Second International. Ben Zvi, one of the outstanding and most talented of their members, was a delegate at the congress in Marseilles, where I met him.

It is important to note that the settlements referred to as communist are that way in the sense that they conduct a communal-cooperative life. This term has nothing to do with Russian Communism or with Soviet Russia, which is perhaps anything in the world except communal-cooperative.

The Jezreel Valley, the pride of Zionism, is part of the Histadrut and all the settlements in it, with very few exceptions, belong to it.

The Histadrut in Palestine is a mighty force and its strength is constantly growing. Its importance and influence increase from month to month. As a small example I mention only the fact that the present mayor of Tel Aviv, Bloch-Blumenfeld, is among its leaders.

Local reality has many interesting facets, which I got to know very well through observation and through lengthy discussions and debates with workers' representatives and leaders. I admit that in certain cases I did not easily get to the bottom of things. For example, it is interesting to know how a communal-cooperative settlement solves the problem of the family and the difficulties such a unit creates in the texture of its life. Such a manifestation as envy or natural daily frictions are normal among the members. Still, there are a thousand things, small and large, that might disturb the harmony of cooperative life. There are so many delicate matters that might disrupt communal-cooperative life.

When I asked these questions I would usually get abstract and theoretical replies. The replies also possessed high moral shadings, but they did not touch on harsh reality. I heard impressive speeches which demonstrated talent and ability, but they all were up in the air, and did not impinge on or deal with the hard shell of the problem. They were also miles away from human nature and real life. You would think that the cooperative settlements were not inhabited by ordinary people but only angels moved by unsullied idealism and self-sacrifice, and who in no way were mere mortals.

Nevertheless, by strenuous effort and circuitous routes I think I managed to learn the true facts that I was seeking. Of course, all this requires a wide-ranging account and full explanations, and this is impossible to accomplish through telegrams. Therefore, I am now at work on a series of articles covering the subjects mentioned and others, such as how the workers contend with the problem of industrialization in Palestine;

the city of Tel Aviv; the new neighborhoods of Haifa, and more . . . The articles will appear in *Forward* as soon as they arrive by mail.

New York, Saturday, 7 November 1925
6.   **Jews and Arabs at the Tel Aviv Market**

I went to visit the Tel Aviv market at 5.30 in the morning. I asked a Jew there what he thought about the future of Tel Aviv. "You call this a city? . . . Maybe, if people of means would immigrate and come here . . . But very few of those are coming now . . . When many of the Jews of Poland immigrated it got things moving and livened up commerce and business . . . Naturally, apartment rentals went up and it was impossible for Jews with little money to find accommodation. On the other hand, you could earn money then, there was work and there was also business in the shops. Now only a few of the immigrants are well-off, and most of them are poor and were brought here by their children. Those live from hand to mouth . . . " He went on to complain bitterly about Tel Aviv. He mocked the "big" business being done here now. Everything was inflated and no one knew what tomorrow would bring . . . You find this kind of attitude to Tel Aviv in anyone who doesn't succeed here. However, if someone has a good week at business and makes a profit it will be a different tune.

. . . The socialists, the local leaders of the workers, find themselves in a strange position on this matter. In their movement there is full cooperation between the working settlement and the urban workers. Members of the kibbutzim and moshavim are an important part of the labor movement and the Histadrut, and these are opposed to Tel Avivism, to coin a phrase. They are vigorously opposed to the air of profiteering and inflation of real estate prices that prevails over the city. They are also against bourgeois immigration looking eagerly toward a trading and business economy, as one of them put it to me.

Here you meet two diametrically opposed positions, and I shall deal with this later in my article. At this stage it is important to stress that for the urban workers employment in construction is important because this is the main occupation of the socialist-Zionists, who are likeable and full of enthusiasm, the ones who did not go to the land settlement but work in Tel Aviv, Jerusalem, Jaffa or Haifa.

As I have already remarked on previous occasions, Zionism, the building up of Eretz Israel – this is the chief goal, while socialism is a secondary. So when a local socialist hears of the growth of Tel Aviv he is pleased and displeased simultaneously. Profiteering and the development of the bourgeoisie – is this possible? This situation will continue as long as the number of Jews in Palestine continues to rise.

I do not want the reader to imagine for a moment that the socialist in the city, or the kibbutz member, or the anarchist farmer (there are some of those too) are not dedicated with all their heart to their ideals. Among them you may meet many people of marvelous character and wonderful dedication. They sacrifice much and are ready for many more sacrifices for the sake of their ideals, and these are not empty words. Thousands of young people and even more adults are ready at any instant to defend the land against enemies. Many of them fought in the War, and they, like others, are ready to fight, and even to die, if this has to be, in heroic self-defense. There is much to be added to this, but this is not the place.

. . . As I was about to leave the market a Jew who was not young ran after me and wanted to talk to me . . . I asked him his opinion on Palestine . . . "My opinion is that in the end everything will be all right. Whatever happens, we have to build up Eretz Israel. If we say it is necessary it will also be done. I won't say that everything is smooth and good in Tel Aviv, where a few have made money but many have lost it, myself included. But one shouldn't despair, and one must try again and again. You know the saying 'If you don't invest all your energy it will never grow'. This is the way every Jew must think about the situation, and only in that way will we build our land."

He had much more to say, in the same spirit. I don't recall all his words, except for these: "It is no great thing to succeed when you have luck, but it is a mighty achievement when you don't have luck and nothing goes your way, and still in the end you make it. This is exactly what has to be done in Eretz Israel. If indeed we are a stiff-necked people, and are able to use this quality in the right way, we will build our land. There is no other path than that. If we follow that path the result will be positive."

What he said interested me in itself, but chiefly because it expressed the mood of many of those I encountered. You do not hear such views stated openly, because voicing them may endanger your status. It is almost vital here to say that everything is fine and nice, and everything is growing and developing like mushrooms after the rain. Still, in private conversations everywhere you hear the opposite opinions. But even among those who express contrary opinions there are many who talk in the same manner as the Jew who kept me company on my way out of the market.

New York, Wednesday, 11 November 1925
7.   Industry and the Future of Palestine
Paris, 10 November

The settlements being established by the Jewish National Fund and supported directly by the Keren Hayesod deserve our very best wishes. Both the cooperative settlements and those based on principles of individualism [*moshavei ovdim* – Workers' Settlements – Y.G.] have to adopt the principle of self-labor by the settlers. Hired labor and exploitation are completely prohibited.

The position of the Zionist movement on this settlement, like its attitude to the labor movement in Palestine, with all its socialist ramifications, is worthy of our respect and support. There are many things there whose beauty is heartwarming, and not only on the cooperative settlements but also in the semi-cooperative settlements of the new kind based on the principle of private property. This is the poetry in the situation.

Unfortunately, with poetry alone you cannot build a land. The hard prose of life cannot be ignored. It is impossible to make a ring out of low-quality gold. The socialist settlement is not the only enterprise in the country. There are the usual private villages. For the present I shall leave aside all the differences and deal with the complex of agricultural settlement as a single factor.

Can agriculture support the population?

The major question is whether, even if there will be agriculture under the best possible conditions, it can be the basis for a large Jewish population. This question was answered negatively by Dr Weizmann himself. In fact, it was answered negatively by several foremost leaders of the cooperative settlements in Palestine.

We talk here of the Zionist goal of turning Palestine into a firmly established Jewish homeland standing on its own merits. This concerns the present and the near future of Palestine. The immediate question is if Palestine can support a large Jewish immigration. There are sufficient people willing to build their home there because they have nowhere to go. But will they find employment in Palestine? Will they have a means of livelihood there? This is the paramount question that absorbed all my attention during my stay in Tel Aviv.

Until now, unemployment has been mild there. Usually the Immigration Department of the Zionist Organization deals with every immigrant, as does the special immigration department of the central workers' organization [the Histadrut – Y.G.]. These handle every newcomer who wants to be a worker in the city or to go to the agricultural settlement. During my time in Palestine the immigrants had no difficulty getting work. Most places of work were connected with the building branch in Tel Aviv or its auxiliary trades. The question is, how long this can last?

The building boom in the last year or two has been due primarily to the immigration of the economically well-off stratum from Poland. This type of immigration cannot go on for ever – on the contrary, all the signs show that it is only temporary. The employment situation is not based on the natural conditions of Palestine, or on its raw materials and all that follows from this.

If the wish is to maintain immigration, industry has to be developed, and industry of the kind that does not depend on fluctuating conditions being favorable, such as the boom in real estate caused by the situation in another country. If Palestine is intended to be a meaningful homeland for the Jews, it is impossible to attain the Zionist goal unless industries of the kind mentioned develop in its territory, all of it on a wide scale. Industry and trade as the basis, resting on the country's natural resources.

Industry in Palestine

Thus, the real question is how far industry in Palestine is based on actual economic circumstances, and how far it is based on unstable and transitory conditions.

During my sojourn in Palestine I devoted much of my time to studying this prosaic question. I visited all the important factories in Tel Aviv and I spent hours in discussions of these issues with various businessmen, hearing declarations and counter-declarations, positions and counter-positions. The most optimistic industrialists, bankers and businessmen whom I met spoke of the economic opportunities of the country only in terms of faith. It is all a matter of hope, of very bold initiatives motivated by idealism or something akin to adventurousness, or both. My heart goes out to those people, because even in the worst cases they are not without a trace of idealism. The most regular milkman I met in Palestine had a note of spiritual idealism in his voice when he talked about his plans as part of the economic project of building Palestine.

During my time in Tel Aviv I happened to meet a rough little wheeler-dealer who had just arrived from the United States. Just the same, when he began to talk about the future of the Jews in Palestine his eyes lit up and his voice filled with awe, and this gave me a feeling of looking through a crack that gave me a glimpse of the best part of his soul. Yet none of this provides any reason to avoid examining Palestine's future in light of the facts and with cold logic.

It is impossible to build industry in the country by declarations alone, and this, apparently, is exactly what they are trying to do in Palestine. From the depths of my heart I wish them success, but industrial initiative in Tel Aviv seems to me somewhat artificial. It brings to mind the way the Zionist philologists created wholesale new words and expressions in Hebrew in order to adapt the ancient holy tongue to its new role as a language of the twentieth century. This way of creating a language is one thing, but to create an industrial country in such a manner is something entirely different.

The biggest plant in Tel Aviv is a brick-making factory. It is very modern with up-to-date machinery and management. The factory has known lean times, and in fact went bankrupt until the APC bank bailed it out and took responsibility for it. The director of the bank, Mr Hoffein, undertook the management of the factory personally. According to statements and rumors it has become profitable. The huge consumption of bricks in Tel Aviv at the moment has come as a result of the large well-to-do Polish immigration mentioned above. In recent weeks this immigration has ceased, and in consequence, activity in the building branch has slowed down. You hear explanations of all kinds, dismissing the present slowdown as only temporary. With all my heart I want the most optimistic forecast indeed to be realized, but there is no certainty of this. People with money came because they heard of an economic boom, and an economic boom developed because the well-to-do people immigrated; such a vicious circle cannot continue and a halt in building activity means a fall in consumption of building bricks.

There is a silk factory in Tel Aviv that attracts the attention it deserves. The place is owned and run by a man called Dalpiner, who has a similar factory in Vienna. As we were staying in the same hotel I had an excellent opportunity for becoming closely acquainted with him. We spent many hours in conversation about his enterprise, and generally about the economic potential of Palestine. His ideas and plans were quite convincing. The first reason he arouses such great interest is that he is not trying to build on changing circumstances but on what he considers to be natural and changeless factors. He hopes to obtain his raw material from Syria and to manufacture the finished product on such a scale as to allow him to undercut the silk manufacturers from other countries, and at the same time to pay his workers good wages. He gives the impression of succeeding in finding markets for his products in Egypt and Syria, and in his expectation of exporting his goods to other countries.

You also get a good impression from a visit to the sock and stocking factory and the paint factory in Herzliya.

Nevertheless, success so far in all these plants is largely still more a matter for hopefulness and expectation than an achievement based on solidity and natural resources. There are another couple of dozen smaller factories producing for the local market, and not one of them is constructed on a firm and stable foundation. All in all, there is an atmosphere of uncertainty bordering on anxiety regarding the entire economic situation.

Yet together with this there is a large degree of hope and enthusiasm. One man highly experienced in industrial affairs said to me, "Dalpiner must succeed. If not, there is no economic future for Palestine. Everybody hopes that he and many others will prosper."

In sum, I wish to point out that the Jews have an inexhaustible supply of vitality. They know how to get things moving even in uncertain circumstances and in the face of obstacles. They are renowned for their ability to turn the impossible into reality. Only thanks to this limitless capacity in their nature have they managed to survive, despite long years of persecution. In spite of all the criticism I voiced above, I hope with all my heart that the Zionist dream will in fact materialize.

New York, Thursday, 12 November 1925
8.   All Kinds of People and Parties in Palestine

No easy task to get to the truth of things in Palestine but it is possible – The labor movement and its great strength – The sanctity of labor – Will there be employment there?

The four weeks I spent in Palestine were passed in observation and listening; now, on my way back to Europe, I can begin to portray the totality of my impressions.

If one wishes to delve into the roots of the truth in Palestine one naturally has to become acquainted with all the factors involved, and this is by no means easy. A person without a sympathetic attitude to the country is in no hurry to offer his views to a journalist. Such a person is afraid of those who hold power and of public opinion. To tell the world about the other side of the coin – this would need a good measure of courage even if the Jewish homeland were flourishing and well established in Palestine.

How much more today, when all the Zionist ambitions are still more an ideal to be striven for than actual fact, and when every step requires sympathy and help.

The help that they need

The more they progress, the more help they need. As the Zionists, the members of the different groups and parties, approach their goal, the more important becomes the help extended to them and the size of the sums without which they will not reach their target. Jews all over the world give money to Palestine, but what they contribute is too little, the Zionists complain, especially those living in Palestine. Therefore, it would be right and proper that everyone should at least have a good word to say! Let everyone proclaim far and wide the Jewish achievements in Tel Aviv, Haifa and Jerusalem. This is the time for the fire to be kindled! Money from America and every state in Europe must flow there, and the sooner the better! All this is heard incessantly and is seen on hundreds of faces. It brings to mind a New York real-estate agent beginning to build a house with too little capital. With every unit added to the building he needs more and more money, more and more credit and goodwill.

One thing that is encountered on coming to Palestine is the thirst for publicity. In recent years events themselves have provided the headlines. God himself seems to have become a Zionist and the publicity agent for Palestine. As if set up to enlarge immigration to Palestine, the Jewish tragedy has grown worse and the gates to America have been slammed shut before them. To date, the Jews who have to escape and migrate have no other destination than Palestine.

Palestine, the last refuge

Millions of Jews clasp Palestine as a drowning man clutches at a straw. How many people can this straw sustain? How many people can find refuge there? The man who has to save himself by any means possible does not think about these questions and the bystander has not the heart to ask them such questions. This psychological situation exists all over the world, so the criticism about what is happening in Palestine is almost considered sacrilege. This is the feeling of Jews all over the world. If this is the case, what can be said about those who themselves dwell in Palestine?

The main element characterizing public opinion in Palestine is nationalism, of a force unequalled anywhere in the world. During the war this kind of chauvinism swept all countries, but now even the French have become more sober-minded and the Americans certainly have cooled their ardor here. Today you find this sort of toxic patriotism only in Palestine.

Zionist chauvinism is so strong that it has become something like a superstition. Free thinking has no meaning here, and revolutionary aims are denied everywhere. The most extreme socialist and member of the communal committees whistles exactly the same tunes as the ugliest patriot in Poland. When he whistles these tunes he works himself up to the sort of feelings that were his grandfather's legacy in the synagogue.

Much of what has been described above has to be attributed to the fact that the Zionist Organization financially supports the kibbutzim and the workers' moshavim, and these play the most important part in this country. Regarding the subject under discussion, it makes no difference at all that in the Zionist congresses there is a large conservative majority that sharply criticizes the policy of excessive importance that the Zionist Organization imparts to the Palestine labor movement generally and to the working agricultural settlement in particular. The congresses are held outside Palestine, and they express the feelings that prevail in various countries but not in Palestine of recent years.

Today the labor movement is the most important force in Palestine, and within it the central factor is those 2000–3000 settlers living in the communal settlements and the moshavim. All of these are supported by the two funds of the Zionist Organization, in both grant of land and grant of money. The Zionist Organization collects donations for its funds from all the Jews in the world, religious and freethinking, capitalists and workers alike.

The fire of Zionist nationalism has melted all the class and ideological conflicts. In such a situation what meaning can there be to declarations on principles, or class struggle or social revolution? When you tell a revolutionary in Palestine that you are going to write about the greed of the property owners in Tel Aviv, for example, or about the depressed economic condition of the workers in Palestine, he finds himself in a quandary. As a socialist he has to insist that you do write about these matters, but as a Zionist he is afraid that to do so may harm the endeavor in Palestine. In the end, he is first of all a Zionist, and all the other "isms" come only afterwards.

In the same spirit, if you tell a worker who is very dissatisfied with the workers' organization (the Histadrut) that you are going to publish the information he has given you, he will not allow you to do so, as he is a loyal Zionist. The labor movement in Palestine fulfills an important role now, with Zionism bound up in all its operations, and your disclosures may damage the prestige of the entire movement. I mention those who are not satisfied, but are loyal Zionists. By contrast, those who are not loyal to the labor movement, or those who are not Zionists, are simply afraid to speak. They are afraid that if they talk they personally will suffer for it. Others keep silent because of the pressure of public opinion. There are of course also those who do not wish to endanger what is being done in Palestine because they live there and do not know if they will be able to emigrate to another country. At the same time, there are still sufficient people who do not fear the consequences and they pour their hearts out to you. After each of my visits to an important public figure, or after each time such a figure visited me, people approached me presenting a position opposite to what I had just heard, or they criticized the situation in Palestine. They would come to me in person or send letters by circuitous routes, mostly letters asking for a meeting to discuss various matters. I always agreed, and I set up the meetings. In many cases these were disappointing encounters. Some of the people were just bitter and troublemakers, or those with personal grudges who were only waiting for a chance to get even. But there were also many who spoke out because of their deep and genuine knowledge of things, and they also had something important to say.

It is of course possible to criticize even the best of things. Most of the qualifications I heard about the workers' organization in Palestine, for example, might also be voiced by those dissatisfied with the finest trade unions in America or Poland. Yet this should not be a cause for closing your ears to every one of those who expresses reservations against the Palestinian labor exchange [of the Histadrut – Y.G.], or against the general workers' organization, or against their collective agreements, or against the cooperative settlements, which constitute a part of this moderate and all-powerful organization. Whoever wishes to see the truth must see it from all its sides, must hear out every factor, and also must not forget that everyone observes things through the spectacles of his party or only through his personal feelings. Even the person who refuses to talk to you freely brings you nearer the truth. At times the truth echoes even in the phrasing by which someone tries to smooth matters over. Sometimes this also is reflected in his behavior and facial expression. When you are dealing with dozens of people of different classes, parties, factions, and groups, or with those who do not belong to any party, faction, or group, you gradually begin to form for yourself a genuine and clear picture of the true situation.

I spent long hours in conversations with the party leaders of the workers' movement in Palestine. It is quite natural that each of them spoke only about the good things that characterize his movement. This is an accepted feature everywhere, but the workers' leaders in Palestine overdo it. The general workers' organization [the Histadrut – Y.G.] includes several parties and groups with different outlooks. One group is social-democratic, the second tends to anarchism, and the third is opposed to both of these. They are not keen to criticize each other in the presence of an outsider. They are hesitant to talk to anyone who might publish his impressions in a newspaper. First of all, these opposing groups are part of the same general workers' organization, secondly – and this is the most important point, all disagreement fades and they all appear as Zionists when engaged in discussions with the outside world. This is especially true when the question at issue is if you are going to express yourself sympathetically or not on Palestine. In such a case all these groups become one body, which sets the subject of the rebuilding of Palestine above all other ideals in the world. A social-democrat and an anarchist? Rightist socialists and leftist socialists? All these differences are within the family, so that outwardly they appear as a single party. A handful of the Bolsheviks now in Palestine who are working on behalf of Zinoviev [the leader of the Communist Comintern – Y.G.] were expelled from the Histadrut. By contrast, there are several Bolsheviks who operate quietly and disturb no one, and these were permitted to remain within the organization.

The diverse outlooks of the various parties are of slight significance. The most lucid platform is presented by Ahdut Ha'avodah, the strongest of the three parties. This is a social-democratic party, and its leaders have a clear and correct grasp of the workers' movements throughout the world. But in Palestine social-democracy has little meaning. At one and the same time they are also the paramount leaders of the Histadrut. This position was achieved on account of the special circumstances that arose in Palestine, and they have very little connection with the workers' struggle as it is understood all over the world. Anyway, I shall deal with this issue in a separate article. The workers' organizations in Palestine now play a part so great that you cannot understand what takes place there unless you are closely acquainted with nature and importance of these organizations. Among the Zionists in Palestine there are many who bitterly oppose the workers' organizations. In conversations among themselves they do not have single good word to say for them, but the moment they talk to a man like me they have something different to say. But as I said earlier, there are other ways to get to the truth.

I mentioned people who are loyal to the Zionist movement: it would be a mistake to think that these are the majority in the Jewish population in Palestine. The great majority, in their heart of hearts, are indifferent or even hostile to the Zionist movement. Most of the new immigrants come here only with the aim of finding a house and a living. If they do not find what they want they become bitter and their anxiety is written all over their faces. The number of dissatisfied people is greater than the number of satisfied, including even a significant number of those who arrive here with certificates showing that they belong to the Zionist framework and were permitted to immigrate by the government by virtue of being Zionists.

Two or three months ago there was more work to be had. Jews of means from Poland also came. New houses were constantly being built and hundreds of young educated people became plasterers and building laborers, and in that way they and others made their living. The real-estate market was very lively, and new factories, businesses and shops were established. The number of dissatisfied people was much smaller then. It does not matter how hard the work is, but as long as you have something to eat you are satisfied because you are not surrounded by the anti-Semitic atmosphere that prevails in Poland, Lithuania and Latvia. Living in a Jewish city like Tel Aviv is paradise.

In recent weeks the number of immigrants with economic means has fallen. At the moment the impression is that they have entirely disappeared. Very few new houses are being constructed, and building has stopped midway on a considerable number of those on which work had begun. Unemployment is steadily growing, and those without a livelihood cannot survive for long only on the spiritual fruits of paradise.

I had many opportunities to learn how much people have changed their attitudes. When I arrived in Palestine they were just about kissing the sand dunes of Tel Aviv, while a few weeks later they were making jokes about their initial enthusiasm. They wore a sad smile on their faces. They made fun of themselves, and attacked without restraint the Histadrut labor exchange, claiming favoritism in giving out jobs, and preference for others, while they were forced to tramp the streets searching for work until their feet were swollen.

Unemployment is the most terrible test for people, and I am bound to say that in Palestine I saw many dedicated youngsters who withstood this ordeal. I saw some who had gone hungry for weeks, and they suffered like martyrs. Their idealism, their loyalty to Zion, gives them strength. Of course, there were many young people for whom this is nothing but partial pretence, but I also met people who were utterly sincere in their devotion.

I mentioned the hard and dangerous work performed by the immigrants. Such a spirit exists only in Palestine, and it is linked not only with the joy stemming from their being free of the curse of anti-Semitism, but also from the joy deriving from the fact that you live in a Jewish city. This feeling is clearly evident.

To work hard, to work and put your life in danger, to work and be content with meager rations – this has become something almost like a religion for the young men and women who have come to Palestine. There is no difference between pioneers and those who are not pioneers, or immigrants without a Zionist background. Naturally many arrive here hoping to become established in business, but as long as you have to go to work you are infused with the idealistic spirit. This preaches to the immigrant that work in Palestine is something sacred, that it is building the Jewish homeland, and therefore the harder the work the greater his happiness becomes.

The immigrant hears this everywhere and in various ways. He hears about the young educated Jewish men and women who break stones and pave roads; about the Jewish youth from pampered homes who died of malaria when they drained the swamps of Palestine, of students who turned stony land into gardens and flourishing fields.

You must labor at physical work. To hire hands to work for you or even only to help – this is like a crime and a plot against the hallowed earth of Palestine. These are the tenets explained to the new immigrant, who also feels that it comes from the heart, and therefore it exerts an enormous effect on him. It is a kind of hypnosis, a kind of magic that enthralls him. The immigrant works and sings with everyone. There are naturally not a few for whom this magic does not work, or those who suffer and suppress their pain; those who sing together with the zealots, but with a trace of despair in their voice. The number of those devoted to ideals is truly great. It is a fine idealism, pure, and indeed sacred. How long it will survive is a question that does not concern us here. At the moment it is a fact, and it would be stupid to deny it. Much as you oppose the chauvinist facet of Zionism, this spirit demands respect. I of course refer to the spirit that adheres those who are working here, but what about those who do not find work? To wander about without work and without food – this is a far harder test than breaking stones and draining swamps, and who knows how many young people will stand up to this test? How long can such a situation go on? This brings us to the question of the kind of work that Palestine can provide. This is in fact the foremost question. But the reader must first gain an acquaintance with the different workers' organizations in Palestine.

I shall begin with the communal settlements, which are the highest form of idealism to be found in Eretz Israel. I shall try to depict for the newspaper's reader their marvelous aspects, and also the features that verify the old saying that all that glistens is not gold. I shall attempt to clarify their present and future problems. This will be the subject of my next article, which I hope to dispatch in a few days.

New York Friday, 13 November 1925
9. The Flowering of Palestine Depends on the Welfare of the Arabs
Paris, 12 November

The Arab question is closely connected with the economic problem of the Jewish settlement in Palestine. The solution to the problem lies largely, as I see it, in providing a living for the Muslim population. Wider economic opportunities and higher wages for farmers and workers, as well as more business for merchants, with the Jews playing a leading role in the improvement of conditions – this will shatter the anti-Semitic propaganda.

This is evident to anyone who visits Palestine and examines in depth the nature of the relations, the different conditions between the two peoples. The propaganda of the anti-Jewish Committee of the Effendis, the secretary of which, the vital force of the committee, I interviewed shortly before I left Palestine, is obviously a constant hazard. But as long as Great Britain retains the so-called Mandate I believe that there is no cause for concern. The leaders of the anti-Jewish propaganda, from their viewpoint, are very serious, more than I credited them. But on the other hand, my stay in Palestine eradicated any belief I had in the virtues of their cause from a moral perspective.

There is no need to take seriously the excessive rhetoric of the Zionists belonging to the extremist chauvinists: the Jews deserve a home in Palestine not because this was once their home, but principally because of their splendid work and self-sacrifice by means of which they are seeking to turn barren tracts into fertile land, and the miserable, decayed and primitive existence that characterizes the country into a land where life is in keeping with modern civilization. First and foremost, it seems to me that this is a question of economic success. If the Jews of Palestine succeed in realizing the major part of their program and build up the trade and industry of this country, as has been done in other countries, then their sense of self-reliance will not be damaged even if Britain leaves Palestine to its fate.

It is also possible to believe that the Jews of Palestine hold the key to the economic activity of a civilized east, including Egypt. It is more than pure surmise that soon Britain will quit Egypt. The moment this happens, Egypt will strive for economic dominance over all the Near East [the term used from the start of the twentieth century to World War II; only then did the expression Middle East come to replace Near East, or the Asian Territories of the Ottoman Empire – Y.G.], but its ambitions in that direction are doomed to failure. A brief stay in Cairo is enough to convince the tourist that the Egyptian people are entirely unprepared for such a role. This, therefore, is the chance for the Jews of Palestine. If indeed their dreams in this direction are realized, Palestine will become their homeland, in accordance with its size and its capacity to absorb immigration. From afar these problems of Palestine appear in one light, but when the problems are studied closely it all appears in a different light.

Furthermore, things in Palestine have been steadily changing. The reality in recent years has created a kind of revolution in its condition, a revolution that it is barely possible to understand merely by reading journals and books. But is this drastic change in the country's circumstances likely to continue, and will it be able to absorb and support large immigration? This is the most important question . . .

New York, Saturday, 14 November 1925
10. The Cooperative Settlements in Palestine

. . . What these cooperative settlements have achieved is of great significance for Zionism. Through their enthusiasm, their hard work, and the spirit of self-sacrifice they are turning swamps and desert into gardens and fertile fields, and this is the best affirmation of the right to Jewish possession of Palestine. It impresses the world. This description applies also to the new kind of radical *moshav* [village] founded on private property but on the principle that the farmer must do the work himself, without hired labor. There is a certain measure of cooperation here too. Every moshav consists of several farmers, each one of whom has his own plot of land which he works as private property. They operate a cooperative system of selling and buying commodities. If one of them falls ill his comrades help him according to a defined method.

The veteran settlers in Palestine also worked hard, but now they engage hired labor, mostly Arab. The Zionist movement assists the two new types of settlers: the communalists and the individualists [members of the kibbutz and members of the workers' moshav -Y.G.] with grants of land and of money. It does its utmost with the little money it has. Land ownership always remains in the hands of the Zionist movement, but as long as the settler works his land himself, as a member of a moshav or as a member of a kibbutz, the land belongs to him or his kibbutz.

The principle is very fine, and really very fine too is the enormous help and great sympathy proffered by the Zionist movement to these settlements. That they are indeed deserving of the assistance given to them in no way diminishes the affirmative attitude to them of the Zionist movement. In truth, if Dr Weizmann and other leaders of the Zionist movement did not possess a progressive world outlook they would not act as they do. Mr Menahem Ussishkin, head of the Jewish National Fund, which purchases and distributes lands in Eretz Israel, is known to be the most conservative among the Zionist leaders. Therefore, I was at pains to learn of his attitude to the communes as regards the land that they require, and the answer to this was always that they have nothing whatever to complain about on that score.

Among themselves, the leaders believe that the commune, as a way of life, is only a transitional stage. Or in simpler words, they will not endure for long. As for the workers' moshavim, their view is that these will gradually forget their ideals and what will count is interests linked to their private property. But in parallel to these views, one hears from the same leaders that the Jewish homeland will be built differently from what is usual in other countries. It will arise on loftier moral principles, on a superior economic system, and chiefly on the basis of the tenets of socialism. "Not merely a Jewish homeland is being constructed in Palestine," one hears constantly from these leaders, "but a higher human society is in the process of being built." This too depends on the mood a Zionist leader is in when he speaks about the working settlement – if his mood is sober and pragmatic, or is one of excitement and idealism, along the lines of the prayer "Thou has chosen us . . . ," in the sense of the Chosen People. In any event, our concern at the moment is not with the future but with the present. And for the present, these settlements are imbued with ideals and the noblest feelings.

The apple is not always as good and as sweet inside as it looks outside, but there is much beauty and purity in the inner life of these settlements. The two kinds of idealistic settlements [kibbutz and workers' moshav – Y.G.] I noted, that now fulfill a most important role in Palestine. They are located mainly in the Jezreel Valley [Emek Yizre'el], called for short "the Emek." If you are in Palestine you hear this name everywhere and it is spoken with pride and love. In the Emek there are fertile lands. It is surrounded by mountains and is beautiful and extends like a vast carpet. The plains are crossed by lines in different colors and in the mountains salient points can be picked out. The successive changes of the landscape produce a kaleidoscopic effect. It looks clearer and purer early in the morning at sunrise, but it is always lovely and crowns every part of the day with a lucent glow.

I spent considerable time traveling in the Emek and I always found it difficult to tear my gaze away from the scenery, the fields, the mountains, the flocks of sheep pasturing on the land, and the camels moving slowly with their cautious and graceful gait. Each mountain crowning the Emek has a biblical name, and the same is true of every corner in the valley. Here were fought the famous battles recounted in the Books of Samuel, Judges and Kings. The most interesting tales a Jewish boy learns in the *heder*, tales that even the laziest pupil learns avidly, are associated with these places. Here occurred the actual events set forth in these accounts, and here were born the legends into which they were woven. A modern *heder* in Poland or Lithuania teaches the Bible with the aid of a map of Palestine. When the children in Palestine learn the Bible they use the landscape itself as a map – the landscape with its hills, its valleys, its streams and its brooks. The Zionist movement has purchased a major part of the Emek and hopes in time to acquire ownership of it all. In Eretz Israel the working settlement is the flower of the Emek.

The two types of working settlement belong to the Palestinian labor movement. They are not merely attached to it, they are an organic part of it. This might appear strange, because, you may think, what connection at all can a self-employed farmer have with the trade unions fighting against factory owners and labor-employing farmers? And even the communes – how do these come to be a part of the movement of paid workers united in their war against the exploiters?

But the labor movement in Palestine is entirely different from that in all countries of the world. What I have pointed out is not the only marked distinction from the rest of the world, but this is not the place to describe its general nature and to introduce the reader to the different parts of which the labor movement is composed. At this stage it is important only to note that the working settlement constitutes an integral part of the Histadrut.

We refer here constantly to the two types included in the working settlement: the communes [kibbutzim – Y.G.] and the workers' moshav. The first type is larger and more important. The original communes played the most important part in Palestine in recent years. The foremost workers' moshav is Nahalal, which was founded by people who had previously belonged to a communal settlement. They became dissatisfied with that way of life and sought a greater degree of personal independence. They fashioned the ideology of a semi-cooperative lifestyle based on private property with several forms of cooperation – a defined combination of individualism and mutual aid. The most important people in Nahalal are Yaffe and Uri. The first, a graduate of the Woodbine Agricultural School in New Jersey, is the theoretician of this type of settlement. He is also a leader of the Hapo'el Hatza'ir party, which competes with the Ahdut Ha'avodah, the socialist party in Palestine. After speaking with him for about an hour, I asked him, "Do you preach a kind of anarchy?" To this he replied with a smile, "Almost." Yet it cannot be claimed that Hapo'el Hatza'ir is an anarchist organization. In general, one may say that it is very hard to understand exactly what its program is. Yaffe's seriousness and integrity are not to be doubted for an instant, and this is true of Uri also. They and other comrades of theirs with whom I spoke, and who also showed me, with explanations, the various parts of their farm, all make a good impression.

The same may be said of the members of Kefar Yehezkel, also a workers' moshav, and of all the cooperative settlements I visited. Judging by first impressions, these are pleasant people and certainly honest. A dishonest person cannot last long in such surroundings, and will undoubtedly be sent away. I have to say that I am certain that the idealism of some of the people in the cooperative settlements is genuine and profound. The work in the communes is hard and the food is poor. You work from the break of day to the setting of the sun, and the food you are given is not enough for the amount of energy required for the work. Life is monotonous. When the bell rings and you return from the field or from the stable you are so tired that sleep is the best form of leisure you could desire. If spiritual sustenance and joy are drawn from awareness that one is serving an ideal, then such a way of life is like a prison.

Not everyone feels this way, and not everyone is happy on the commune. Far from it, but there are many for whom the gray life of the communal settlement is lit up by spiritual rays of happiness. Many leave and others come in their place. The number of members remaining after several years is not large. The oldest commune in Palestine, Deganya, is almost 15 years old, and of the 55 members living there today only five are founders, and even this is high. The other communes are much younger. The largest of them is four or five years old and the percentage of those who have been in it from the start is tiny. In recent years the number of cooperative settlements has grown so much that their influence is felt in certain circles not only in Palestine but also in Russia, Poland, Germany, Czechoslovakia, and even America. A kind of communalistic mystery radiates from them, and young men and women who feel confined in the cities where they live, and have nowhere to migrate to except Palestine, sense this radiation.

. . . How long these cooperative settlements will survive, what effect there will be on their existence if industry develops in Palestine – these are questions I shall deal with in future articles. At present the communalist settlements are flourishing chiefly in the spiritual sense.

The leaders of the communalist settlements and of the labor movement tell me of thousands of young people, boys and girls, in Russia and Poland who are preparing themselves for the farming life on the communalist settlements. In Poland there are young Jews working as hired hands on farms for this purpose. The same process is taking place in Russia, although in a different way. There the Zionists planning for communal life [the Hehalutz movement – Y.G.] are being persecuted by the Cheka and they are facing this heroically, in the hope of emigrating to Palestine and living on a cooperative settlement.

The numbers of those getting ready for communalist life are perhaps exaggerated, but there is no doubt that such people exist. Special conditions have been created that impart to the communes in Palestine an attractive force for young men and women of a certain kind. How long this state of affairs will last is another question.

Altogether there are 16 to 18 communes in Palestine, with about 2000 members. Their leaders usually give a higher figure of 3000 members, although one of them set the number at 2500, yet this too is apparently exaggerated. The communes are divided into two organizations, while some of them are independent. It is an old rule that wherever there is activity parties and factions develop. In Europe this is a more widespread manifestation than in England and America, and it is also a more common feature among Jews than among other peoples. All the social bodies mentioned are communal, and there is no reason for them to be divided into factions, but their leaders have different ideas, and perhaps in part different ambitions, hence the split. All these groups belong to the Histadrut mentioned above. The two biggest communes are Ein Harod and Tel Yosef. The first has 280 members, the second slightly fewer. Ein Harod belongs to a different organization than Tel Yosef. All the other communes are smaller, with between 40 and 80 members. The organization of Tel Yosef arouses special interest. The organization is called Gedud Ha'avodah [Labor Battalion] and three communal settlements and three urban communes belong to it. When Gedud Ha'avodah was founded Ein Harod joined it also, but later left, and now several urban communes are connected to Ein Harod . . .

New York, Tuesday, 17 November 1925
11.   Mendel Elkind and Gedud Ha'avodah

In my last article I wrote about the important role played by members of the communalist bodies in Palestine. What causes their growth and what is their future to be?

A member of a commune whom I spoke to during my travels in the Emek made a comment related to the subject. I asked him if he had been a socialist before he immigrated to Palestine, to which he replied, "No. I was just a Zionist. Here, the moment I became a laborer I became a socialist. The work itself caused that result." His answer interested me but I did not take it as a guiding rule. For that young man socialism means that one has to work in a communalist body; but only a few hours earlier I had visited a settlement that was not cooperative. There too the people work very hard and there too the people are dedicated Zionists, yet for all that, they wish to live on the basis of private property. Thus, the same reality does not necessarily bring everyone to the same awareness. Not everyone becomes a socialist because he works, and certainly not every socialist here has an inclination for life in one of the communalist bodies. Socialism means the organization of every country on the tenets of socialism or communism, meaning the operation of large-scale industry on cooperative foundations.

When the communal bodies were first organized in Palestine the leanings and ideals of people presumably played an important part, and the ideas of the stronger-minded people influenced the others. But this is only one of the factors that produced the cooperative bodies and led to their influence. There is another factor embedded in the conditions themselves that surround the young farmers. Nature in Palestine is very harsh, and it does not favor the pioneer. He is obliged to work very hard, and the work is accompanied by dangers. He toils long until the earth yields any crop at all. In time, if he has invested much energy in the goal of his labor, the land becomes fertile and the farm becomes as dear to him as a sickly child is to its mother. But during the first years they have to be prepared just for work and danger. The peril lies not only in the illness associated with draining the swamps but also in an attack by some Arab or other or raids by many Arabs. All this has befallen more than one pioneer, and more than one pioneer has fallen victim during the course of his pioneering work. These are the circumstances that cause one to avoid being an isolated farmer.

When I talked to people during my time in Palestine about the agricultural settlements, I sometimes compared the English and French pioneers who went to America and settled the Atlantic seaboard with the Zionist pioneer who immigrates to Palestine with the aim of becoming a farmer. There is one very great difference between them: in America nature is abundant, the open space was full of trees, and the forests were full of wild birds and game to be hunted. The pioneers there needed only an axe to hew logs, out of which they built their cabins, and rifles to hunt for their sustenance. That rifle also helped them to defend themselves against the Indians.

By contrast, in Palestine timber is sparse, and rare it is to find an animal to hunt. The rifle is not a highly effective means of defense because the Arabs have the same weapon. Hence it is very difficult for the pioneer to get by through his own resources at any godforsaken spot in Palestine. It was essential to settle in groups. The people naturally became close to each other. Work and common dangers draw hearts closer.

No one usually becomes a member of commune without having an inclination for it. This is not an absolute rule although it is generally correct. There is a flood of excitement here. The deep feelings, basically religious, are manifested in movements that express group interests, not private concerns. To tell the truth, this holds not only for movements but for anything a person does for another and not just for himself. When you help others you feel a warmth in your blood – a sensation that may be defined as excitement.

The Zionist movement has grown greatly in recent years because of the tragic condition of the Jews on the one hand, and the Balfour Declaration on the other. The flame of excitement has flared up, chauvinism has intensified, but in parallel the willingness for sacrifice has intensified also.

There were times and places where children died like flies because of the terrible hygiene conditions in certain regions, but the people did not leave their farms. They did not relent despite their grave situation, they jeopardized their lives even more, but they continued to toil day and night. Now these places are no longer infested with disease, and the farmers can point them out with pride. The swamps are the next target for attention. The ardor has reached such dimensions that a certain group declared that it was its duty and purpose to work only the worst and most dangerous places, and also to carry out only heavy physical labor and not only to farm. They told me that "there are certain occupations, certain kinds of work in which Jews are not usually to be found, such as breaking stones, for example, or paving roads. Let us show that the Jews can do these kinds of work also, and they are willing to do them. Let us turn the most desolate and swampy regions into the healthiest areas. Let us show that no obstacle and no danger will stop the Jews, who love the Land of Israel and are willing to sacrifice themselves for it."

This kind of talk was heard in the past too, but as the official program of a movement it was presented only five years ago. This movement is called Gedud Ha'avodah [Labor Battalion] and it exists, under this name, up to the present. Gedud Ha'avodah is the Jewish pioneering corps, the avant-garde which goes first to the front line. The Gedud consists of several communes distributed in various places. It does not restrict membership only to agricultural communes, but welcomes into its ranks urban communalist bodies also. In an earlier article I listed six communes: three agricultural and three urban. I did not note two communes engaged in industry but not in town. The total number of communes now in Gedud Ha'avodah is eight. When the organization decides that one of its members must transfer from one agricultural commune to another, or from one urban commune to another, or the opposite, he must comply. At first the Gedud tried to create one common purse for all: for example, if a certain urban commune suffered from unemployment, it was temporarily supported by the other communes in the Gedud. In other words, all the communes of the Gedud formed a kind of single large commune. But it was hard to implement this policy as the agricultural communal settlements, for instance, are still economically weak and themselves need such assistance to stand on their feet. If these were obliged to cover the deficits of the other communes it would place a heavy burden on their resources. Because of this state of affairs the largest commune, Ein Harod, left the Gedud; the second largest, Tel Yosef, has remained in the Gedud, although at the moment it refuses to carry the weight of the deficits of the other communes. The principle remains on paper because economically each commune of the Gedud at present constitutes an independent body, although in other respects they are united.

The Gedud was established on the basis of the ideology of always going first to the front line, and it remains loyal to its oath. It is not the only body to undertake such a mission. Ein Harod and the communes connected with it and also the independent communes all serve the communalistic Zionist ideals exactly like the Gedud. In all the organizations the members work from morning till night, eat poor food, never recoil in the face of danger, and expect no personal material reward for themselves. Whatever you have to say about their attitude, or about the relevance their goals have, this kind of life must evoke respect. Therefore it is entirely natural that the other Zionists, perhaps apart from the ignorant or the extremely orthodox, hold them in great honor. These, the communalist Zionists, are the true pioneers. These are they who by their toil have won for the Jews the right of possession of Palestine. These are the true heroes of Zionism. Nahum Sokolov is very far from communism or socialism, but when he happens to talk to important and influential Poles about the achievements of the Jews in Palestine, what does he point to with special pride? The communalist bodies there.

It should be noted that the difference between the communes of the Gedud and the communes linked to Ein Harod lies in their attitude to political issues. Ein Harod supports social democracy, while the Gedud does not engage in politics. Just recently we heard that the Gedud altered its position. During my stay in Palestine I heard of Mendel Elkind, the leader of Gedud Ha'avodah. Active members of the Histadrut told me that in his political program he now leans definitely toward Bolshevism, although he does not recognize the Communist International because of its stance against Zionism. Elkind's influence on 600–700 members of the Gedud is absolute, therefore the feeling prevails that sooner or later he will attract his followers to Bolshevism and its destructive policy. So young a man with 600 faithful adherents, I thought to myself, can destroy everything that Zionism has built.

His political opponents in the labor movement in Palestine did not talk of him as of an enemy. At first I thought that this was because they were careful not to speak frankly with me. It was quite evident to me that Elkind's policy was wrong. I wanted to see him personally, but just then he was ill, and I did not have time to travel to where he was staying. But I did not want to leave Palestine without hearing his political platform, so

I did not relent until I got my way. A day before I left I saw him and we
spent several hours together.

Elkind makes an excellent impression. The moment you look at him,
especially when he smiles, you take a liking to him. When you sit and talk
with him, you become increasingly exposed to his charm. Elkind is 28,
tall with broad shoulders and clear eyes as guileless and as direct as a
child's. He was wearing a loose shirt of the kind that all the young radicals of Tel Aviv and the settlements wear. All in all he was dressed like a
poor man, an ordinary hired laborer. He completed high school in the
Crimea and also two years at the polytechnic at Ekaterinoslav. Needless
to say, he is extraordinarily intelligent, possessing excellent qualites and
a keen, clear and logical mind.

After listening for an hour and a half to his political program, which he
set out before me, I said to him, "You must have been considered highly
talented in mathematics at high school and the polytechnic." "Yes," he
replied, with his charming, open smile that dispelled all resistance. He
continued his lecture, myself interrupting from time to time with a question. His platform was very logical and brimming with idealism. As a
chain of arguments it had a good ring to it, but the conclusions he reached
and the very quality of his theory bore more than a shade of immaturity
owing to youth rather than real contact with life. A little more life experience, a little more acquaintance with the world and its people, with the
pitfalls and the shadowy areas of real life, and he will set aside, smilingly,
his present philosophy. But the Gedud is composed of people far younger
even than he, so when I witness the magnetism of his personality and his
ability, I can see how naturally he enthralls them.

The role of Elkind in the Gedud, and also the role of the Gedud in
Palestine, are so interesting a phenomenon that it is important, I believe,
to bring to our readers' knowledge Elkind's thinking, principles and platform, which also constitute the platform of the Gedud. "We are a political
party, not in the usual narrow sense but in the broad philosophical sense.
This means that we do not limit ourselves to being content with the fruit
of our labor, but we intend to cooperate with the workers for the ideal of
the liberation of mankind. This is the difference between us and the other
communes. We have two goals; one is nationalist – to help in the building
of Palestine, and the other is socialist – to help in the establishment of a
communist society in the world. At present it is impossible to establish
social communism in Palestine, and this will be possible only after the
social revolution. In this sense Palestine is no exception, and it is like any
other country. The Keren Hayesod and the Jewish National Fund are not

large enough to put vital necessities in the hands of the settler, so private enterprise in Palestine is inevitable. Without private enterprise it will be impossible to settle a large Jewish population here. In addition, in conditions of larger immigration the two national funds will not be able to restrict their activity to extending assistance to the communal settlements and communalist industries, but will have to support private property owners too." I asked him what the attitude of the national funds was at the moment, and he replied, "At the moment their attitude is excellent. In practice we have kind of monopoly over them, but how long can this last? Representatives of private property are raising their heads and demanding their share. In short, Palestine will have to undergo the same stages as the other countries, namely the path of the socialist revolution. Otherwise it will never achieve equality and genuine economic freedom. Therefore we see it as our task to join the class war until the advent of the social revolution. This can be done only through our urban communes, whose members are employed mainly in private enterprises."

At this point I asked him about the attitude of the Gedud to Solel-Boneh, the Histadrut company that functions as a cooperative. This company is big both in the number of tasks it sets itself and also in its power. At present it has undertaken to construct buildings, highways, bridges and the like, and it divides the projects up among work crews belonging to the trade unions. The urban groups of Gedud Ha'avodah work with this company. Do they perhaps consider the wages too small? I asked. To this Elkind replied, "With Solel-Boneh we don't strike. We strike only against private capital. Even after the socialist revolution it will still be a long road to attain a communist society. This will only be the first way station, and the transition from this station to true communism will take more work and time than the revolution itself. This effort [after the socialist revolution – Y.G.] will have two goals: first, to create a genuine basis for the economic life of communist society. I refer to a system that will organize labor and the mutual relations among people in respect of labor. Capitalism has its own system in this matter. The capitalist system is built on the principle of fear of hunger on the one hand, and on the other on the element of profiting from others. The worker must work, otherwise he will have nothing to eat. By contrast, the capitalist is set on industry because it provides him with new sources of wealth. These two motivations do not exist in communist society, therefore it is necessary to find other motivations. This leads us to new life forms, in communist society. The family is crumbling, and together with the other pillars of society it must collapse. Therefore, the new conditions create new demands and needs in the cultural life of society.

"In its social platform the Gedud has three goals: (a) the class struggle; (b) to create an internal basis for communist society; (c) to construct the special culture and special relations among people in communist society. The world labor movement is leaving (a) and (b) until after the socialist revolution, because it has no possibility of creating communist cells like those we have. In this sense we are in a particularly favorable situation. Moreover, as Russia is already making a start in realizing (a) and (b), these two goals have special significance for us; as part of the world's working class we see these measures clearly."

Judging by the path of his explanations, I thought that he would end with the usual Bolshevik speech, but this did not happen. Elkind said that he regarded the Bolshevik Revolution as a failure (this was his phrase, speaking in Russian), and secondly he began to organize the facts so as to prove that the Gedud was not obligated to, and could not, take part in politics as a political party in the accepted sense. He went on to argue: "We are in the midst of the class war but this is not so clear in our case as in respect of a political party with a defined political platform. We have no platform, as a party, for election day. Our political function, we believe, concerns only the preparatory work being conducted in our communes for the sake of future communist society."

In that case, what will you do when election day comes? I asked. To this Elkind replied: "We will allow our members to vote as they see fit. About 40 of them belong to Ahdut Ha'avodah; about 40 are sympathetic to Hapo'el Hatza'ir or Left Po'aley Tziyon. We accept members from all parties: Bolsheviks, socialists, and international socialists, but we do require of our members a definite stand on the future of society, because we are already conducting experiments for the future. We do not reject preparation for the future, as do the workers in other countries. The future form of the society in which human society will exist demands attention and we are already preparing for it.

"This is another reason why we cannot be a political party. A political party confines itself to the opinions and outlook of its members; if a member accepts the party platform it is enough. By contrast, this does not satisfy us, for we require every member to carry out a total revolution in his way of life in the moral and cultural sense, as well as in his economic outlook. We demand of him an absolute and total reversal in his entire daily life. And this is by no means an easy matter. It is impossible to require this of tens or hundreds of thousands of people, and a political party must necessarily attract thousands and millions."

Talking of the Communist International, Elkind explained why the Gedud could not belong to it. "Firstly, we are not a political party, so we have no ties to this organization. Secondly, we cannot accept the views of the International on the national question. Thirdly, we cannot support its policy on colonialism, since because of the International's ambition of destroying the British Empire it is willing to take advantage of the feudal-bourgeois Arab movement. We, of course, cannot submit to such tactics."

Replying to a series of questions I asked him at the end of our interview he said: "Many are leaving us. Not everyone is suited to a way of life like ours. Today we have 650 members. In the last five years we have had a turnover of about 2000 members. I agree with you that Palestine will not be built without capitalism. We are a microcosm, a tiny world, but we are conducting the experiments that all the world will have to carry out. Our experience will make the expected future process smoother. The failure of the Russian Revolution is not proof that it is impossible to realize our plans. We are living, generally, in revolutionary times, and what happens today to the working class in England is more important than what happened in Russia."

I presented him with the following arguments: Mankind does not develop according to the social experiments of small groups. It shapes itself as an entirety or according to nations, and social laboratories cannot contribute anything to this. Even if a few small communes live an ideal life this will in no way ease society's giving birth to communism. My arguments made no impression on him, and I had no desire to get into a deep debate with him. My purpose was to listen to what he had to say and not to dispute with him.

It was easy to see that even though he called the Bolshevik Revolution a "failure," and despite his opposition to the Communist International, he is under the influence of Bolshevik literature. What he lacks is the room of the Bolsheviks to destroy and to annihilate. The Bolshevik poison and the spirit of barbarity are not his legacy. His platform is the mental expression of an inexperienced man ready to sacrifice himself for his ideals and who demands a similar sacrifice from others.

New York, Friday, 20 November 1925
12. The Future of Palestine Depends on the Success of Industry
Paris, 19 November

In earlier articles I wrote that the Jews are safe as long as Great Britain remains in Palestine, and I also wrote that the Arab question is connected to the economic problem. There is a firm link between these two elements in the given situation. It seems to me, from what I have seen in Palestine, that the economic condition of the Jews there will most probably not only determine the attitude of the Arabs but also the ability and the will of the mandatory government to use drastic measures to give the Jews a sense of security.

I am absolutely convinced that Great Britain is determined not to allow pogroms to happen. Among the Jews of Palestine the feeling prevails that the events of Jaffa four years ago were directed from above, but this is an exaggerated charge. The officials at that time simply failed in every way to understand the situation and made one mistake after another. Since then they have learned a few things, and now the Arabs like their Jewish neighbors are convinced that any attempt to organize new slaughter will be nipped in the bud.

Still, there is security and there is security. The Arabs are not so rebellious as to challenge Great Britain in the form of wide-scale disturbances. But isolated small-scale outbursts of violence and rioting against the Jews are certainly within the realm of possibility.

The anti-Jewish propaganda of the Arab committee [the Arab Executive Committee – Y.G.] in certain conditions might be far more effective than the Zionist leaders believe. Likewise, we cannot ignore the mood of the Arabs in the neighboring countries. That they condemn the Balfour Declaration and the use the Zionists tried to make of Lord Balfour – this has been highlighted by them in many ways. Their hostile attitude has been felt by the Jews living among them in Syria and Egypt. I saw evidence of this situation when I was in Egypt.

Nevertheless, if the Jews in Palestine succeed in building the trade and industry of the country, a new situation will develop generally in the attitude to them of the Arab masses. The indirect result of this will be that the interest and goodwill of Great Britain towards the Jews will grow. It will also wish to demonstrate to the entire Arab world how seriously it treats the subject of the establishment of the homeland for the Jews, and will not tolerate any opposition. This also involves the question of how much prestige the Jews of Palestine will win in their relations with Great Britain.

The Zionists in Palestine with intelligence and common sense, and who understand that the British officials are not to be accused of causing the Jaffa disturbances [of May 1921 – Y.G.], believe that the British do not appreciate the importance the Jews have in Palestine. These Zionists nevertheless go too far in their interpretation that London wishes not to arouse the enmity of the Arabs by non-implementation of the Balfour Declaration. An influential Zionist put it this way: the British officials in Palestine at present are backing the wrong horse. They believe that the Jews immigrating to Palestine are not worth much, and therefore a little flirting with the Effendi leadership is the right policy, at least for the time being.

This state of affairs provided support for the critics among the Jews, who saw the pogrom [of May 1921 – Y.G.] as the result of British policy as described.

Since then the British officials have realized their error. They have come to understand that the Jews in Palestine constitute a factor of greater significance than they believed at first, and in any case things went too far. The Commissioner [of Jerusalem – Y.G.] Storrs is now aware that he backed the wrong horse. Being not only an educated man, but also a wise and astute man, he has altered his position considerably. I heard this also from responsible Zionists. I held an interview with Commissioner Storrs himself on the subject. After having a short talk with him in Tel Aviv I was received at his office in Jerusalem, where we held a long conversation. He totally rejected rumors that he had anti-Semitic biases. He complained jokingly that he had to fend off attacks from both sides: the Arabs accused him of hostility to them, while the Jews accused him of being anti-Jewish. Storrs mentioned a series of cases in which he demonstrated his fair attitude to both sides and his sympathy for the Jews. A young man from Brooklyn has a post in his office as Secretary of the Jewish Department, and he was present during our conversation. The Commissioner noted several issues that he had decided in favor of the Jews and against the Arabs. Among others he recalled that he had expelled from Palestine the ringleader of riots organized in Syria against Balfour shortly after the inauguration of the university in Jerusalem [the cornerstone was laid in 1925 – Y.G.]. This Arab, a Jew-hater, went to Haifa with the aim of staying in Palestine, but his expected arrival was made known to Commissioner Storrs a few days in advance, and when the Syrian arrived he was told that his presence there was not desired and he must return to Syria. Obviously, in this concrete incident Storrs took action because of the attack on Balfour, and not because of the threat the Syrian constituted against the Jews. Commissioner Storrs assured me that the chief factor leading to his decision was indeed the Jewish interest.

All in all, Commissioner Storrs impressed me as a man of keen judgment and it seems to me that there are no grounds for accusing him of any schemes against the Jews. There is certainly no reason to accuse him of inciting the Arabs who work openly against the Jews. True, he acted with great insensitivity at the time of the disturbances, but this was because he was not fully aware of the situation and certainly did not expect matters to go as far as they actually did – again, owing to the fact that he did not learn the nature of things. As Commissioner, he is a man of rare knowledge and is extremely well read. It is interesting to talk with him and it seems to me that the attacks on him were largely the result of misjudgment. If Commissioner Storrs is guilty of lack of proper behavior four years ago, then one may make the same accusation against a number of Zionists about their attitude to him today.

I spoke to several Arabs on this subject, and I also listened to all sorts of accounts and views of Jews in Tel Aviv, Jerusalem, and the communes. The sum of my main impressions is that in most cases where the economic condition of the Arabs has improved because of the presence of the Jews, the Arabs' enmity toward them has decreased.

The Arab is smart, and he is highly aware of what is best for him. He knows which side his bread is buttered. When he realizes that the arrival of the Jews means more money for him he will prefer this to the propaganda of the anti-Jewish Effendis. In this situation their propaganda will fall on deaf ears.

Clearly, the industrial activity, the flowering of Tel Aviv and the marvelous accomplishments of the Jewish settlement have made a great impression on the mandatory government in Palestine. They are also showing how impressed they are, and the Arab population understands this. The conclusion is self-evident: commercial and industrial success of the Jews will most probably create the right mood among the Arabs on the one hand, and in the British government on the other.

Yet precisely here lies the problem: the great question is if commercial and industrial success in Palestine is assured. Is the Zionist leaders' optimistic forecast based on real foundations? Unfortunately, I do not feel certain enough to answer these questions affirmatively. What I saw in Palestine strengthened the sympathy I have for the enterprise there. I wish them a vigorous continuation of all their burgeoning endeavor, I wish them prosperity with all my heart – my heart's desire, which I never cease to repeat. But the last few years do not seem to me a promising sign of what is in store for the future.

The mighty expansion of the building branch, which provided so many jobs in Tel Aviv, and indirectly elsewhere, was only a temporary event. I fear that this was a development that zealots will tend, quite naturally, to interpret as a sign of steady success that will continue to grow. By contrast, sober people free of sentiment that clouds judgment will not be able to accept this position. If indeed the existing situation of industrial and essential activities comes to an end, if indeed as a result of this immigration declines significantly, then the resistance of the Arabs will weaken considerably, and the presence of a small British force will suffice to ensure safety.

At the same time, one cannot overlook the question of the duration of the British stay in Palestine. No one can foresee, concerning the continued existence of the British empire, what the future will bring. Recently serious questions have arisen on this subject. If indeed Great Britain one day leaves Palestine to itself, a difficult situation will ensue. Again, this is a question of economic opportunities. If by then the Jews will have constructed wide-scale industry and commerce it is possible that the Arabs' feelings toward them will differ from what their anti-Jewish leaders expect them to be.

The part played by the Palestinian labor movement in the Arab question may greatly influence the economic situation. The workers' leaders do not agree with the Zionist position, which is concerned only about jobs for the Jewish workers and rejects any investment in improving the conditions of the wage-earning Arabs. In the view of the workers' leaders, the economic interests of the Jews are bound up with those of the Arab workers. This is how it was presented by David Ben-Gurion, the Secretary-General of the Histadrut, in one of his speeches: "If we wish to achieve an eight-hour working day it is impossible to leave the Arab worker outside such an arrangement. If he remains unorganized he will continue to work 12 hours a day for a pittance. He will work as a strikebreaker and will bring all our achievements to nought. As a matter of plain logic, and for the interests of our people, we are organizing the Arabs, who work for slave wages. "If this creates the impression in some people that this position is opposed to Zionism, then it's a pity. From our viewpoint this is the best thing we can do for our homeland. Among other good things, this policy, of forming a trade union of Arab workers, leads us to closer ties with them, to greater understanding, and to better relations. In this way we are acting against the anti-Jewish campaign being mounted against us by the Effendis."

One may pose some difficult questions about these words of comrade Ben-Gurion. But this is only a part of the totality of the economic problem that the Zionists have to contend with and the solution of which is still hidden in the mists of an unknown future.

New York, Sunday, 22 November 1925
13.   Solel-Boneh and Big Industry in Palestine
Paris, 21 November

If Palestine ever becomes an industrialized country, the fine things we see in it now are doomed to vanish. The enthralling idealism of the communes and of the individual semi-cooperative settlements [workers' moshavim – Y.G.], as well as this essence of labor and self-sacrifice that constitutes the religion of the Jezreel Valley – all this is condemned to death. Even the leaders of the communes understand this, because they talk all the time of ways to forestall the advance of capitalism. In parallel they are aware that without capitalistic development large-scale immigration will not be possible. Therefore they admit and accept, from the national point of view, that the development of capitalistic industry, at the present stage of Zionism, is a most desirable thing. All this sounds like praying for rain and then finding means of protecting the plants against getting wet.

One of the leaders of the communes hopes that the process just noted will pave the way to the socialist revolution, which he sees as already knocking at the doors of Palestine, like everywhere else in the world. But if indeed capitalism does appear it will devour the communes before the socialist revolution has broken down the doors. Other leaders hang their hopes on Solel-Boneh, the cooperative union of building workers, which itself accepts contracts, that it will successfully contend with capitalism. In other words, they hope that Solel-Boneh will build socialist enterprises under the very nose of capitalism. But to compete with capitalism Solel-Boneh will itself need capital. Wide-scale industrial enterprises need millions of available dollars, and where will they get these from?

Solel-Boneh is a marvelous organization, one of the finest things you can find now in Palestine, but it is short of capital to realize its goals. The young generation that go out to the settlements look upon the veteran settlers in Palestine as swindlers who are exploiting the hired laborer. But there were times when those veteran settlers, about 40 years ago, were themselves young idealists, full of ardor. Now these veterans answer the criticism hurled at them like this: "Wait a bit, young people. Time will tell. You are wrong if you think that you are made of different stuff from us."

True, the veteran idealists established their settlements on the principle of private property while the young men and women of the communes are organized on the principles of socialism. In their society they have eliminated the personal interest and the egoism of the individual. This is more or less right, but the vision is that socialism must come simultaneously to all civilized human society, not piecemeal in the form of isolated communalist settlements. If indeed capitalism invades Palestine these communes will have to contend with a different psychology.

Jacob Lestchinsky talks of Tel Aviv as though it were a new Berdichev, implying that the spirit of speculation has infiltrated into Palestine, just as it possesses the various cities and towns of Poland and Lithuania. This is true, but the speculative spirit that he so complains about is not the great danger, as people tend to think, because the obsession with speculation in real estate is only temporary. It will not of course solve the problem of immigration. If there is going to be immigration, this will become possible through industry and not through land speculation.

All in all, there is a conflict here of a special kind. On the one hand, we have those fascinating communes as well as the wonderful spirit of honest labor in the building of Palestine, but on the other we have the lust for capitalism, which will quite obviously cause the destruction of all this. Even the senior Zionist leaders who had no connection to socialism, such as Shemaryahu Levin and the poet Bialik, speak in terms of building an ideal society in Palestine, one that will escape all the curses of capitalism. Yet these very people are perfectly aware of the necessity for capitalistic industry if Palestine is to develop any meaningful industry.

It is like having your cake and eating it. Here lies the tragedy of the entire situation, where an attempt is being made to blend two irreconcilable opposites: on the one hand the splendid idealism today manifested in the Jezreel Valley; on the other the desire to create the most highly developed economic life, without which significant immigration is inconceivable.

New York, Wednesday, 25 November 1925
14. What Do the Jews of the World Find in Zionism?
Paris, 24 November

The purpose of this telegram is to deal with Zionism and the position to adopt on it in the given state of affairs. I feel that this is necessary in order to complement the impressions and opinions I have presented on the situation in Palestine.

The popularity of Palestine is growing everywhere. If previously its attractive force was only for Zionists, now it is winning general recognition. True, it appeals more to imagination and emotion than to the cold logic of its inherent possibilities, but still, its attractive power has greatly expanded and it is genuine. There is a feeling that wide-scale and active sympathy can produce surprising results in the creation of a wealth of unenvisaged opportunities, and in turning the impossible into a living source of hope. This is entirely a matter of the mood emanating from the eternal Jewish tragedy. Today it is perhaps greater than before even though it is reflected in less drastic ways than at other times in the history of Jewish suffering.

Anti-Semitism is spreading in fresh directions, and as a result a great surge of national feelings has welled up in Jews all over the world. Therefore, when one hears of one corner on the face of the earth where there is a chance that Jews will build their home and will not feel like strangers, the heart warms to it. The news from Tel Aviv in recent years has caused an intensification of these feelings because the impression has formed that at long last the Zionist dreams are being realized.

Nothing succeeds like success, and Palestine has begun to look like a successful realization of national dreams. In addition, so much is heard about the wonderful idealism of the pioneers in Palestine, and also of the praiseworthy position of the Zionist movement regarding these settlers. Every method of buying and selling land to Jews in Palestine is based on the estimable principle of working it directly, without graft in any form. This, as well as the support given generously by the Jewish National Fund and the Keren Hayesod to the cooperative settlements and other idealist companies, has enhanced the prestige of the Zionist movement among the left-wingers.

In consequence of all the foregoing, socialists all over the word have nurtured an attitude of warmth to Palestine in their hearts. After Mr Ramsay MacDonald visited Palestine he wrote an enthusiastic report about what he witnessed there, and his name has been added to the list of personalities sympathetic to Palestine. These also include Mr Philip Snowden, Mrs Snowden, and Colonel Wedgewood. A similar position is evinced by people such as Edouard Bernstein, Léon Blum, and other socialist leaders of Jewish origin.

But it is different with the Jewish socialists in Poland, and there is nothing unusual about that. The hostility to Zionism of our comrades from the Bund arises principally, but not exclusively, in local affairs. The two movements are in conflict over various political problems, which have nothing to do with the subject of Palestine. Therefore, the bitterness of our comrades in Warsaw, Vilna and Grodno is understandable.

Still, for us in the United States it would be utterly absurd to be guided by feelings that have no connection with our political life. We can afford to be free of preconceptions and to be clear-minded – and such we must be. If Palestine does not convince us we cannot be moved by the impression that it creates through its marvelous goals and the self-sacrifice that underlie the work being done there. We are better placed to understand what is going on between the Bundists and their Zionist opponents in Poland. Our comrades in Poland are of our bones and our flesh, and they are ever assured of our spiritual, material, and moral support. But regarding the events in Palestine – we cannot permit ourselves to determine our position on it in light of conflict in Poland.

Perhaps the present enthusiasm for Palestine is just a temporary wave of excitement. But as matters stand this is a reality filled with heart-warming content that imparts to it the right to our sympathetic concern. Of course, the truth must be told even about Palestine, but the tone is what makes the music, as the French saying goes. Whatever our criticism, it has to be expressed in terms of amity and brotherliness, and should be as remote as possible from the spirit of hatred.

In the course of my present tour I met all kinds of Jews. In many cities and in every place I found great support for the idea of a Jewish homeland in Palestine. On various occasions unfavorable comments about the idea are received in the way a mother hears negative criticism of her child. It may be that the child suffers from an incurable disability, and it is also possible that the mother is entirely aware of this, but she does not allow a stranger to refer to it. Moreover, an incurable disability in her child provides good cause for the mother's complete devotion to him.

This is the kind of feelings I found towards Palestine in many cases. The Jews reject criticism about its future. The notion has been firmly adopted, and it is very dear to their hearts. It is good to hear that there is a refuge in the world, a corner for the Jews. Therefore, they will cast aside all hostile criticism about Tel Aviv or the settlements. Almost every Jew in the world suffers terribly over what is befalling the Jews in many countries. Millions of Jews feel great anger in their hearts, with a profound sense of anguish; whether they express this in one form or another they hold it in their hearts. They long for a remedy and they grasp the straw of the creation of a Jewish homeland in Palestine. A religious Jew goes to the synagogue to pour out his sorrowing heart in prayer. Modern Jews seek relief for the same feelings in the form of zealous support for Palestine.

I talked to an interesting businessman in Paris, a man with much experience and a penetrating pragmatic outlook, and he expressed the matter in this way: "My father is happy with his faith, and his great consolation is his belief in the advent of the Messiah. It is not only his World to Come, but also a source of comfort for all the troubles in this world. When I was young I tried to taunt him about this, and that was stupid of me. Why destroy the only comfort he has? This is the feeling I have when I talk to a fervent Zionist. I am dubious about the future of Palestine, but I don't have the heart to tell him this. Palestine is their Messiah and there are very many Jews who have had no connection with Zionism who feel this way."

Naturally, there is a limit to this approach. It is impossible to suppress a person's criticism, but at the same time the many fine things one finds in Palestine are not be belittled, nor are the admiration and sympathy that has lodged in his heart.

New York, Wednesday, 9 December 1925
15. The Labor Movement in Palestine

The labor movement fulfills an extraordinary function. It is of outstanding importance, first as an organized movement of wage-earners, and secondly because it plays an important role in the industrial activity of Palestine as a supplier of jobs. At one and the same time it is a militant union of wage-earners and a big entrepreneur of cooperatives. In addition it has certain elements that have developed in it, which all together give it a character different from any other workers' movement in the world.

Four years ago, when the Histadrut sent three representatives to America [the first Histadrut mission, which traveled in 1921, consisting of Berl Katznelson, Yosef Baratz, and Manya Vilboshevich-Shohat – Y.G.], I discussed with them the peculiar nature of their movement and I stated that "our workers will not find it easy to understand the nature of your movement, because it has a different character from that of the workers' movements in other countries. In other places the workers' movement is organized and unites the wage-earners in a struggle against the employers. This is its essence and this is its purpose. It is class war and it is also the essence of the Jewish workers' movement in America. By contrast, in your movement there is a high percentage of people who work for themselves. It makes no difference if they are organized in communes or in other groups. Or if they work as individual farmers – all of them don't have a boss on their heads. They don't have anyone to fight against.

In such a situation, how can they be part of your movement?"

The only clear answer I managed to get from them was that every member in their movement had to work himself, and was not allowed to employ hired labor and to exploit others. This of course is a very nice ideal, but it alters nothing regarding the question of the class war. The fact that a certain farmer or someone else does not exploit anyone is still not sufficient reason for accepting him into a workers' movement. He has to be exploited by someone else, because the purpose of the trade unions and their organs is to unite the exploited against their exploiters. These who have no one to defend themselves against may be good people but they have no place in an organization the purpose of which is a defense pact and struggle.

The Palestinian labor movement has a single ideal: to build Palestine and turn it into a Jewish homeland. Therefore, for the accomplishment of this goal the farmer or associations of farmers who work for themselves are no less important than the hired hands who work for an exploiting employer. But that's another story.

Regarding the workers' movement in the sense that this term is used all over the world, the Palestinian labor movement is not like them at all. The Palestinian labor movement has a twofold nature with a twofold purpose: (a) to unite the wage-earners in their struggle against their bosses; (b) to organize and invigorate all the workers for the building of Eretz Israel as a Jewish homeland.

Of the two foregoing aims, the second is the more important. The great majority in the labor movement are socialists, and the others too are left-leaning. But for all of them the realization of Zionism constitutes their primary goal, while socialism is a secondary target. They would like to achieve both goals together, and they are completely serious in this quest, but priority always goes to the building of Eretz Israel. They, like the non-socialist Zionists (apart from Mizrahi), want in Palestine only people who work honestly, and they wish to prevent the entry of exploiters. Yet at the same time, from the Zionist viewpoint every immigrant is important because the arrival of each immigrant enlarges the Jewish settlement. If the immigrant also has money to invest in industry in Palestine this is even better, and in such a case he may even become an exploiter. From a pragmatic Palestinian viewpoint this entire approach is understandable, but our interest here is a comparison with the world workers' movement.

If in America you raise the question of the assistance that should be offered to the workers of Palestine, the answer usually will be "Assistance? Yes. But proportionally no more than that given to Jewish workers in other countries. Why, for example, should we give them preference over Jewish strikers in Warsaw or Grodno?" Whoever believes that the workers' organization in Palestine deserves more attention than a similar Jewish organization in another country holds that view because he sympathizes with the movement the goal of which is to create a place where the Jew will feel at home. But this has hardly anything to do with his sympathy for the labor movement.

When I arrived in Palestine the situation there was in many ways different from what it was four years before, but the nature of the labor movement has not altered. The movement has grown and has brought into its ranks urban wage-earners, but in parallel it has added many settlers who work for themselves and are not employees. In addition, the number of employees who do not work for private employers has risen. I refer to those whose employer is the Histadrut itself through the Solel-Boneh company, which contracts to pave roads and build bridges, buildings, and so on. It is part of the Histadrut. In this case the paid worker, again, is not associated with the class war because he does not have an exploiter. As members of the Histadrut the paid workers who pave roads and construct buildings are at one and the same time employees and their own contractors. If they call a strike, for example, this means that they are striking against themselves.

The number of workers in Palestine today is not large, less than 20,000, including members of the cooperative settlements, the workers' moshavim and also private farmers who do not employ hired labor. If this number grows significantly, it is possible that the nature of the entire movement will change. Then it will almost certainly assume a character more like that of the workers' movements in other countries. A considerable wage-earning population can develop in Palestine only if trade and industry develop there, and in turn the development of trade and industry will in many senses affect the changes.

The existing communes, with the fine idealism and courageous self-sacrifice, will not be able to last long in conditions of a country with developed trade and industry. Greater opportunities will be created for a better living and a better life than on the communes. Those who now remain on the communes do so in the first place because it is hard to find work elsewhere. When the situation changes they will leave. The fervently idealistic members who live on the communes will then be vulnerable to the lure of better and fuller lives in the city, an attraction that only few will be able to withstand. The question is what effect will such development have on the sense of excitement with which Palestine is now being built? But this has nothing to do with our discussion of the present. I wish only to note that trade and industry are more effective means of building the country than excitement. This is not a nice thing to say, but what can you do when it is also the truth.

Our concern here is with the present reality, and not with what may be expected in the future. Today the labor movement in Palestine is different from the workers' movement in Europe and America. Today a large part of it has no connection with the workers' struggle. The fact that they are sympathetic towards this struggle and participate in international workers' congresses only points to their idealistic interest, while our concern is with material things, the kind of things connected with the daily life of the worker.

Therefore the labor movement in Palestine is a mixture of trade unions in the usual sense and cooperative settlements, workers' moshavim, farmers owning private property of a different kind, and paid workers in cooperatives such as Solel-Boneh. All are involved and united in the same workers' federation . . .

New York, Thursday, 10 December 1925
16. The Labor Movement in Palestine (continued)

The workers and farmers in Palestine are organized in three parties: a social-democratic party, which is Ahdut Ha'avodah; the semi-anarchist Hapo'el Hatza'ir; and Poaley Tziyon Left, three-quarters of whom are Bolsheviks. All belong to the Histadrut. There is a group that are one hundred percent Soviet communists who work for Moscow's interest and take orders only from there, but they were expelled from the Histadrut in Palestine. The name Po'aley Tziyon refers now only to Po'aley Tziyon Left, those communists who were not expelled from the Histadrut. The socialist Zionists do not use this name, and their leaders, referring to themselves, use the name Ahdut Ha'avodah . . .

 . . . The Histadrut and the Zionist movement usally work in concert. As far as I could see during the four weeks I stayed in Palestine, relations between them are most cordial. I was especially interested in this point. My impression was that even if all the Zionist leaders were members of the socialist movement they could not treat the Histadrut better than they actually do.

In my last article I presented this view in relation to the communes, but, as stated, this attitude of the Zionist movement holds for all the labor movement in Palestine. At the last Zionist Congress in Vienna, when a vote of confidence in the Zionist movement under Weizmann's leadership was taken, the workers' delegates abstained. After the vote they said to Weizmann: "You know how dear you are to us, but in the present situation . . . ," and they pointed out the various reasons that had made them abstain. In any event, afterwards they voted for him and helped him obtain a significant majority.

Before my arrival in Palestine, when I heard of this incident, it did not make a good impression on me. I was dubious as to the honesty of their support. I thought it was part of the political game. But when I reached Tel Aviv I found out that the expressions of amity to Weizmann voiced by the workers' delegation were not empty words. On one occasion I put it to a workers' leader in Tel Aviv: "You lose nothing by the nature of such relations with the Zionist leadership. They do everything you ask of them. They help the communes and your other institutions. They give you land and money, and on your account they have to suffer at the hands of the orthodox religious Zionists."

The workers' leader did not deny the fact that the Zionist movement treated the Histadrut with great fairness, but he also pointed to the disputes between the two bodies. For example, Weizmann was opposed to the activity of Solel-Boneh, and he believed that this cooperative constituted a barrier to private enterprise – what is more, just at a time when it was impossible to build Palestine without private enterprise (I shall write more on this subject when I write about Solel-Boneh). It is important to note here that Weizmann, despite his reserved attitude to Solel-Boneh, supports it, and the cooperative also operates on the basis of the assistance granted to it by the Zionist Organization.

This same workers' leader stated his views to me as to why the Zionist Organization was so amicable towards the Histadrut and supported all the agricultural settlements and the urban organizations associated with the Histadrut: Eretz Israel could become the homeland of the Jews only if it was able to attract a large Jewish population. It was a question of mass migration, of many people, and masses of immigrants meant Jewish workers. Zionism was obliged to contend with the problem of cheap Arab laborers, who worked for a few pennies a day. Therefore, if you want to make mass Jewish immigration possible you must give the Jewish worker the opportunity to organize, otherwise cheap Arab labor will destroy him and this will eliminate the likelihood of wide-scale immigration by the masses. A large Jewish settlement cannot grow only out of a population of merchants and industrialists.

When the inhabitants of Palestine talked to me they often referred to Dr Ruppin, the famous Jew of German origin who is also an important personality in the Zionist movement. They ascribed to him a weighty share of the major ideas and achievements. This is also true in all respects of the labor movement. In this context the workers' leader said to me: "Dr Ruppin was the first to understand this notion. He understood the huge importance of our movement in connection with the complex of questions concerning the development of Palestine."

I also spoke on this subject with young people on the extreme left wing of the labor movement, although not counted with the Bolsheviks, who are totally spurned here. These young people's view of the Zionist movement was identical to that of the labor leader I cited above. The foremost people among these youngsters went even further, stating that "at present we hold a monopoly on the resources of the Zionist movement." Their uncertainty concerns only the future. They have no idea how long these friendly and most sympathetic relations will continue.

The orthodox religious Zionists maintain a different attitude to the labor movement. Many members of Mizrahi believe that they are behaving correctly when they break strikes by workers belonging to the Histadrut. This position is not typical of them all, for example, the rabbi from Yablonka and his band wish to join the Histadrut. When I was in Tel Aviv I held a number of interesting conversations on this subject with several orthodox Zionists; unfortunately they did not permit me to publish their names. One of them argued: "The Histadrut is ruining trade, meaning it is ruining Eretz Israel. They talk incessantly about building the land! But how is it possible to build it if they do not allow you to do so? If you are able to employ cheap labor, which makes it possible for you to sell your goods, along comes the Histadrut with its overseers and it forces you to take on the people it wants you to take on, and to pay them wages according to its demands. In such circumstances how can anything get done?"

I asked him if he meant that the Histadrut did not allow the employment of cheap Arab labor. He did not give me a direct answer to this question. He said that he was referring to Jewish workers who were not obliged to be organized in the Histadrut. He also stated that the Histadrut was closing every path before the industrialists and confining them in such a way that they had no room for maneuver. When we spoke of immigration he said that were it not for the Histadrut more immigrants would come, and it would be easier for the Jewish worker to find a job.

A veteran resident in Palestine defended the system of employing cheap Arab labor on the moshavot. He himself was a city-dweller and not a farmer, but he opposed the criticism made against the farmers of Petah Tikva who tended their orange groves with the help of Arab workers. In his youth the veteran settler had studied political economy, and he was familiar with the law of supply and demand, and also the principle of laissez-faire, that is, the possibility of engaging in commerce without restrictions, and he based the thrust of his argument on this foundation. I commented on his words: "But if you want to obtain a Jewish majority in Palestine, is it not essential that labor in the Jewish sector be reserved in order to provide work for Jewish immigrants? If the work is done by Arabs, the masses of Jews will not have any livelihood in Palestine; is this not your Zionist outlook?" He replied by pointing out that at the moment the Histadrut itself was organizing and receiving the services of Arab workers.

To tell the truth, the problem is difficult and complex. Regarding the organization of Arab workers, the Histadrut must do this, whether it wants to or not, because unorganized Arab labor will destroy any Histadrut effort to shorten the working day and to increase wages. If the Arab workers are organized and accepted by the trade unions their right to conditions equal to those of the Jewish workers must be recognized. Here we get back to the problem of jobs, which from the Zionist view-point are vital for the livelihood of Jewish immigrants who will come and will swell the Jewish population – and it is these very jobs that are liable to be filled by Arabs organized by the Histadrut. This is a situation full of contradictions, but is the Histadrut solution the right one? Has it adopted a certain solution of its own free will or not? In any event, the Histadrut is now functioning as a socialist movement should in fact function.

The most important and renowned figures in the labor movement impressed me as honest and earnest people, absolutely devoted to the cause. I saw them and spent time with them often. On various occasions I posed questions to them and debated with them. I heard all their arguments and in general they made a very good impression on me. Of course, on many matters I do not agree with them. For example, I greatly regret their chauvinism, their fanaticism about Hebrew, and similar issues. I also entirely disagree with them on several Zionist tenets. But I must comment that it was a great joy for me to see them at their work and to gain an acquaintance with their character and the nature of their toil.

The reader already knows that I spent many hours listening to opposition people. I made special efforts to establish contact with the opposition camp and to give them full opportunity to present their position to me and their points of controversy with official Zionist politics. On several subjects the opposition people impressed me. Anyway, in sum I left Palestine with a sense of the most profound appreciation and a feeling of the greatest warmth for the Zionist leaders.

New York, Saturday, 12 December 1925
17. The Work of Solel-Boneh

I have frequently mentioned Solel-Boneh, namely the Histadrut cooperative . . . This is an unusual workers' organization, and it plays an imporant part in the present situation in Palestine.

The institution appeared on the scene in an unexpected way and its size is unusual. The fact of its existence and its success were so surprising that the labor leaders in Palestine now expect miracles of it. They believe that it can revolutionize the economic process in Palestine. Essentially, Solel-Boneh came into existence on account of the unemployment that prevailed after the war . . .

The vital problem was how to increase Jewish immigration. By God's grace there was the Balfour Declaration, and there was the Mandate and a chance for a Jewish homeland, but efforts had to be made for a rapid growth in the Jewish population and also that it should change from a minority to a majority. The assumption was that if a way were found to provide a living for the Jews in Palestine they would migrate there. But the great question was how to supply work to masses of immigrants.

In a more concrete and immediate sense the problem emerged in a very harsh way after the war [World War I – Y.G.], mainly in respect of the young Zionists who migrated to Palestine. For them, it was not a theoretical political question but one of urgent sustenance for thousands of Jews . . .

In the five years of its existence Solel-Boneh has built about 50 percent of all the buildings constructed in Palestine, at a value of about $6 million. During my stay in Palestine it had building contracts for $1 million more.

The building workers' union in Palestine covers about 4500 members, and about half of them, some 2500, worked in August and September [1925 – Y.G.] with Solel-Boneh. Eighty percent of the construction of Rutenberg's electricity station [in Tel Aviv – Y.G.] was done by Solel-Boneh. The cooperative also subcontracts to smaller cooperatives belonging to the Histadrut, and in special cases to private tradesmen. A

large part of the work is carried out directly by the company. The great majority of the building workers in Palestine never worked at that trade in their countries of origin and they learned it on the job with Solel-Boneh
. . .

At the Solel-Boneh headquarters there are 51 engineers and technicians, 17 of them holders of diplomas from universities in Germany, Switzerland or France. The company has a head office and four local branch offices. The head office is in Tel Aviv, and the branch offices are in Tel Aviv, Jerusalem, Haifa and Tiberias. The salary of a qualified engineer is $125–150 a month; that of a technical engineer is $60–100, and that of managers is $60–110. The total number of employees in the five offices, including bookkeepers, is 126. Every month the company pays out about $8500 in salaries, not including, of course, the workers' wages. The hired workers are divided into four wage categories: three categories for various kinds of skilled workers ($3/4/5 a day) and one category of unskilled laborers ($1.75 a day). These figures were given to me by Comrade Remez, who manages the head office and the company as a whole, being one of the foremost leaders of the entire labor movement.

When I asked him about private contractors against whom Solel-Boneh has to compete he stated, "Until recently we have had to compete only with small companies, Jews who came from Poland with a little money. But lately in Palestine foreign capital has begun to appear belonging to companies with large resources – and this is a great danger for us. We shall have to expand and we shall need capital. This danger is linked to another: our new big competitors will employ cheap unorganized Arab labor, so it is even more important for us to take control of the builidng of industry as quickly as possible, before the Arabs enter this field."

. . . Solel-Boneh has many critics and enemies. Businessmen in that field hate it because the cooperative is a fearsome competitor, while other businessmen condemn it on the grounds that it is a socialist enterprise. A "Bolshevik" concern they call it, with venom in their voices. Those who use this sobriquet would like to include the entire Histadrut in it, with its institutions. Mizrahi, for example, is convinced that Solel-Boneh and the trade unions are destroying Palestine. Mizrahi also breaks strikes on principle, and this at once reveals its political position. More attention should be paid to the criticism by progressive Zionists, who respect the labor movement and even support Solel-Boneh. This is the essence of the criticism: Solel-Boneh, as a part of the Histadrut with its trade unions, enjoys advantages over its competitors in the private sector. For example, it controls the labor market, and at any time it so desires it can hire as many workers as it wants, and the best of them, while contractors in the private sector have problems in this area. Solel-Boneh gets the cream of all the contracts because of its size and its power. Let us assume that someone wishes to build a building or a factory, and he happens to know that a private company can do the work better and cheaper than Solel-Boneh; he still has to give the contract to Solel-Boneh because he personally will have less to fear from strikes, and secondly it is generally better to be on the right side of those who wield power. These are the arguments of the businessmen opposed to Solel-Boneh.

To this criticism the Histadrut leaders respond that their organization treats everyone fairly and does not show bias. They find ridiculous the claim that the Histadrut initiates strikes in private building firms in order to promote Solel-Boneh. "They talk as if a strike in Palestine were child's play," one labor leader retorted when I repeated the arguments voiced against Solel-Boneh. "Industry as a whole is still in such a fragile state that we reconsider a thousand times before deciding on a strike. This is no small matter. There is also the constant fear that the Arabs will break the strike. So these accusations are a foolish distortion."

A certain businessman complained to me that the Histadrut labor exchange was ruining his business because it did not provide him with the number of workers he needed. It did this to serve the interests of a certain well-based group of workers, so he told me, so that they would get high wages. This businessman did not link his claim to the questsion of Solel-Boneh, but several other businessmen made similar complaints, and they blamed everything on Solel-Boneh, which they saw as the root of all the problems in Palestine. An intelligent Zionist, not in business but a critic of Solel-Boneh, "simply as a friend of Palestine" as he put it, said to me, "Cooperatives are cooperatives and trade unions are trade unions. These are two distinct categories, and when they are merged into a single framework the cooperative is bound to harm the quality of the trade union. If a private factory employs workers belonging to a trade union and pays them salaries as required by the union, it thereby creates the right relationship with the labor movement and it merits its support and its protection. But here the workers' organization is not its protector but its competitor . . . We still do not have socialism and the Histadrut is mixing up its role as a fighter against capitalism with its role as the creator of a socialist society in Palestine. This is not a natural mix, and no good can grow out of it."

Much criticism is also heard on the part of the workers, and their claims are the opposite of those outlined above, namely that Solel-Boneh is responsible for the strikes that erupt among its competitors. The workers complained to me that the company does not allow strikes, with the goal of keeping wages down and so preventing competitors from carrying out the work more cheaply. As a capitalist, Solel–Boneh is interested in contracts.

These are the complaints of the workers who are dissatisfied with the Histadrut leaders and with Solel–Boneh. Solel–Boneh operating as a sort of capitalist body is in conflict with itself functioning as a socialist institution and as part of the Histradrut. The workers who are not affiliated with the Zionist movement accuse Solel–Boneh of siding with the Zionist workers, to whom it supplies more and better work.

The Solel–Boneh leaders reject all these charges. As for the complaint that they want to build a socialist industry in the country even before the rest of industry has become established, they argue that the conditions in Palestine are quite different from those in other countries, so economic development too has to be different. They are not at all certain that with the help of Solel–Boneh it will be possible to skip the capitalist stage in Palestine.

Solel–Boneh builds in a fortuitous manner. In this context as in others, the leaders of Palestine are controlled by circumstances more than they control circumstances.

One of the chief things that has to be borne in mind in respect of Solel–Boneh is that it is first and foremost a construction company. Much of its rapid growth has to be attributed to the building frenzy, which in a few years led to the enlargement of Tel Aviv from a small town to a city of 40,000 inhabitants. Is this a permanent source for development? If not, what other kinds of activity can be found for Solel–Boneh to undertake? What will happen the moment building ceases?

I studied the cooperative very closely, and in the present circumstances I got to know it very well. Despite all its flaws and the inimical criticism, which more or less stems from these flaws, this is an institution that deserves the greatest feelings of sympathy on the part of every socialist.

New York, Tuesday, 15 December 1925
18. Is There a Future for Eretz Israel?

Building Eretz Israel! The zealous settlers in Palestine believe in this slogan literally. When the settler works his land he feels that he is building Eretz Israel, namely the land of the People of Israel. He is doing it with his own hands. He invests his toil in the soil that is so dear to him. As a mother nurses her child, so does he nurture the land with tenderness. When a little greenery appears in the sandy soil, when desolate land is covered with trees and becomes fertile, the settler is suffused with the consciousness that this is his precious land being built, through his own labor and with his own hands. Every farmer speaks lovingly of the crops he has produced, but the Jewish settler in Palestine speaks of his crops with double love. It is always a joy to see the fruit of their labor, and in this case the fruit is not of any soil, but the soil of the Land of Israel, the land of the People of Israel. I sensed these emotions in my conversations with every settler in Palestine who showed me his farm. In the case of a fervent man like Levkovich [Lavi – Y.G.] of Ein Harod this emotion has become a burning flame. He does not forget for an instant that he is working that same land where Gideon gathered his army [for the war against the Midianites – Y.G.]. He does not forget for a moment that the little spring rising out of the hollow rock is the very spring [Harod – Y.G.] mentioned in the Book of Judges. It is the same land that he is cultivating. He is helping to build that same land and likewise to reclaim it as the homeland for the Jews . . .

. . . The word *eretz* means land, so agricultural work brings the Zionist, in the most tangible way, into contact with the land, and this perception of the importance of the land becomes rooted in his consiousness. When immigration swelled and Tel Aviv was constantly growing, the subject of settlement of the land was the talk of the town. Those young Zionists abroad who had prepared themselves for immigration were ready, on arrival, only for the farming profession. These ambitions, of course, were connected with the motivation to acquire more and more land in Palestine. In the city a large population can develop on a small area, and a large Jewish population is necessary to achieve a Jewish majority as quickly as possible. The acquisition of as much land as possible is no less important for the establishment of Eretz Israel than the gathering of a large Jewish population. To reach the first goal you need more and more settlement. The focus of the Palestinian idealist's interest is agricultural settlement. Cultivating the land gives him supreme spiritual satisfaction. He learns farming with the goal of being able to tend the land of his dreams, the land of Israel . . .

. . . For various reasons it became an accepted principle that the land acquired is to be the land of the people, and that no one has the right to purchase even the smallest plot from the Jewish National Fund. At the same time cooperative settlement began to develop and the ideology grew up that there may not be private ownership of the land. Concern for the interests of the individual, talk of "mine" and "yours" – for people like Levkovich this is sacrilege. He is working and cultivating the land where Gideon was born. For members of the cooperative settlement, work on terrains mentioned in the Bible appears as the only right way of building Eretz Israel . . . These people work hard and make do with the humblest food and lodgings. They invest all their energy in working the lands of the people and they do so without generating material goods for themselves or their children. They are simply building Eretz Israel. What can be greater? Every settler of this kind is a living poem. The question still remains as to whether Eretz Israel can be built by poetry.

Palestine is a small country. Even if it were possible to convert every patch purchased from the Arabs into fertile Jewish land, the Jewish population in the cooperative settlements, and settlement as a whole, would remain limited. If it ever becomes necessary for a million or even a million and half Jews to be in Palestine this will be possible only through the rapid growth of the Jewish cities. The rapid growth of Jewish cities in Palestine has very little to do with agriculture.

Unfortunately, the ceaseless toil and steadfastness of dedicated farmers will not build Eretz Israel. This is the harsh and bitter truth. Again I am obliged, greatly against my will, to state that for the building of great cities cold, hard prose is more effective than poetry and idealism.

When Tel Aviv began to grow quickly it seemed to have set out on the road to success. This is the impression it makes from afar on those who have not gained an acquaintance with the reality from close to. People have compared it to those towns that grew up fast in America, but there is a great difference between America and Palestine. In America, when a town grows quickly, like mushrooms after the rain, this state of affairs somehow is continuous. The rapid growth has some basis in reality also. It stems from new economic factors, new sources of trade and industry. Perhaps new mines have been opened, and as a result new factories have been set up, or new railroad junctions have been built out of demand created by the activity of industrial concerns. Next, new streets are set out, with houses on either side, because the new industries attract crowds of new residents: thousands of workers, hundreds of merchants, agents, and the like. All this new community needs a roof over its head, so entire new neighborhoods are constructed. Hence the building branch grows as a function of the development of new industrial plant, commerce, mines or railroads. This is the history of the fast-growing American town.

By contrast, in Tel Aviv building activity is not the result but the cause.

People rushed to build hundreds of houses not because industry attracted masses of immigrants but because many people moved to Palestine or heard that hundreds of houses were being built there, so there was a living to be made by workers in the building branch.

A number of well-to-do Jews immigrated from Poland, and the first thing they did was to build homes for themselves. From an interview I held with Mr Hayimson, head of the Immigration Department of the mandatory government, which I conveyed in a telegram from Paris, the reader has already learned that building homes swallowed up too large a portion of the immigrant's capital. Too little money was left to invest in industry. But for the moment jobs were created in brick manufacturing and for builders, carpenters, glaziers, and so on. These workers brought their parents or friends over. New immigrants arrived, and this again created a demand for houses and the real estate branch flourished. And once again a few Jews arrived with some money, which they invested in real estate in Tel Aviv because they had heard that this was a flourishing field . . . So why did people immigrate to Palestine? Because many new houses were being built there. And why were many new houses being built there? Because people continued to immigrate to Palestine.

Even in America not every town that sprang up suddenly had a real foundation. There were many towns of this kind the prosperity of which had no basis. But America is so large and rich that even agriculture alone laid the foundation for a very large number of towns, for thousands of miles of railroad track, and for successful enterprises of every kind. By contrast, Palestine is a small country. The amount of arable land is limited and this is poor land that suffers from a shortage of water. The agricultural industry can support only a small number of towns. Even Jerusalem, if the pilgrim trade is taken away, will drop to the level of a small town . . .

. . . The building of Palestine cannot be dependent on its agriculture. Nor can it be founded on the Tel Aviv building craze. Anyone examining its economic opportunities must concentrate on the question of whether the possibility exists of developing commercial and industrial centers in it based not only on the local market but also on the neighboring countries and even more distant lands. Pragmatic people in commerce and finance in Palestine point out that the country is situated in the heart of the East, among Egypt, Syria, Mesopotamia, and Turkey. This fact, they believe, offers some chance of success.

One should not rush to reject the view, nor should one should rush to confirm it, that a splendid industrial future is ready and waiting for

Palestine. It may certainly be assumed that the Jews will build something there, because they are rare people, talented and unusually industrious. Given the opportunity they will move mountains.

The countries surrounding Palestine can be developed. As their inhabitants approach civilization more closely their requirements will expand and grow. The neighboring Jews possess a great civilizing influence. In parallel it is possible to develop the natural resources of the bordering countries under the direction of Jewish entrepreneurs. It is possible to develop an active manufacturing industry there, as well as commerce, with the Jews playing a leading role in all matters. Then they will become the masters of the situation. They will also hold the key to the transport of goods from the east to Europe and the key to the entire life of the east. In such circumstances the danger from the Arabs will diminish to a minimum.

If Great Britain remains in Palestine, which is strategically very important for it, it will come to recognize the practical importance of the Jews. The Jewish homeland will be recognized everywhere as a fact. The Arabic-speaking peoples will become accustomed to this fact as something that their interest is to connect to and affirm. If even then a troublemaker appears who instigates pogroms, the Jews will have adequate means for self-defense.

This is an optimistic picture of the future, but no one can know if it will come to pass. Whether the course of events and conditions in fact lead in the direction indicated, we will be able to see in the coming years.

Yet again the question arises of what will happen if there is no meaningful industry in Palestine that can sustain a large Jewish population, and if the Jews do not become masters of the economic situation. The answer to this question, as to others, can be got only in the course of time with the development of things. But it is reasonable to assume that Palestine will in any case remain a Jewish center. It perhaps may be small, but in the present world circumstances Palestine will always play some part in Jewish life.

As long as the situation in Poland remains grave, even though the Jews are no longer leaving the country in such large numbers as before, they continue to emigrate and must reach Palestine as there is nowhere else for them to go. Even if they do not take much wealth with them, they carry a huge amount of Jewish vigor and gifts and Jewish devotion; something must grow out of this. Even Bismarck was obliged to state: "You have a very difficult problem when dealing with the Jews. Once they decide on something they cannot be moved from it."

It is unthinkable that everything that has been built in Palestine will melt like snow on a warm day. Bismarck did not believe this, and I too find it hard to believe. Anti-Semitism has resulted in the appearance of a large class of Jewish nationalist intelligentsia, and for them Jewish Palestine today is like the Western Wall and the tombs of Maimonides and Meir Ba'al Haness for the orthodox Jew. So far the interest shown in Palestine has been great, and this of course has major importance. How long this interest will continue I do not know, but it most certainly will be a long time.

As for the idealists who sacrifice themselves for the building of Eretz Israel and the agricultural settlements, those among our comrades who live a life of selflessness on the communes, they deserve, whatever the case, the warmest sentiments and the best wishes of every socialist.

New York, 16 December 1925
19. What Is the Meaning of "To Build Eretz Israel"?

Even in America there were many cities that sprang up overnight – boom towns, mirages, and the growth of many of them was not rooted in healthy soil. But America is so large and rich that even its agriculture alone provided an economic basis for large towns, for the development of thousands of miles of railroad track, and for flourishing businesses. By contrast, Palestine is a tiny country. Its agricultural land is sparse, dry and of poor quality. In the best case, agriculture can support only a few small towns. If Jerusalem loses its pilgrim trade it too will fall to the level of a small town.

When I was in Tel Aviv I visited the building of the the workers' movement (the Labor Lyceum as it would be called in America). I formed the impression that the building was the center of a busy workers' movement. The rooms were indeed small, and everything was poor, but there were many of them, and everything seethed and bubbled with activity like a boiler. I was interested to learn which branches were represented by trade unions and how many members there were in each union. I requested the secretary of the Jaffa (i.e., Tel Aviv) Workers' Council to provide me with a list of names of all the trade unions of Tel Aviv and to note the number of members in each. Now, as I write the article, the sheet of paper lies before me. It transpires that of a total of 7245 organized workers, 4550 belong to unions concerned with construction. One union is indeed called "building workers," and it has a larger number of members than the total membership of the two unions that come after it. These two, and the four subsequent unions, are also connected chiefly with the construction industry. I do not count two more unions connected indirectly with building. The following are the details in the list I was given:

Building workers	2400
Clerks and commercial clerks	500
Woodworkers	700
Teachers	70
Metalworkers	530
Musicians and singers	80
Electricians	180
Opticians	60
Building material workers	450
Hospital workers and nurses	75
Technicians	130
Ice workers	35
Painters	160
Carters	250
Cakeshop workers	100
Camel drivers	200
Hotel and restaurant workers	100
Porters	90
Garment workers	85
Railway workers	200
Printing workers	190
Leather workers	60
Cardboard workers	90
Gardeners in Tel Aviv and vicinity	10

It emerges that the building industry is not only the foremost branch but in fact the only one in Tel Aviv. Workers in other unions make their living directly or indirectly from those employed in construction and all that is connected to this branch.

The future of building of Palestine cannot be based on agriculture, or on the building boom in Tel Aviv. Anyone wishing to examine its economic possibilities must refer to its ability to develop industry or a commercial center that will be based not only on the local market but mainly on the markets of other countries – in the first place the adjacent countries or even on those further away.

Practical men of finance and business in Palestine point out that Palestine is situated in the geographical center of the East: of Egypt, Syria, Mesopotamia and Turkey. Here they believe lies the future opportunities of Palestine. One should not be too quick to dismiss these arguments out of hand, just as one should not hasten to say that Palestine may expect a splendid industrial future. It certainly is conceivable that the Jews will do something. The Jews are a gifted people and possess extraordinary building ability. When the opportunity is granted them, they can move worlds.

Progress may be brought to the countries surrounding Palestine. The more their inhabitants develop, the more their requirements will grow. Their Jewish neighbors will exert great influence on this process. In parallel it will be possible to develop, under Jewish direction, the natural resources of the region according to the new needs and by modern means. It will be possible to promote wide-scale industrial and commercial activity, in which the Jews will play a major part and may perhaps be those who set the tone. The Jews could hold the key role in the relations between the east and Europe, and also in all the economic activity of the east. In this situation the force of the Arab menace will decrease.

If Britain remains in Palestine (the country is extremely important for it strategically), it will learn to appreciate the important role of the Jews. The Jewish "homeland" will then win general recognition, and will be accepted as a fact. The Arabic-speaking peoples will grow accustomed to this reality, to which their economic interests will be linked. If then someone appears who creates problems and incites against the Jews, they will possess adequate means to defend themselves against such a possible danger.

This is an optimistic picture of a possible future, although it is hard to promise that it will become reality. Only in the coming years will it be possible to see if the processes and conditions that emerge are leading in the direction depicted.

The question arises as to what will happen in Palestine if no large industry grows up, capable of providing a substantial basis for a large Jewish population. What will happen if the Jews do not become those who set the tone of comprehensive economic development in the region?

The answers to these questions lie only in the bosom of the future. But it is already perfectly clear that whatever the case Palestine will continue to exist as a Jewish center. Presumably, it will also be a small center, but nevertheless it will always have great significance for the Jews.

The present situation in Poland is terrible, and even if the Jews are not emigrating from there to Palestine in the same numbers as previously, they are emigrating, and they must go to Palestine because there is nowhere else for them to go. Even if they do not take great wealth with them they carry much Jewish energy, talent and enthusiasm, and out of all this something is bound to grow.

The Christians assert that anything to do with Jews is unusual. When the Jews get hold of something, they do not let go of it until it is finished. Even Bismarck expressed this concept in an interesting way:

> You can hang an innocent Christian, and no one will make a sound, but if you arrest an innocent Jew even for a few days, this is liable to cost very dear.

I recalled these words of Bismarck when I was reflecting on the Jewish saying "Next year in Jerusalem." Another nation that loses its land forgets it in the course of generations, but with Jews things are different: they do not forget.

For almost two thousand years the Jews have been in exile, but they never cease to lament their land. When a Jewish child just begins to speak, he is already taught to say "Next year in Jerusalem." I came to know the name Jerusalem long before I heard the name of Petersburg or of Kovno – a city only 3.5 kilometers from the town where I was born.

Is it at all possible to imagine that everything the Jews have built in Palestine in recent times will disappear like snow on a warm summer day? This is hard to believe.

The Jewish tragedy has given rise to a large class of nationalist intelligentsia. For this class the new Palestine constitutes the same value as that of the Western Wall or of the tomb of Meir Ba'al Haness for the orthodox Jews of the old type. Objective reality is helping Palestine, and there is meaning in this. I do not know how long the situation described will last but it is certainly possible that it will last a long time. The Jews of the world seem to be shouting through thousands of windows to the Jews of Palestine: Do not lose your vigor and your hope.

Will Palestine solve the Jewish problem? It certainly will not! Millions of Jews no longer have a home, but Palestine is a tiny country and it does not possess the means to absorb and maintain large Jewish immigration. It is also hard to point to potential resources that will provide it with such means. But for those hundreds of thousands of Jews who feel strong sympathy for Palestine, there is no question whatsoever of a solution to the Jewish problem, or the possibility of turning it into a home for the masses of the Jewish people. For them it is a part of their Jewish essence and emotion.

None of this concerns our socialist movement. Our socialist movement is a world movement, and a movement that stands on the ground of reality, while Palestine constitutes a focus for modern religious fervor.

When you see the Palestinian idealists in the place of their abode it affects the mood in the same way as the feeling created when observing the religious Jew – likeable, decent, and filled with faith – as he pours his heart out in the synagogue. You know that his religion has no reality, but you sympathize with and respect his belief and his heart's feelings at that moment.

Whatever happens to the idealists who are sacrificing themselves at the altar of the building of Palestine in the agricultural settlements, or to the socialists who live a life full of austerity on the communes, they deserve our warmest feelings and the best wishes of every one of us; and the workers' movement, as such, merits our love simply because it is a part of us. The Zionist movement is worthy of our appreciation because of its fine attitude to the workers' movement.

I wrote the entire series of articles on Palestine in Palestine, Italy, and Paris, and on the liner *Majestic* that brought me back to America. I have more material and pictures connected to what I experienced in Palestine, but before I publish them a debate will take place in the pages of *Forward* about the ideas and feelings I have presented in my articles. Comrade Zivion, for example, disagrees with me, so I have asked him to set forth his position in one or two articles. Subsequently other comrades will express themselves. Then I shall reply to their reservations after the debate is completed I shall publish more of my impressions.

Part Two

The Debate

New York, 28 December 1925
1. **Zivion**
The Debate on the Articles about Palestine

Comrade Abe Cahan declared that despite the fact that the work being accomplished in Palestine aroused powerful emotions in him, he has not become a Zionist.

If this is indeed so, then I actually have nothing to argue about. You understand that I will not try to persuade Comrade Cahan that he is a Zionist when he himself admits that he is not. First, this is not my concern. Secondly, I myself do not believe that Comrade Cahan has become a Zionist. As far as I understand from his letters from Palestine, which I re-read in preparation for the debate, it is entirely clear to me that he does not believe in Zionist realization. In his articles he stated more than once that he sees nothing real about the work in Palestine, and this is because everything there is built on sand, without foundation.

Generally, Zionism is not based on awareness and truthfulness; mostly it rests more on emotions than on awareness. It may be said about the majority of Zionists that their Zionism is founded on emotions. From this viewpoint, such emotions are to be found in Comrade Cahan's letters too. Here originates the impression people got, that on his journey to Palestine, Cahan was influenced by Zionism and became a Zionist. This is also the source of the fact that Comrade Cahan's articles from Palestine made such a great impression on the Zionists. All this occurred without their noticing that he wrote expressly that he does not believe in the possibility of the realization of Zionism. His articles are being exploited for pro-Zionist propaganda. They do not convince the world by means of facts, but by means of an appeal to the emotions, especially on the subject of Eretz Israel, which is all a matter of emotion.

The Jewish masses would be concerned for facts if they were planning to emigrate to Eretz Israel. If this were the case, people would be seriously interested in the nature of the country and how one could live there. The Jews regard Zionism as something that is good for others but not for them. Ex-King Ferdinand of Bulgaria once said this: A Zionist is someone who tells another to move to Palestine. Can you argue about feelings? You can argue about concepts and opinions, but you cannot argue about feelings. All that may be said about feelings is that they should not always be exposed, unless one wishes to achieve a particular goal. We do not usually expose all our feelings in public but keep them to ourselves, or share them only with those closest to us. Feelings are, in general, like religion – a personal matter as long as they remain private. Religion is a personal matter as long as one observes it privately at home, but when, for example, someone goes to a socialist meeting, and wishes to hold prayers there, then it is no longer a question of privacy. I myself doubt that religion is a personal matter: it is supposed to be that, but in reality it is not. Religion is mixed into every sphere and it is forced on us despite our struggle to get free of it. Therefore, perhaps the comparison I made between religion and feelings was poor, but it is clear that feelings cannot be argued over. Sometimes it is indeed hard to explain them. Myself, I find it hard, for instance, to explain why Jerusalem evokes such deep feelings in me, while the Western Wall does not arouse such feelings. The mountainous Holy City affected me deeply, but the Holy Wall did not awaken any feeling in me. I think I have an explanation for this, but it is difficult for me to express it clearly because it is very difficult to express emotions.

Furthermore, least of all do I wish to discuss the question of what is allowed and what is forbidden, namely may a socialist be a Zionist or not. We do not have a set socialist code to help us hand down a decision in problems of this sort that arise, regarding what a socialist may or may not believe. The question before us is different: is it logical for a socialist to believe in Zionism? If our subject were what a socialist may want, or could want, we might say that he may want the Jews to have a state of their own, not only in Palestine but also in America. But the question is whether this is feasible, and this is the subject under discussion. The question to be considered is how should a socialist treat Zionism if he is convinced that it is not attainable, but exists in the realm of dreams only.

From Cahan's articles from Palestine it is not at all hard to understand whether he liked the country. He described what is taking place there in detail. As far as I recall, he did not find anything good there except the cool evening breeze after a heatwave during the day. True, he also wrote that in spring beautiful flowers bloom there, so he was told, although he himself did not see them as his visit was in the late summer. If so, what else is to be found in Palestine apart from the cool evening breeze after a hot day and nice flowers? With a cool evening breeze and spring flowers alone, pretty as they may be – with these alone it is not possible to exist in any country, and the core of our subject is the question of whether Jews can find sustenance there.

Comrade Abe Cahan described in glowing colors the ideal-filled life of Jewish workers there, as well as the pioneers and their communes. All this is pure poetry. What counts is the nature of real life. Are the pioneers actually able to exist on their communes? Not at all! The prose, in contrast to the poetry, is very dismal. Comrade Cahan tells us what sort of poverty-stricken and primitive life they lead there. They are able to maintain even this kind of life only on the basis of the support they receive from the Zionist movement – all this because the poor land of Palestine cannot provide a basis for minimal existence. It is almost certain that life in the commune has fine aspects, and I can also understand the uplifting effect one can have from the communes in Palestine, but what connection is there between this and the question of whether Palestine can be turned into a Jewish homeland? Communes of Jewish farmers may also be set up in Mexico or Cuba, if money is lavished on this purpose. Without doubt, in Cuba they would cost less, and could be more easily established than in Palestine. But it is impossible to convert either Mexico or Cuba into a Jewish homeland.

I understand that the problem of creating a national home for the Jews in Palestine did not interest Comrade Cahan so much. In the first place he was concerned with the question of how Palestine could become a destination for migration by Jews, and how many Jews might build their lives there. The moment one removes from Palestine the national element and the idea of turning it into a national home for the Jews, it becomes nothing other than that sucked-out lemon that is not worth talking about. If the discussion were only about a suitable destination for Jewish migration, namely the countries where Jews are still allowed to enter, then any of the following countries would be better than Palestine: Mexico, Brazil, Cuba or Argentina. If such large sums were invested in Mexico for the settlement of Jews as in Palestine, then without doubt the results would be better and on a larger scale.

Comrade Cahan devoted a large part of his letters to a description of the communes, but the more he wrote about them the more convinced I was that he does not believe in their ability to exist. I too have seen the communes of the pioneers in Palestine. In me too they aroused sympathy, but I knew well that they are nothing more than soap bubbles. A soap bubble is a very pretty thing; it has a wealth of colors, a marvelous play of shades – but what good does this do? The moment you touch it it bursts. There are more pioneering communes there today than when I made my visit, and they are bigger. From Comrade Cahan's letters it appears that the poverty and the primitive conditions are still the same as they were four years ago. It is certainly understandable for a socialist to be caught up by an elevation of spirit on seeing how the people living on those communes uphold the rule of "what's mine is yours." At the same time, it must not be forgotten that on the communes in Palestine there is nothing whatever to discuss in the sense of "what's mine is yours." Not only in practice do they have no property, but even if they wanted they would not acquire any. Their members have barely enough bread to satisfy their hunger, and they only get this by virtue of support by the Zionist Organization. When life is primitive it is easy to live on a commune, and indeed, in ancient times, when the human being's needs were minimal, then, too, people lived in communes. When I visited the pioneers' communes in Palestine I saw that the whole issue of "what's mine is yours" found expression only over a slice of bread or another bowl of soup; the problem under discussion did not exist at all in respect of any other sphere. All were poor to the same extent. All covered themselves with the same paltry clothing, which can hardly be imagined. And there all life's necessities on the commune ended. I would like to see a commune with a high living standard, where people can enjoy modern human culture, and also lead a modern and civilized way of life. On such a commune I would like to see how people live and distribute their property. This greatly interests me, because I would like to get an idea of how one day people will live in a socialist society. I imagine future socialism only as a society possessing a high level of culture, a rich and variegated life with a wide range of requirements by the people living in it. But the sparse and primitive communism existing in Palestine arries no good tidings or innovation: it already existed once. True, the people on the present communes are different from the people of ancient times, because in the ancient primitive communes the people were primitive too, while today the members of the communes are civilized people. But here precisely lies the factor that will not permit the existence of the communes. In the best case, to continue living a communalist life, the people will have to lower their cultural needs to the most primitive level, the level of the communes now.

The things I have said are quite harsh, but Comrade Cahan also expects a similar fate for the communes, although he says so in a more delicate way, so delicate that not everyone discerns it. In his articles on the communes, Comrade Cahan did not maintain the correct proportions because at first he so lauded them that doubts about their ability to exist, which he expressed later in his articles, were not adequately stressed. Nor must we forget the chauvinistic spirit with which the members of the communes are imbued. It is not at all clear to me how these fanatical chauvinists may be regarded as socialists. True, Comrade Cahan mentioned several times the fanatical chauvinism of the Zionist workers and the pioneers in Palestine, but he did so offhandedly and so gently that it was hardly noticeable. Would he treat the fanatical chauvinism of the Poles in such a manner? Now the Polish chauvinists, like the Zionist workers and pioneers in Palestine, are internationalists. Do not the Polish chauvinists brutally suppress the Yiddish language in Poland, as do the Zionist workers in Palestine? These – the Zionist workers in Palestine – are they who placed a ban on Yiddish and forbade its use in public.

Not to be forgotten either is the reactionary chauvinist ideology of the "conquest of labor" – the concept of labor in Palestine being only in Jewish hands, expulsion of Arabs from the Jewish villages, stopping Arabs from working in Jewish industrial or commercial enterprises – this is the ideological meaning of the idea of "conquest of labor." How do we react when the reactionary chauvinists in Poland fight for their "conquest of labor," meaning prevention of Jews working in Polish industrial and commercial enterprises? How do we respond to the "conquest of labor" of the Romanians?

It seems to me that in his articles Comrade Cahan does not refer at all to the reactionary, chauvinist aspect of the "conquest of labor." I certainly understand why Comrade Cahan is so restrained on this issue. It is because the communes in Palestine are the only enterprise that can excite the socialist who visits there. If one were to remove from Palestine the few communes built there, through major financial support by the Zionist movement, there would be nothing left to show. In any event, in reference to the communes it must be said, in the sharpest and clearest manner possible, that they have no future. In the best case they are just a kind of game, and cannot influence the life of the Jewish people to the slightest degree. The communes cannot build Palestine as a Jewish national home. But this subject is not so important. It must be borne in mind, when we debate whether Palestine is good or bad and whether the Jews can settle there or not, that we are dealing with a particular ideology and a particular movement, which regards Palestine not merely as another country for settlement by Jews, but as *the* country for the Jews. Today, when referring to Palestine, we must do so in connection with the Zionist movement.

Comrade Cahan asks if Palestine is good or bad for the Jews, if it can or cannot absorb Jewish immigration. For the Zionists these questions do not exist. For them, Palestine is *the* land for the Jews, and the future Jewish national home. When Comrade Cahan learns that Palestine cannot absorb Jews, while Mexico, for example, can do so, he will support the Mexican solution. By contrast, a Zionist, irrespective of circumstances, will always support the Palestinian solution. The renowned Zionist Ussishkin expressed this clearly once. In Palestine, he claimed, one should not look for bread, one should be sated even by stones.

At the present time it is not possible to detach Palestine from the Zionist ideology and the Zionist movement. Therefore, the only question to be discussed is how far the Zionist idea may be realized there. Let us forget for a moment the poetic aspects of life, and consider real life in Palestine. Let us see what indeed the Jews may expect from Palestine.

New York, 29 December 1925
Zivion
The Debate on the Articles about Palestine (continued)

In my opinion there is a difference between Eretz Israel and Palestine. Eretz Israel is to be found, as far as I am concerned, in the realm of romance. The term "Eretz Israel" moved me to weave a wealth of fantastic dreams in my boyhood *heder* days. Even today this phrase has still not lost – for me – the attractive force inherent in it. The name Eretz Israel yet retains that ring that arouses in me the association with a wondrous land, a land full of magical tales and miracles, a land that is more a legend than reality. Regarding Eretz Israel, everything is possible. In Eretz Israel, no miracle is impossible. Eretz Israel is a dreamland lying somewhere far away in a world more in heaven than on real earth. By contrast, Palestine is a small country, presently under British domination, where dwells a backward Asiatic people that is totally alien to me.

The name Palestine for me is a dry political word that gives rise to an association with a political movement the goal of which is to establish the Jewish state by actual earthly means. Eretz Israel lies in the domain of poetry, while Palestine lies in the domain of real life. One may treat poetry poetically, but prosaic real life has to be dealt with on the level of reality. As for Eretz Israel, all fantasies are permitted, and an abundance of emotions and poetry may be expressed, but regarding Palestine we are obliged to adopt realistic attitudes and at once to ask the question: Can it be done? What can Palestine give to the Jewish people? What needs of the people can it satisfy?

In face of these questions, the Zionist comes up with his old foolish argument: Why are all the nations on earth allowed to have a land and state of their own while the Jewish people are not? This foolish and dumb question is asked with such hysteria, as if someone were actually saying that the Jews are forbidden to have their own land and their own state. I want to state unequivocally that the Jews *may* have a land and a state of their own, just as other nations have. The question before us is different: can they achieve this? The question to be asked is what can the Jews obtain in Palestine and what can that country give them? The Zionists claim that the Jews can get everything in Palestine, that this country can give them everything. As far as they are concerned, Palestine can provide the answer to all the problems of the Jewish people – in the economic, political, and cultural spheres. Similarly it is the answer to anti–Semitism. Some say that only foolish Zionists who make this claim, while a clever Zionist will not utter such a statement because he knows that Palestine cannot solve the problems of the Jewish people. This division into clever and foolish Zionists is very convenient. For purposes of propaganda and persuasion among the masses of the people, the foolish Zionists are needed, they who in the name of Palestine promise everything and claim that this country will indeed solve all the troubles of the Jewish people. When it comes to debate based on logical proofs, means to demonstrate that it is impossible to realize these assurances given to the Jews, they reply that all the exaggerated promises have been made by the foolish Zionists only, while the clever ones know that the possibilities of Palestine are very limited. The actual truth is that the so–called clever Zionists turn foolish when they engage in propaganda, promising the people everything in the name of Palestine.

What is the reality in Palestine? The dreamers of wild dreams may seek the solution to the economic and political problems of the people there. Even in the most ideal circumstances and in the best conditions, namely if Zionism had sufficient capital to invest in developing the land and the British government likewise opened the gates of the country to permanent Jewish immigration – even then Palestine would be able to absorb only a small number of Jews. The area of the British Mandate in Palestine is 10,000 square miles, less than half of the area of small Switzerland. In Palestine there is a population of just over 800,000, of whom 600,000 are Muslim Arabs and almost 100,000 are Christian Arabs. There are only

120,000 Jews there, and a few thousand people of other nationalities. For such a small country this is a very considerable population. I mentioned Switzerland, one of the most cultivated and fertile lands in Europe, and still it has a population of less than four million even though it is densely populated. This means that even if Palestine became a cultivated and fertile land like Switzerland its population, in proportion to Switzerland's, would hardly reach 1,900,000 people. Let us even imagine that the stony mountains of Palestine magically brought forth grasslands and woods like the mountains of Switzerland. Let us imagine that the dry land of Palestine became fertile land like Switzerland's. Let us imagine that Palestine would be cultivated from end to end, like Switzerland. That the swamps there were drained and malaria was eradicated, and enough good potable water was found, and in this way the other diseases were subdued. In short, that Palestine turned into a second Switzerland: could there be a lovelier fantasy? Even then, Palestine, relative to Switzerland, could contain a population of up to 1,900,000 people only.

Let us assume that such a reality might not be so bad, namely the possibility of absorbing 1,100,000 Jews, which would make Palestine a Jewish country. But this is not enough, because for the future miracle necessary to turn Palestine into a kind of Switzerland another miracle is needed: the Arabs there would have to decide not to multiply any more. Otherwise natural increase of the Arab population in the coming decades, before Palestine could be converted into a second Switzerland, would double their numbers. Moreover, apart from the Arabs in Palestine there are masses of Arabs throughout the region, and these most probably would wish to settle in a developing land promising an abundance of opportunities. In sum, even if Palestine became a second Switzerland it would be Arab, not Jewish.

Fantasies must be set aside, and we must return to reality, which is many times more bitter. True, there are parts of Palestine that can be made fertile, and for this purpose labor and money should not be spared, but in no way is it possible to convert Palestine into Switzerland. The soil and climate needed for this does not exist there. Therefore, Palestine cannot contain a dense population. The Jews cannot hope to develop a large-scale agricultural population because the land suitable for agriculture is limited, and that which exists is already settled by Arabs. By this I am simply reinforcing the argument of Comrade Cahan as this emerges from his articles, that he does not believe in the future of Jewish agriculture in Palestine.

If there is no future in argiculture, perhaps there is a future in industry:

are the Jews not capable of developing industry there? Jews indeed are capable, but Palestine can provide only very few opportunities for the development of industry and becoming an industrial country. Everyone knows that an essential condition for the development of industry is the presence of raw materials, and these are not found in Palestine. It buys raw materials from other countries, and this even includes the timber to manufacture the crates in which the goods are shipped. Not only raw materials, but also the machinery has to be bought from other countries. So how can it compete with other countries that do possess raw materials, and also manufacture machinery?

In addition to all this, we must not forget that Palestine is a British colony, and Britain has no interest whatsoever in the development of industry there: the opposite is the case. The colonies primarily serve as a market for British industry. This is the reason why Britain does not permit industry to develop in its colonies. In fact, these words only strengthen the opinion of Dr Magnes, expressed to Comrade Cahan, that he does not believe in the industrial future of Palestine. (Comrade Cahan reported Magnes's view in a telegram describing his meeting with the Jewish leader at the latter's home.)

In fact, I have nothing to debate with Comrade Cahan regarding the possibility of realizing Zionism in Palestine. He himself, in both his telegrams and his articles, and especially the last of these, entitled "What is the meaning of 'To build Eretz Israel?'" proves in the clearest and most cogent manner that it is impossible to settle any considerable number of Jews in Palestine. He points in the clearest manner to the limited possibilites of the country in the domain of agriculture as well as the domain of industry. But Comrade Cahan is alarmed by his grim prediction, so he softens it by indicating the elements of the energy, talents and strengths of the Jews, by means of which it is possible to move mountains.

If our concern were compassion for the Zionists, namely that because they work so hard for an ideal that cannot be realized we must give them a word of encouragement, this is really very kind of Comrade Cahan. But the problem arises from the fact that when people read these words of encouragement they may make the mistake of thinking that Comrade Cahan himself believes that with the help of the strengths, energy, and talents of the Jews it is possible to move mountains, including overcoming the limitations of Palestine.

The argument that the Jewish people are capable, by its strength of will, energy and talents, of overcoming the limitations of Palestine is an old Zionist claim. Even in this claim it is possible to discern the true nature of Zionism. Their claim is nothing more than a modification of the old Jewish saying "God will help," except that instead of God now there are the will and strength of the people. If we are concerned with the level of hope and faith, then it would be more logical to rely on the will and strength of God than on the will and strength of the Jewish people. All this is not because I think little of the strength and talents of the Jewish people, but because as a socialist I was trained to think that first and foremost suitable economic conditions have to exist, and only on the basis of these may the will, the strength and the talents of the people be able to erect the enterprise. Incidentally, it seems to me that we exaggerate regarding the will, strengths and talents of the Jewish people. True, the non-Jews complement us on being a special kind of people, but we must be sober-minded and not intoxicated by these blandishments.

Moreover, if indeed the Jews are a marvelous people, they became so not necessarily in Eretz Israel but in the Diaspora. As long as the Jews were in Eretz Israel, they did not excel in anything. There the Jews created very little, owing to the lack of opportunities to create. All their energy and strength were sunk into backbreaking toil on Palestine's parched and poor soil, in order to draw from it some little sustenance, and also in defending themselves against the nations that surrounded them and attacked them constantly. Jewish cultural creation, such as the Bible and the Talmud, were produced, from antiquity onwards, not in Eretz Israel but in exile, everywhere the Jews were expelled to and wandered. In Babylonia a far higher culture existed than in Eretz Israel. Babylonia was an extremely fertile country, and it was easy to live there, so the Jews could dedicate themselves to cultural productivity. It is a fact that even now we do not hear that cultural assets are being created in Eretz Israel. Jews sit there and study. Thousands there devote themselves to Torah and to labor, but when they need a rabbi they are obliged to bring him from the Diaspora. For some reason, nothing grows out of the studying in Eretz Israel. In Eretz Israel there are already Hebrew high schools, they already speak Hebrew there, there are already many people there whose mother tongue is Hebrew; yet for all that Eretz Israel still has not produced any Hebrew writer of note. The writers of note who live in Eretz Israel got their education and their renown in the Diaspora.

The Jews have produced a large number of gifted and famous celebrities because the Jews in Europe, in the countries of the Diaspora, could absorb the culture of the nations among whom they dwelt. Personalities such as Doctor Hertz, Doctor Einstein, Doctor Bergson, and so on could arise because they grew up and were educated in the developed culture of

Germany and France. By contrast, we do not hear of Jewish men of intellect in Turkey, Bulgaria, Serbia, and the like. This is because these people are still at a low cultural stage and they themselves do not yet have an intelligentsia.

God did not create Jews more gifted than other peoples, but the Jews developed their qualities because they lived among nations in possession of high culture, and also because they were obliged to live in cities, where culture is constantly on the rise. But if the Jews go back to Palestine, where the culture is backward, the struggle for existence is very harsh, and the economic conditions are limited, then Jewish talents will gradually deteriorate.

Let us refer to reality as it is at present. We do not know what talents the Jews have for building a country. The Jewish people have displayed the strength to bear suffering, but we do not know at all how great are their strength and qualities for building a country that lacks land. In any event, I do not believe that the Jews can move mountains in a place where they do not even have a foothold. The problem of Palestine is that there is no living space in it. If we are to deal kindly with Zionism, this obligates us to take into account our old socialism, which taught us that with goodwill alone not only is it impossible to move mountains, it is even impossible to carry out a revolution in human society.

It seems to me that Comrade Cahan has also been affected by the Zionist adage "Next year in Jerusalem," a phrase that the Jews have uttered whenever the occasion arose for two thousand years. Comrade Cahan mentions this saying and asks, "Is it even possible to imagine that everything the Jews have built in Palestine will melt like snow on a hot summer day?" This should not be considered imaginary: the opposite is the case. I certainly can imagine that the Zionists will build more in Palestine. I certainly can accept that the Jewish population in Palestine will grow significantly. I can even imagine that with time a Hebrew university will arise in Jerusalem, a real university with students and professors. But is our concern really with such matters when we talk about Zionism? Does anyone argue that the Zionists have not established any project in Palestine, or that they are incapable of building anything there? By no means; but the question should be stated otherwise, namely *what value* does the Zionist enterprise in Palestine have, and what are they capable of constructing there in the future?

There would be no need whatsoever to argue with the Zionists if they came forward and said: the Jews are suffering terribly in Poland, Romania, Russia, Lithuania; in light of this, let us settle a few tens of thousands of Jews, or more, in Palestine, where they will live decent and free lives. But this is not the Zionist attitude! The Zionists come to us with tidings of redemption, namely Palestine is not just another state where the Jews may settle, but *the land of the Jewish people*, which will solve all the troubles of the people and will heal all their wounds; therefore Palestine is above everything and everything has to be mobilized for the sake of Palestine. Here we must of necessity say to them in the clearest possible way: You are deceiving the Jewish people! Palestine cannot give the Jews what you promise them. Your movement is wrong in that you claim that Palestine is above everything and before everything. You are not only creating a delusion, which will be followed by disappointment, but above all in the name of your imaginary Palestine you are hindering all constructive work in the countries of the Diaspora. You do not always hinder this work directly, but you are always a hindrance indirectly, because you arouse imaginary hopes about Palestine, and thereby paralyze the Jews of the Diaspora to the point of their being incapable of accomplishing any constructive work.

Only one kind of rationalist Zionist is to be found, and they are those who claim that a few hundred thousand Jews in Palestine are dearer to them than the millions of Jews in the Diaspora. First, they are not certain that the Jews in the Diaspora will retain their Jewish identity, while with the several hundred thousand Jews in Palestine they are sure of the continued maintenance of their Jewish identity. Secondly, they believe, the Jews of the Diaspora are of no great importance because they are already in a process of assimilation and they are not preserving their Jewish identity, while those hundreds of thousands of Jews in Palestine will preserve their full Jewish identity: they are Hebrew speakers, and they possess Jewish culture and spirit.

These museum-Zionists, who wish to preserve in Palestine, as in a museum, a few hundred thousand Jews, may hold a reactionary viewpoint, but we must admit they there is logic in their Zionism. Zionism of this kind can also be realized. I permit myself to doubt if Comrade Cahan will view this kind of Zionism with favor. We must admit that we live in an age when nationalism is very strong, to the point that many socialists and radicals are being swept along by this plague. There is indeed a tendency to swim with the tide, but how far away may one go with this tide?

Zionism is a form of nationalism that hauls us backwards. Zionism draws its strength from the Jewish past and drags us back toward that past. It pulls us back to a past full of moldiness that has long been forgotten.

Zionism cannot exist together with socialism, and in places where an attempt has been made to connect them, Zionism has swallowed up socialism.

If we are talking about commitment to the Jewish people, then our duty, as socialists, is to explain again and again, unremittingly, that the Jewish people, which now number more than 15,000,000 people, must remain, and indeed will remain in the countries of the Diaspora, because Palestine can absorb only small numbers of Jews. Palestine is not able, even in the best conditions, to bring about a change – economic, cultural or political – in the life of the Jewish people. Hence the Jews must remain in the countries of the Diaspora; they must therefore root out of their hearts the Zionist dream and fight for their rights in the places where they live.

It is by no means necessary to commiserate with the Jews over the fact that the Zionist dream is unattainable. This dream, of the return of the Jewish people to their ancient land, is not the first dream or the last. The Jews always prayed "Next year in Jerusalem" and will continue to do so. Zionism, meaning the belief in the possibility of our return to Zion, has changed its image more than once in the past, and this image will change yet again in the future.

I have repeatedly argued elsewhere, and I argue yet again, that Zionism will continue to exist as long as the belief in the Messiah exists. If the Messiah had indeed appeared it would have passed away long ago. The continued existence and power of the messianic belief derives from his non-appearance. Zionism likewise will continue to exist, for the reason that it cannot be realized.

New York, 2 January 1926
2. Max Pine
The Debate on the Articles on Palestine

Zivion, master of the facile pen and one "good at his job," opened the debate on Cahan's articles using the "simple" method: he set the debate so that his opponents would be forced only to defend themselves. Instead of treating Cahan's articles from the viewpoint of a socialist and of a socialist's attitude to Palestine, namely what the worker's attitude is to this issue, he twisted the subject into a debate with the orthodox Zionist position. At the moment he is certainly enjoying the trick he has played.

Zivion opens with a quotation from Cahan: "Comrade Cahan declared that although several things aroused excitement in him, he has not become a Zionist." Therefore, Zivion claims, "I have nothing to debate about." It turns out that Zivion has no basis for a debate except with extremist Zionists of the kind who will not rest until in Jerusalem once again a king sits on David's throne of glory and the last of the Jews is redeemed from exile and ascends to the Land of Israel. Zivion applies a clever device here, by which he adheres to his positions but he places an obstacle before his opponent to catch him out.

And true enough, why should he trouble himself to delve deeply into the complex reality out of which new sympathies and hopes regarding Palestine are now growing up among the masses of Jewish workers in America? – the faith in its ability to absorb the Jewish masses; a place where the workers' movement has been founded to serve as a model for the world. Why should he refer to Cahan's articles, 90 percent of which describe working Palestine, when he can demolish all that with the few words "Cahan is not a Zionist" therefore he has nothing to debate with him. But he does debate the basic Zionist ideology, which can be easily dismissed! What is this like? It is as if Zivion has piled up a heap of snow and built snowman on top of it, and then has rolled up his sleeves declaring, "You see this hero? Well, I'll show you how I can knock him down." Zivion is fighting his own snowmen which he himself made, breaking them to bits and looking like the victor.

To get to the heart of the matter right away, I state at the outset that we are not Zionists in the sense that he wishes to attribute to us, but we are certainly Jews! As Jews, our concern will always be drawn to the condition of the Jews. Therefore, even if we are not Zionists we have something to discuss on the subject of Palestine. Zivion could have written what he did without resorting to Cahan's articles. He could have written what he wrote a year ago, or five years ago. He has not produced anything new. With him, nothing has changed.

On the seashore, Jewish workers have constructed a marvelous city, with tall buildings and all modern facilities. Zivion has never seen it, nor has he been influenced by it. Naïvely, I thought that when he wrote about the settlements that Abe Cahan portrayed so well, Zivion would try to show that not a single remnant had survived of those settlements that he himself saw four years ago. But on the contrary, Zivion writes that these settlement have grown and expanded. If so, is there any greater sign of progress than this? Obviously, Zivion would like the pioneers there to go about in tuxedos, but still, it is remarkable that in the course of four years they have succeeded in multiplying and enlarging the communes. Here, in wealthy and civilized America, it took us decades until we managed to bring the workers to a situation in which they work less but earn more.

Zivion goes on to argue that the subject of the national home has no connection with the energy and the enterprises being developed in Palestine. Cahan, so Zivion claims, is interested in Palestine only as a country of immigration for Jews, but if the national element is removed from it, it will then be like that dried-up lemon. As far as he is concerned, Mexico, Brazil, Cuba or Argentina could offer better results on the matter of Jewish settlement if such large sums of money were invested in them. In writing this, Zivion did not even sense the truths that he elicited, and that serve as evidence against him. It transpires that the idea of the national home is the driving force for youth to work under unbearable conditions, and it stirs in them the belief that they are building a center for their unfortunate people there, a center in which the Jews will be able to show what they are capable of, and that through these efforts the Jews will also win respect.

It is doubtful that the Jews, as settlers, would obtain better results in Cuba or Argentina. In Argentina such an effort was made on a large scale, in which Baron Hirsch's fund invested much money, and the business fell through. If you wish to build a large enterprise, then money alone is not enough. In addition to money, there must be vision and spiritual uplift, and these are present only in Palestine. There, in the communes, they cannot stop to count the finances, as Zivion would like. They are seized by a great ideal that instills strength and power in them, and accompanies them on their way. They are conscious of the fact that they are striving mightily not only for the moment to put a few dollars by in the bank, but they are preparing the land for many new immigrants with whom they gladly share their last slice of bread.

In his approach, which discards everything under the sun, Zivion is like that "greener" father whose son shows him the wonders of New York: he shows him railroad tracks suspended in the air, but this does not faze the old man, who tells him disdainfully, "Big deal! So they raised them up higher a bit." The son persists, and takes him to the aquarium, pointing out to him all kinds of fish with gorgeous colors. Again the father makes little of it: "So – you're showing me a few little fishes?" The son goes on, and takes him to a Chinese resaurant where they are served noodles. The old man tastes them and declares, "So what do you think – you can't get lockshen like this in Lemberg?"

You show Zivion that the members of the communes live a life together, despite the hardship of existence, and then he says that they do not quarrel because they have nothing to quarrel over. And again Zivion, who not for a moment has parted company from Karl Marx and always bases himself on him, states: "Sure – what is there to quarrel over, a piece of bread?" But it is clear from the laws of economics, and from common sense, that it is harder to live peacefully in conditions of poverty than in conditions of wealth. It is very important to divide up the thin slice of bread in amity rather than in strife. The war of existence takes place around a slice of bread. Zivion tries to fortify his arguments by indicating that in a primitive way of life people can live fairly easily on a commune. Certainly, in ancient times people could live more easily in communes, but in the actual case before us we are talking of people who have already lived in better circumstances. Many of them, if they wished, could even now live in luxury. Only as a result of the ideals that motivate them have they dedicated them to a certain course, with the greatest self-discipline. Incidentally, regarding the future of the Jewish settlement in Palestine, I prefer to believe those who live there and realize themselves by hard work than to believe Zivion. All this is because he may split hairs on the subject as much as he likes without it costing him a red cent, while the people living there make sacrifices in order to realize the ideals in which they believe. In this case we are talking facts and not beliefs.

Zivion does not relent and demands that we choose between absolute commitment to Zionism or abandonment of the subject of Palestine, and in his article he states: "As far as Comrade Cahan is concerned, the question is whether Palestine is a good country or a bad one, if it can absorb Jewish immigration or not. But for Zionism these questions do not exist. For Zionism Palestine is the Jewish land. It is the unquestioned future Jewish national home." Yet again he reminds us that for Zionism only Palestine exists as the country of the Jews and their future national home.

There might have been room for this entire approach if Zivion had disputed with Zionists. The debate here is not between us and the Zionists. Cahan really is only interested in the question of whether Palestine can or cannot absorb Jewish immigration. He also shows great concern for the future existence of the enterprise established by the workers. I will take the liberty of trying to represent Cahan, but I do wish to state my position and that of many comrades who think as I do. We are greatly concerned by the question of what influence a large Jewish concentration in Palestine will have on the condition of the Jews in other countries.

To show that Palestine is not worth dealing with, Zivion presents the following points: 1 The British Mandate in Palestine covers only about

10,000 square miles, an area on which lives a population of almost 800,000, of whom only 120,000 are Jews. Similarly, Palestine is about half the size of small, fertile, wonderful Switzerland, which is densely settled by 4,000,000 people. 2 Even if in Palestine the same amount of land could be prepared as in Switzerland, it would still be able to absorb only about 1,000,000 Jews. 3 If this indeed took place, the Jews would then constitute a majority in Palestine. But for this to happen the Arabs would have to decide not to reproduce. There are likewise masses of Arabs in the neighboring countries who most probably would wish to settle in Palestine if it were to flourish and prosper. 4 The Jews will not be able to develop industry in Palestine because there are no raw materials there. If these raw materials have to be purchased from other countries, Palestine will not be able to compete with them. 5 Palestine is a territory under British rule, and Britain is entirely unwilling to develop industry in its colonies.

These are the reasons given by Zivion to show that it is impossible to realize Zionism in Palestine. Next in his dispute with the Zionists he states: "We would not have to debate with the Zionists if they were to come *forward* and say, The Jews are suffering, and here is a land called Palestine where it is possible settle a few tens of thousands of Jews who will be able to live there in a reasonable way. But the Zionists do not define their position in this way." Zivion does not cease debating with the Zionists who come *forward* with tidings of redemption and with Palestine, which they believe will resolve the troubles and sufferings of the Jewish people. Against this, Zivion immediately lets loose a cry, declaring, Palestine cannot fulfill what you promise, so you are deceiving the people. Again, like the story of the snowman, Zivion is shooting in the wrong direction. Instead of addressing Cahan's articles, he goes back to his old tunes. To complete his arguments, Zivion once again brings out the old chestnut that Zionism is a nationalism that drags the people back to their past, and also that whenever Zionism encounters socialism it swallows it up. The conclusion is obvious: it is necessary to fight against Zionism, which endangers socialism.

Instead of disputing Zivion's positions, I would like at once to assure him sincerely that we do not believe that Palestine will in fact solve the entire Jewish problem. I hope that he does not think us so simple minded as to believe that this small country is capable of absorbing the 14,000,000 Jews that there are in the world. He need not worry. We can assure him that not all the Jews, not even all the Zionists, will emigrate there. To tell the truth, we should not even wish that all the Jews will settle in Eretz

Israel. Do all the Greeks live in Greece? Only two and a half million Greeks live in Greece itself, while throughout the world there are seven million more Greeks. Why then should all the Jews, to the very last, have to settle in Eretz Israel?

In parallel to the above, it has to be clearly stated to Zivion that the old refrain – that we are not Jews but Yiddish-speaking socialists – that refrain is over and done with. The first pogrom wiped out the propaganda about assimilation, claiming that we are plain secular internationalists with no concern for the fate of the Jewish people.

In addition, the facts prove that although in the last eight years many Jewish workers, and also many of the best-known socialists, have been active in extending help to the bloodied Jewish people, this has not mitigated the class war in the slightest. Moreover, it has been proven that the Jewish socialists do possess national awareness. They have certainly tried to deny this, but the facts are obvious to all. For example, at the same time as Jewish blood was being shed in the pogroms, the Turks were wading in the blood of the Armenians. The slaughter of the Armenians was on such a scale that only one third of the Christian Armenians were left. It cannot be argued that we Jews did not know these facts, which were published by the Allies as it served their interests. I would like to know how much and in what way help by Jews, particularly American-Jewish socialists, was offered to the Armenians drowning in their blood? Did the world's conscience rear up, even once, and shout out against the slaughter by the Turks? The answer is no. The Jews were busy with their own troubles. The heart of the Jews was heavy, filled with the sorrows of their people, who were sick and starving.

So it is clear that the interests of the Jewish people are closer to our hearts than the interests of other peoples. Why is it necessary to deny this, and to complicate matters?

And again, why do we maintain Jewish socialist schools? Surely socialism can be learned better in other languages? But since we do, this means that there is something that binds Jewish socialists to their people and their language. Clearly, then, it is impossible to disclaim national feelings. What after all is the crime in wishing to help Jews wherever they are? I wish to point out that Zivion's zealotry is directed against Palestine and he cannot join in those feelings of sympathy of the body of socialists.

Why is it that many workers and socialists have begun to take an interest in Palestine? The answer lies in the fact that conditions in the world have changed, and many hopes have been shattered. The pogroms in the Ukraine were carried out with the assent of Petlura, who was thought to be a social democrat. He, in order to keep his soldiers constantly busy and to stop them from going over to the Bolsheviks, "fed" them continuously with the property and blood of the Jews.

The great hope for a free Russia, for whose realization generations of Jewish socialists shed their blood, has not materialized. That Russia, on which just a few years ago all who suffered turned their gaze, that Russia now, after all, is as before a vast prison.

All countries large and small that were liberated from Russia, including Austria, celebrated their independence day with persecution and pogroms against the Jews. America closed its gates to immigration. The chances for the realization of socialism – the great hope of the oppressed – have receded.

In the Near East there is a land, albeit small, but which is steadily developing, in which the Jews for years have fought their Arab attackers. There Jewish heroes fell, weapon in hand. Those people there have struggled greatly, and no longer fear pogroms. They have also succeeded in opening the gates of the land to new immigration. There in the land a glorious and upright workers' movement has been constructed, demonstrating in practice and realizing in exemplary fashion life on the basis of socialism. Why should all this not stir the heart and awaken sympathy for the workers?

Now to Zivion's reasoning. He claims that mandatory Palestine, which has been allocated to the Jews, covers only about ten thousand square miles, that is, about half the size of Switzerland. My question is, why must he deprive the Jews of two-thirds of what the British took unjustly?

By the example of Switzerland, where despite the fertile soil only about four million people live in very crowded conditions, Zivion wishes to prove that the scale of agriculture determines the scale of population. This is absolutely wrong. Russia had, and has, vast terrains of good land, but nevertheless there never was in any country so much hunger as there is there, not only now under the Bolshevik regime, but at all times. By contrast, Holland is a small country with poor soil, covered with marshes that are drained day and night as the land would be inundated if they were not, and still, the produce that the Dutch farmer draws from his soil is ten times greater than that of the Russian farmer. The Russian is barely able to produce a single yearly crop, while the Dutchman gets three crops a year. In every Dutch village there is an elementary and an agricultural school, and from a young age the pupils study farming, while in the Russian villages the children are not even taught to write their names.

Regarding Switzerland, it should be noted that it is not based solely on agriculture and industry. A considerable part of its economic existence is founded on revenues from tourism. Eretz Israel could also base itself on this branch, perhaps even more so.

While Zivion wishes to show that it is impossible to settle many Jews in Palestine, I would like to prove the contrary. True, I do not believe that within a short time a Jewish majority will arise there, but I am convinced that a large Jewish minority will develop, and it will exert great influence in shaping the country. Let us set aside all talk of a Jewish monarchy and the gathering of all the Jews there, but the creation of a Jewish settlement of half a million will have major implications for the future of the Jewish concentration in Palestine, and also for Jews in all other countries of the world. It may even have the same value as several million Jews in America have in respect of the Jews of the Old World.

And again, Zivion argues that if the Jews wish to reach a majority, this is possible only if the Arabs stop reproducing. I wish to faithfully assure him that the Jews too have not forgotten the commandment of "be fruitful and multiply." The combination of this and Jewish immigration will create a reality in which the Arabs will be unable to exceed them.

Zivion asks how will they make a living there? He states that the Jews will not be able to develop industry because of the lack of raw materials, while buying them abroad will make it impossible to compete with goods of other countries. He likewise points out that Palestine is a British colony, and the British will not permit industry to develop there. Since on this issue Zivion does not base himself on Karl Marx, I will be so bold as to point out the great opportunities that exist in Palestine for the development of trade and industry.

Eretz Israel is situated between the Suez Canal and the Mediterranean Sea, so experts assert that because of the ports that are to be built on the coast, Palestine will become a junction through which goods destined for all the markets of the East will pass. As for Britain, presumably it will wish to move its factories closer to the markets for which the products it manufactures are intended. Therefore, it most probably will in fact allow the establishment of plants in Palestine. Zivion's argument regarding the lack of raw materials in Palestine is not sound. America itself purchases its raw materials for the rubber industry from India, and it is still able to compete with the entire world in its finished rubber products. Not by chance has tension arisen between Britain and America, as the British want to reduce the export of these raw materials to America. Russia buys cotton from America, and it sells the textiles its produces from it all over the world.

From the developing Jewish population in mandatory Palestine a great Jewish settlement will arise. As noted in Cahan's articles, the Jews will be able to settle in Transjordan (where there is abundant land and a small Arab population), in Mesopotamia, and in Syria. Palestine will become a large Jewish center with enormous economic and political significance for the Jews.

No one claims that because not all the Jewish people will be able to migrate to America it will be necessary to reduce migration there.

Zivion is incapable of allowing the Jews the reputation they enjoy of being a gifted people. Even this he wants to take from them. He is unwilling to recognize the falsity of the claim that the Jews were not capable of carrying out hard labor and were not suited for agricultural work. Not only are they indeed capable of performing these tasks, they have leveled mountains, broken rocks, paved roads, and built modern cities.

That is not all. To pump up the claim that the Jews are not so talented as they are made out to be, and that they have not created anything in Palestine, he goes still further, and states that even the Bible was written in Babylonia, as a far higher culture existed there than in Palestine. It seems to me that the origins of the Talmud composed in Babylonia were rooted deep in the culture of Eretz Israel, and it was influenced by it. It would be unreasonable to suppose that scholars would publish Jewish books in America under the influence of the local culture. The opposite is the case. The accumulation and consolidation of the Talmud protected Jewish culture throughout the long years of exile and prevented assimilation and intermixing with the population of the countries where the Jews lived. Regarding the Bible, Zivion wishes to rob Eretz Israel of its rights. The fact simply cannot be denied that the books of the Prophets and the Hagiographa bear the stamp of the Land of Israel.

Then Zivion compounds his error by asserting that against this Eretz Israel, despite the fact that Hebrew is spoken there, has still not produced a writer of note. This is a childish thing to say. What does he want – that in just a few years gifted minds should appear among the Jews? Just as, in the space of four years, he wants communes to have developed Jews brimming over with happiness. In fact, he wants the impossible.

Let us take the example of America, which undoubtedly is a country of a very high cultural level, yet it still has not produced a Darwin or an Einstein, a Shakespeare or a Thackeray, no Georg Brandes or Ibsen, or Sarah Bernhardt – not even a Lloyd George. All this is because as a nation it has existed, on this side of the ocean, only about 150 years. And what do we find, in the domain of talent, in the Jewish community in America? Journalists, poets, artists, playwrights – all immigrants, "imported" goods. Why is this so? It has to be understood that great talents are not born at regular intervals. It takes a long time. Is any better proof needed than the fact that Zivion clutches at anything just to attack Palestine? Obviously, fifty years of migration there could not have given rise to great talents.

Now for the subject of the workers' movement, which Zivion carefully sidestepped. The debate is about Comrade Abe Cahan's articles and impressions. He dismisses these in a word, writing that Cahan had heard that in the summer flowers grow there, and that in the evenings, at the end of a hot day, a pleasant breeze blows – and that's all. Does this indeed summarize everything that Cahan found in Eretz Israel?

In his article of 14 November, Cahan wrote:

> Because of special conditions the communes now fulfill an extremely important role in Palestine. I refer to genuine communes, not those of the kind that the despotic Bolshevik regime established in Russia, which they call "Communism." The endeavor of the communalists is of great significance for the Zionist movement. Through their enthusiasm, their hard work, and the spirit of self-sacrifice they are turning swamps and desert into gardens and fertile fields, and this is the best affirmation of the right to Jewish possession of Palestine. It impresses the world. This description applies also to the new kind of radical moshav (village) founded on private property, but at the same time on a foundation of socialist elements: the farmer must work himself, without hired labor. Similarly, life there is based on certain cooperative elements (the moshav consists of a certain number of settlers. Each of them has a plot of land which he works as his private property. Buying and selling are cooperative. When one of them becomes ill, his comrades provide him with help according to a defined method.) On the veteran moshavot too they worked hard, but today hired labor is employed there, mostly Arab.

The Jewish workers are accomplishing another great thing there. While the old colonists, and the capitalists, prefer to hire cheap Arab labor the workers organize those same Arab workers into unions according to their trades, and to that end the Jewish workers publish the relevant literature in Arabic. All this is intended to improve the lives of the Arabs. By his stance Zivion does not contribute in any way to the workers' cause.

Elsewhere Cahan writes:

> The work on the communes is hard and the food is sparse. They toil hard from sunrise to sunset and the food is by no means sufficient even to furnish the strength they need for such back-breaking work. Life is monot-

onous. When the bell rings for the end of the workday in the evening, and they return from the fields or the children's houses, or the cowshed, the people are so tired that sleep is the greatest joy they could wish for. If this way of life were not based on spiritual satisfaction, on awareness that they are serving an ideal, their lives would become merely unbearable hard labor. Not all of them live with such feelings, not all the members of the communes live there and feel joy in their hearts. Far from it. But there are sufficient people there whose gray lives are lit up by spiritual rays of sunlight.

There is no possibility of migration and settlement in Cuba and Mexico. Even if there were, people would not be motivated there by the same lofty spirit that is theirs in Palestine – a spirit of dedication and elevation, which can move mountains.

And again, Cahan wrote in his articles:

There were times and places where children died like flies because of the diseases that were rampant in the places where they settled. But they did not run away from their land. They overcame all, and again threw their souls into their labor day and night on their land. These lands are healthy today. Today the settlers are proud of their land. Today once more they are harnessed to the task of making new terrains healthy. They have reached such a level of enthusiasm that a particular group announced that it was its duty to work only the harshest and unhealthiest of tracts, and also to accomplish the hardest work not only in agriculture but also in town. There is such un-Jewish work there as breaking stones and laying highways: they want to show that the Jews are capable of carrying out this work and they also wish to do it. They declare: Let us go and work the most deserted and marshy lands! Let us show that the Jews are not deterred by any obstacle or danger, and that they are ready struggle against them! Such words were heard earlier too, but as a formal program of an organization they appeared only five years ago. This organization, called "Gedud Ha'avodah" (Labor Battalion), still exists today. The Battalion is the Jewish avant-garde, marching before the camp into the fire . . .

All this marvelous reality and self-sacrifice Zivion dismisses, and does not consider.

And Cahan again, describing his meeting with the rabbi from Yablona, cannot free himself of the impression left on him by the rabbi's words; he writes, "I recalled his saying that the Jews were always the middle class. The situation that has arisen recently shows that as a middle class they no longer have any place in Poland."

How true these words are! In Russia they certainly have no place. For that reason the proposal of agricultural settlement by Jews in Russia has evoked such great excitement. This is so even though no one believes that this will solve their problem, and even though many fear that potential pogroms will destroy everything that was constructed. Nevertheless, they welcome the chance to save even a few through the project. The economic basis of Jewish existence in Russia having been destroyed, they must be given at least the chance of getting a living from whatever possible, and they have to be afforded some kind of hope in the possibility of their continued existence. If this is not done, they will succumb to demoralization from the fact of having no work, and they will die of starvation.

Obviously, here in America we do not need settlement and communes. We sit here over the fleshpots, and so are sated and free of concern. But the Jews in Europe are suffering and in need of a solution. Large numbers of them set their sights on Palestine. Much of this hope is justified. Should one be so cruel as to trample their aspirations?

Zivion shows very little faith in socialism when he argues that socialism and Zionism cannot live together, because wherever they meet Zionism swallows up socialism. Why is it that the socialists of other nations in no way fear that their nationalism will devour their socialism? They do not wish to destroy their nationalism since that would be unnatural, yet their ambition is that their nationalism will have the correct content.

I must apologize for stating that Zivion put forward no new argument. This is not the whole truth. He has released us from the vow not be Zionists. He does not yet know what a mighty impression his words have made on devout socialists. I repeat here, word for word, what he wrote on this subject:

> Least of all do I wish to discuss the question of what is allowed and what is forbidden, namely may a socialist be a Zionist or not. We do not have a socialist code to help us hand down a decision . . . regarding what a a socialist may or may not believe. The question before us is different: is it logical for a socialist to believe in Zionism?

True enough, it is not logical to believe in that Zionism that Zivion insists on referring to, namely that which believes in the immigration of all Jews to Eretz Israel. But it certainly is logical to believe that many Jews can be settled there, and that the workers there will fulfill a very important role, and that the enterprise of the Jews there will force the world to recognize, in time, their right to live and work in Palestine.

The fault of Zivion is that he distorted the debate, so that no room was left to analyze Cahan's articles. I am certain that the contributors to the debate who follow me will do that. But I cannot refrain from saying a few words about them. The articles made a great impression not only because of their level of journalism, but also because each and every word is stamped with truth and integrity.

In the past too we had no hesitation about sympathizing with the workers in Palestine and being amazed by their energy. Cahan's profound journalistic gaze simply brought out, in a very fine way, the wonderful areas of life there. Cahan's descriptions only deepened our sympathy. Now that it is permitted, as Zivion himself says, it seems to me that in the very near future a great change will take place in the minds and hearts of our workers regarding their attitude to our brothers, the workers of Palestine.

New York, 9 January 1926
3.   Baruch Charney-Vladek
The Debate on the Articles on Palestine

We are engaged in a debate on the articles by Comrade Cahan. Comrade Cahan traveled to Palestine and saw there things which left a deep impression upon him, and he has published these impressions. Like all good journalists, Comrade Cahan was himself influenced by what he wrote, and therefore his articles turned out so compelling and vivid. When an artist paints a picture he exaggerates in comparison with the actual subject. If he did not do so there would be no need for him, for then a photographer would suffice, who would do the same job but quicker. If Comrade Cahan, as a journalist, were merely a plain craftsman he would have presented his readers with the material he collected in a straigh*for-ward* way. But there is no certainty that it would have been read. But he is not a plain craftsman, and because he introduced into his articles so much character and verve that they had to be read.

That same element that made his articles so interesting was also the source of the unease that arose in many comrades. They were irked by the fact that Comrade Cahan was influenced and excited by a matter which to us is deemed alien. What is this like? Like a woman who displays jealousy when her husband shows interest in another woman. Who knows, the comrades thought (just as a wife would), what might grow out of this?

From the warm looks sent in the direction of the other woman and also from the exchange of ardent words between the two, a real love affair may develop!

From a close reading of all the telegrams and articles sent by Comrade Cahan from Palestine, it may be stated with certainty that for the time being the affair between Madame Zion and Comrade Cahan is up in the air. Comrade Cahan did not go beyond making a few compliments. For a couple of charming remarks you don't get the electric chair. On the contrary – it has to be admitted that the material sent from Palestine is worthy of him and of *Forward*, and there is still nothing to complain about.

The problem becomes more complicated when the sympathetic tone wafting through Comrade Cahan's articles is united with the overall problem of Zionism. The issue grows more serious because the Zionist movement and our movement at times maintain reciprocal relations and at times are in conflict with each other. Therefore we are obliged to act with greater caution and in a more calculated manner.

For example, Comrade Cahan wrote with great enthusiasm about the pioneers on the communes. All comrades who are sympathetic to Zionism are more moved by this part of Comrade Cahan's descriptions than by his other descriptions of life in Palestine. I must confess that the articles impressed me both in the manner of Comrade Cahan's writing and because of the seriousness and fire bound up in them, but the subject itself makes no special impression on me at all. Idealism is always a fine and exhilarating term. Obviously, I feel enormous respect for those men and women who have given up the comforts of social life and have devoted themselves to the ideal of building a home for the Jews. But this is nothing new among Jews. We always had, and still have, more rogues and more idealists than any other people. The entire history of Jewish youth in recent decades is a history saturated with idealism. This is true of the Biluim and the Jewish Narodniks, it is true of the pioneers of Jewish migration to America and the Bund, of the young Jews who established the Jewish trade unions and the *Arbeiter Ring* in America, and of the Jewish youth who burned with the fire of the Russian Revolution. Jewish youth has always evinced the highest degree of martyrdom for the ideal. Within our movement in America too there are many people who have sacrificed their personal careers for the sake of a noble ideal.

The sacrifice alone for the sake of an ideal still does not make the ideal itself good and precious. In Russia today there are more idealists than in any other state – idealists in the purest sense of the word. Nevertheless, their ideal is not acceptable to us. Quite the reverse, we find it entirely wrong that such a defective ideology is adhered to by fine, idealistic, zealous human material. In the Zionist movement there are many idealists but this still does not make Zionism right.

It is not my task to delve deeply into the fine details of Zionist ideology, as Comrades Zivion and Pine have done. Zionism is a cry of despair; it is like one of Gorky's tales about a girl who writes letters to her lover, who does not exist. It makes no difference to her. Suffering and wretched, she invents, if only in her imagination, the lover, in order to stop herself committing suicide by leaping off a bridge into the water. It is impossible to convince a religious man of the non-existence of God, or to persuade an invalid that he is going to die. If God did not exist it would be necessary to re-invent him – so, I believe, said Voltaire. If Zionism did not exist it would be necessary to invent it for those who see no future and no possibility of relieving the troubles of the Jewish people except through their having a land of their own.

Jewish identity and belief in the Jewish people do not depend on any conditions. In our own way, we Jews are just as good as our fathers and grandfathers. Our children and our grandchildren will be Jews according to their way. When there is no longer any Jewish newspaper or Jewish theater in New York, there will still be centers, clubs, and schools. My grandchildren will know that their grandfather was a Jew, just as I know who and what my grandfathers and their fathers were. We must support the Jewish spirit in all its expressions and aspects. That is why I would support the Hebrew University in Jerusalem, and that is also why I would give Bialik the respect that he deserves when he comes to America: this is so despite the fact that I am not a supporter of Hebrew and he is coming with a Zionist delegation. None of this has anything to do with Zionism as a movement that aims to win a country for the Jews.

Furthermore, I believe that Zionism has done much to arouse and sustain national awareness. What the Bund did for the Jewish workers in awakening their consciousness of their Jewishness, Zionism has done for the Jewish middle class and intelligentsia. I am vey pleased when I see an assimilating Jewish attorney or physician taking an interest in Jewish problems, without being afraid of losing everything by preserving his Jewishness. But this too has nothing to do with Zionism as a movement, as a promise made to solve the Jewish problem, in a practical manner, by means of the Jewish national home. Today we are obliged to adopt a measure of caution when we speak about these subjects. Zionists and communists have one thing in common – both are extremist fanatics to the point of madness. Like all those whose ideology is based on belief, they consider any opponent a mortal enemy. Nevertheless, let me say that not only do I not believe in the practicality of Zionism, even if it were possible to realize Zionism it would be a catastrophe. When I observe what is taking place in Lithuania, Latvia, Estonia, Romania, Poland, Bulgaria I thank God that we do not have a state of our own. A Jewish kingdom led by Jewish politicians (leaders of states are always politicians and not idealists) within a large Arab population and defended by British rifles . . .

It is hard to determine whether Judaism is a sickness or a bounty from God, but thousands of years of Jewish history have shown that Judaism has stupendous vital force, and when it is pushed out of the door it re-enters through the window. Just as I am unwilling to accept the position of the Yiddishists that the sole basis for the continued protection of Jewish identity is the Yiddish language, or the position of the orthodox that this basis consists of the Jewish religion, so am I unwilling to accept that the only basis for the continued existence of Jewish identity is a Jewish country. As one who always was a Jew and has never encountered a conflict between his Jewishness and socialism, the arguments of Comrade Pine sound empty and childish to me, when he tries to argue that anyone who cares about the troubles of the Jews and is involved with Jewish subjects is a Zionist. Comrade Pine belongs with those American comrades and worker activists whose awakening has remained stationary at Jewish issues and pogroms. Hence they are so sentimental but devoid of logic.

In my humble opinion the city of Brownsville has done more for Jewry than the Zionist movement during its 30 years of activity, except for one small difference – the Jewish policemen in Brownsville do not have Hebrew badges on their lapels. Brownsville is not eternal, just as Spain was not eternal, just as Poland and Russia were not eternal, and this holds for the Jewish state too. Even when Eretz Israel was our land, history treated us worse than a New York landlord treats his tenants, and it imposed on us pressures, expulsions, and all manner of other disasters. No one on earth can give us any guarantee as to the duration of our control of a small city [such as Brownsville – Y.G.].

Zionism, as a movement striving to establish a Jewish national home, is built only on the basis of emotion and not on a pragmatic perception, on facts. It is like the sentiment that causes the poor tailor to invest the few dollars he has managed to scrape together in the remotest plot of land in Long Island. It is nothing but a substitute for a genuine goal that is unattainable. But there are those who will claim that Zionism is not just a movment striving to retain Jewish identity and to establish a Jewish national home: its concern is for the present, and it seeks to bring succor to the masses of Jews being choked in Poland, Russia, Romania and throughout Europe! In general, the Zionists have lately been talking a great deal about the many opporutnities inherent in Palestine as a land of migration that must be exploited, and this quite detached from the longer-term goals of turning the country into a Jewish state.

It seems to me that the weakness of Zionism is exposed here more than anywhere else. Political Zionism has existed for about 30 years. These years were perhaps the worst in all Jewish history, and what has Zionism done throughout these years? Every country to which Jews migrated in these years has done more for them than Palestine. In these years even in Argentina a bigger Jewish settlement has grown up than in Eretz Israel, and this is true also of Canada and, I think, even Brazil. The figures published by the Zionists are highly exaggerated. According to their calculations between three and four thousand people migrate to Palestine each month, meaning 40,000 new immigrants yearly. According to Zionist estimates and forecasts, in recent years, since the Balfour Declaration, there should have accumulated there a Jewish population of close to a quarter of a million; but in fact, the Jewish settlement numbers only 125,000 Jews. Even in the last few years, when Jewish migration to Palestine reached its peak, the Jewish settlement increased only by 18,000 a year – the same as the number of immigrants entering America annually despite all the restrictions that have been imposed on migration here. A similar number of Jewish immigrants, if not more, entered France last year, if I am not mistaken.

What kind of land is this Palestine, as a land meant to absorb immigration? A land that has no water, a land without natural resources, without industry and without an infrastructure of modern civilization. Of course, we must not go to extremes. If Jews actually do migrate to Palestine, if they actually wish to remain there, if they are drawn there by sentiment or national ambitions, then they should be helped as much as possible, but to the same degree that help is given to Jews everywhere else. The truth is that even we "comrades" have assisted Palestine more than it deserves according to the number of Jews located there; this was through the JDC or by other means. At the same time, we object to Palestine being set before us as the center of our being and our purpose. This would be brutal and utterly unjust in respect of Jews in other countries. What right have we to argue, as indeed the Zionists argue, that the Jews located in other countries are the generation of the wilderness and therefore there is no meaning to all their effort and their struggle, and the only meaning lies in the enterprise being conducted in Palestine.

The condition of the Jews in several countries is now truly catastrophic. This applies particularly to Poland, Romania and Russia, although in Russia, so it appears, the situation has improved recently. There they need credit, tools, and aid. I am not willing to assume responsibility for taking from them the little that can be raised for them in order to invest it in Palestine. Comrade Cahan is excited and moved by the pioneers certainly – but what about the 2000 Jewish teachers in Poland who are, quite simply, dying of starvation while conducting a struggle for Jewish schools, which they consider a struggle for the continued spiritual existence of the Jewish people? And what about those being martyred in Romania, sacrificing their lives in order to maintain our institutions in Bukovina and Bessarabia? And what about our activists in Poland, Romania, Lithuania, Latvia, and Estonia, who die three times a day together with the masses of the Jews who are growing constantly weaker?

In recent years terror has been applied against Jewish life by two movements: the communist and the Zionist. Both these movements are struggling for things that are not connected with real Jewish life, and each is willing to sacrifice the Jewish people on the altar of its fanaticism. If there still are comrades who are against Palestine just because it is Palestine, they are wrong, and behind the times in their attitude. Palestine should not be discrimimated against. It is necessary to help every place equally, as far as we are able. But it will be the bitterest day, for the Jews and for Jewish identity, when the Zionists become those who set the tone in our circles. Here sentiments do not count. Everyone may possess national awareness of one sort or another. But the most important thing is the answer to the question Palestine *also* or Palestine *alone*!

Comrade Cahan for the time being expresses himself along the lines of "Palestine also." No one can say anything against this position. But the unease felt in our circles will be entirely justified if someone in our movement should wish to compel us to accept the formula "Palestine alone"!

All this is because Zionism, as a party concerned with Jewish matters, as a mechanism for collecting and distributing the people's money, does not have at the center of its philosophy the Jewish masses but an abstract Jewish identity. It is absorbed by its politics more than by the vital needs of the masses. Zionism has become a despotic movement, barren and embittered, which looms up as a stumbling block and an obstacle whenever the Jews attempt to do something for themselves outside Palestine and without accepting its direction.

New York, 15 January 1926
4. Dr Isser Ginsburg
The Debate on the Articles on Palestine

I admit that I do not set great store by debates. In my humble opinion
they are wasted effort. In any case, each side sticks to its views. I am
convinced that no on has has ever been persuaded to shift positions by
"causes" or "proofs." Debates turn into a kind of cockfight, with each side
getting pleasure from his own bird.

The reason is that we reach our positions and views through thousands
of diverse factors and influences, and very rarely through our intellect.
We ourselves do not know how our views take shape within us.
Sometimes they are the result of our temperament or our feelings, and
sometimes they are due to the influences of a friend, the environment,
tradition, and so on. In any event, the particular opinion appears first, and
only afterwards the set of reasons. In this our mind acts as the servant, not
the master, of our opinions. If as a result of a variety of factors we do eventually formulate a certain position, we continue to hold it. No reasoning
or proofs, rational as they may be, will make any difference. Each person
will remain firm in his views. Even facts from daily life will do no good.
Our mind will find a way of dealing with them and explaining them in
such a way that they blend neatly into the framework of our attitudes. We
are willing to twist and subvert the facts, but not to change our positions.

Such is my position on debates. But the debtate on the articles by our
friend Cahan on Eretz Israel is entirely incomprehensible to me. What in
fact happened? Our friend Cahan journeyed to Eretz Israel to see what
was taking place there. He wished to view it all with his own eyes, to
examine in person the situation there, and to explain it. So he was there,
he made his study, and published in *Forward* the truth and the whole
truth as he saw and understood it. You may like or dislike the truths that
he published, but he could not present any other truth but his truth. Nor
should one expect any other truth than his. If he were to set down things
in which he did not believe that would distort the truth. "Truth" tailored
to the positions of some group or other is not truth but falsehood.

Forward is not a Zionist newspaper, but it is not irritatingly anti-Zionist
either. It is a more or less neutral paper, and to tell the truth, much less
than more. Its neutrality is like that of America before it entered the war.
It was neutral then, but with sympathy for the Entente. *Forward* was
neutral toward Zionism but sympathetic to the anti-Zionists . . . For the
moment it is immaterial why this was so. Most probably it was due to the

supposition that the old generation of socialists took for granted, like two plus two equals four, that socialism and Zionism cannot coexist. It is easy to explain how such a position crystallized among Jewish socialists when you know the history of the development of socialism in the Jewish street, its early character, and the battles it was forced to fight. But that is another story. In any event, *Forward* was more or less neutral.

Forward is the Jewish paper with the widest circulation, and this is a fact whether you like it or not. Zionism, regardless of what you think of it, is one of the most important phenomena in Jewish life in our age. There are perhaps people who think that Zionism is the most important phenomenon. Therefore, it is so natural that the biggest Jewish newspaper should take an interest in one of the most significant manifestations in Jewish life. It is none too soon. Being a neutral paper regarding Zionism, it had to send to Eretz Israel a person known for his neutral attitude, insofar as this is possible. I, for example, would not have been suitable for such an assignment because for my many iniquities I must confess to my sympathy for Zionism. My reports, willy-nilly, would have been too rosy because no one can change his skin. My colleague and comrade, Zivion, would certainly not have been right for the task because he is known to be an ardent anti-Zionist and he has made it his life's mission to wage a bitter and obstinate war against Zionism. A person may adhere to his views and fight against things which, in his opinion, are wrong. But it is entirely clear that if he had been sent, his reports, willy-nilly, would have been shrouded in black. Therefore, it was necessary to find a man relatively free of suspect attitudes and dyed-in-the-wool prejudices. Such a man was our colleague, Cahan.

Therefore, Cahan made the journey and studied the situation closely. He committed his findings to writing. It transpires that he found things there that he liked, others that aroused his sympathy, and some things that excited him and fired him up! The content of his articles jolted the "elders of the movement," all of whom are nice people, and they let loose cries of despair: "Oh no! The man is leading us to heresy, he is taking us to Jerusalem, to the Land of Israel, to Zionism. He is bringing troubles upon us, and he must be forbidden from doing so!" Cahan defended himself against these charges, and stated that he is not a Zionist, nor does he believe in the possibility of the realization of Zionism. At the same time, he cannot deny the feelings of sympathy that were awoken in him by those noble-hearted and idealistic people who gave up careers and personal desires to dedicate themselves to their ideal. This declaration by Cahan did not appease the "elders," and they never ceased tearing out their hair as if they have been struck by catastrophe! What do they want? you may well ask. Did they expect that Cahan would write things other than what he saw and felt? In other words, did they want him to write lies? No: presumably they did not want that. The truth is cherished and dear to them, but it is a different truth, not the truth expressed by Cahan. For some reason it does not suit them that Cahan is a man possessing sentiment and feelings, a man who can reach spiritual exhilaration and excitement. Did they need a man devoid of feelings and without the capacity to be affected by what there is there, and to be enthralled by it? Presumably, if Cahan had written against Zionism everything would have gone smoothly. I would not have enlarged on this subject if our friend Zivion had not addressed it – naturally in a more literary and polished manner.

Zivion divides everything into poetry and prose, into feelings on the one hand and a rational stance on the other. On the basis of this division he gets into a mass of hair-splitting, argumentation and sophistry. It would take me years to reply to every one of the quibbles he presents. Therefore, I shall deal with only one issue: the distinction that Zivion has made, between poetry and prose, between emotion and reason, does not exist in reality. It never has and it never will exist, because the two are always intertwined. Life is a blend of the spiritual and the material, and they cannot be separated. For centuries, people considered the question of what comes first, the spiritual or the material. Science concerned itself with the matter lately too, and concluded that such duality does not exist in human beings . . . I take the liberty of doubting that my colleague, Zivion, is moved only by the rational. I sustain a grave suspicion that his incessant attacks against Zionism are driven by very strong feelings . . .

I beg the reader's forgiveness for dilating on the subject of mind and emotion. It seems to me that this matter is the foundationstone of the debate. The underlying error of the opponents of Zionism lies in the fact that they address Zionism by a pragmatic approach only, with "cold logic." For them it is merely a question of costs or profitability, whether Zionism is good business or not. They, the anti-Zionists, totally ignore the millennia-long feelings of the people, as if they are of no value or importance in life. One must recognize the fact that these feelings, for good or ill, wise or devoid of understanding, exist in at least a large number of the people. Perhaps, in future generations they will disappear, but for the time being they are a fact, which even the rational approach must take into account . . .

New York, 16 January 1926
Dr Isser Ginsburg
The Debate on the Articles on Palestine (continued)

There is an old truth: love is blind. Lovers do not see the flaws that exist in the object of their love. A youth falls in love with a girl, or she with him, not necessarily because the beloved is objectively the best, the cleverest, or the gentlest of creatures, but because the lover believes her or him to be so. They are not "neutral," and cannot be, because they do not act solely on the basis of the purely rational approach . . . All the foregoing is a fable, the characters of which stand for the Jewish people and Eretz Israel . . . The love of a single individual is different from the love of a people. Moreover, the love of the people for Eretz Israel is not as strong as the love between a couple, but it is constant. This is not love of the kind that is consumed in its own fire, but it is a love that has endured for 3000 years. Perhaps it is a foolish love – fanatical, crazy, hopeless, but it exists. You might say that it would be better if the people had a sober approach, and stopped dreaming about their land. But in such a case they would have assimilated into the nations of the world long ago, or found themselves another country and saved themselves the martyrdom of two millennia. All this might have happened, but the fact is that it did not. With unmatched determination, the people clung to the dream they had dreamt for generations. Perhaps the dream is unrealizable, but the dream itself is a fact that must be taken into account when Eretz Israel is compared to other countries. Whoever disregards this is not considering the facts, and his approach is not and will never be scientific. This is the mistake of all who treated the subject of Eretz Israel only on the basis of rationality.

For the latter, the subject was encapsulated in a sort of formula: since there is a people without a land, it must be provided with such a land. And sure enough, proposals were put forward – Uganda, Argentina, China, and so forth. They just forgot one small thing – they forgot to ask the party concerned, to ask the groom if he had a liking for the bride. It turns out the groom is as stubborn as a mule, and rather "stupid;" he won't accept what is offered to him. It turns out that life does not move forward on the basis of pure rationality . . .

There are people who are not in love with Eretz Israel. For them, Eretz Israel is a country like any other. The "romantic" dimension in them is expressed in other domains. For them, Eretz Israel is not a stepchild, yet it is not an only daughter either. From their viewpoint the attitude to a hundred thousand Jews in Palestine or in Poland or in Romania has to be the same. This position is already a great advance, because in the past Eretz Israel was treated worse than a stepchild, and the Jewish workers there were treated as if they were not human beings. Thank God that times have changed. I am convinced that in our midst there are tens of thousands who hold this position of reservation about Eretz Israel, but the question is not what they or I feel, but what the people feel.

The numbers game is misleading, because the attitude to the numbers is subjective, not objective. The Bundists' attitude to a hundred thousand of their comrades will not be the same as it is to a like number of Zionists. In the eyes of the people, a hundred thousand Jews in Eretz Israel do not stand on the same footing as a hundred thousand in any other country. Most of the Jewish people look toward the Jews of Eretz Israel with expectation and hope, with trembling in the heart and with fondness. All this is not because the individual Jew in Eretz Israel is better than the individual Jew in the Diaspora, but because the people consider them the builders of their future. It is a fact that the Jewish people, on all levels, contribute to Eretz Israel more, and with greater readiness, than to the Jews of other lands. Not without grounds does my friend, Zivion, complain about the fact that the Zionists are rolling in money. Where do the Zionists get it from, if the people are not giving? Zivion is wrong when he compares Eretz Israel to Mexico or any other country. The persecuted and tormented Jews, who have no place for a night's sleep, who suffer oppression and hunger, flee anywhere possible: Mexico, Argentina, Brazil, Africa – any possible corner where they might eke out a living. They will peddle matches, rags, old iron. They will become owners of sweatshops, physicians, advocates – even journalists. In sum, they will become anything but *halutzim*!

Halutzim – pioneers, as our friend, Cahan, described them, can only be in Eretz Israel. These are pioneers filled with heroism, who with their fingernails tend the poor, desolate, dry earth of Eretz Israel. These are the pioneers who saturate the soil of Eretz Israel with their heartblood and their tears – pioneers such as these cannot be anywhere else in the world. Rabbis such as the rabbi from Yablonka with his hassidim can be found only in Eretz Israel. All this arises from the fact that for the sake of Eretz Israel there is uplift, enthusiasm, faith, hope and love. The work of the pioneers there is replete with love. They see themselves as the builders of the future. They are working for an ideal.

Some argue that their idealism will not last long, and in the end they will disperse. Naturally, no on can give any guarantee. Perhaps some, possibly even the majority, will leave the present way of life, for it is easier to die as a martyr than to live as a martyr. But they are not isolated and without continuation. After the first ones others will come, and after them their successors, until the wasteland is rebuilt. The Jewish people is rich in spiritual strength and initiative when it comes to Eretz Israel. This derives from the people's special attitude to Eretz Israel, which is different from their attitude to all other countries.

Zivion's joke about the Bulgarian king who said that "a Zionist is someone who tells others to go to Eretz Israel" is misplaced. Not all the Jews can or should migrate there. Only the select few with the pioneering spirit and ideals should immigrate. The right people for the enterprises and possessing faith – only those can be the builders of the land and the society. They will be the pioneering avant-garde, and others will be able to follow . . .

One can understand those lacking romance about Eretz Israel. They state openly that they are not in love with Eretz Israel, and for them it is a land like any other. No romance and no emotions. The only posture to adopt against them is to ask why they do not take the feelings and behavior of the people into account. For Zivion it is different, because he makes a distinction, and writes: "For me Eretz Israel is in the domain of romance. The very combination of words Eretz Israel, which conjured so many fabulous dreams in my heder days – even today these words have not lost their attractive force. For me this phrase still has the ring of my youthful dreams, a land filled with miracles and wondrous acts." Zivion understands the romance of Eretz Israel, but he distinguishes the term Eretz Israel from the term Palestine. (Vladek agrees with Zivion on this, but he calls the romance "sentiment" and he belittles it by comparing it to the behavior of the Jew who rushes to buy worthless land on Long Island. In general, Vladek's article turned out more Zionist than he perhaps intended. He recognizes the rights of Zionism, which stirred feelings of Jewish self-awareness and pride. He even admits that if Zionism did not exist it would have to be invented. He only objects to what he calls "Zionism alone," but he does not object to "Zionism also.") As regards Palestine, Zivion argues that the question is "what can the Jews achieve in Palestine, and what can Palestine give them?" This position is reminiscent of the story about the young man who was deeply in love with a girl, but because she had no dowry he did not want to marry her . . . The vast majority of the Jewish people are not renowned for such a pragmatic approach, and I am not at all certain that this should be seen as a fault . . . . Zivion's arguments are those of one who wants too much, not of one who wants nothing. In Jerusalem, a university is being built, but Zivion is displeased with the humble beginnings. He wants something right away along the lines of Columbia or Harvard. I too would wish for that, but I know that Rome was not built in a day. Eretz Israel is a small and poor country. Of course it would be better if it were large and rich, and I would very much wish for that. But what can we do if it is small and poor? Obviously, it might have been better if Moses had crossed the Atlantic Ocean instead of the Red Sea, and had led us to vast, rich America instead of poor, small Eretz Israel. Things did not work out that way, and there is no cause to get riled with a man who has long been numbered among the departed. Nor is Zivion happy with the multitude of Arab inhabitants in the country: neither am I. But this is a fact and it will be necessary to come to terms and to live with them. The same applies to Zivion's arguments against the British . . .

Among his arguments, Zivion states that in Eretz Israel the Jews actually created very little. In his view, Jewish culture, including the Bible and the Talmud, was created in exile, not Eretz Israel. This concept is entirely wrong. Not only was almost all the Bible created and fashioned in Eretz Israel at the time of the First and Second Temples, but also the Mishnah, most of the Talmud, the earliest Beraitah and some of the ancient *aggadot* were formulated in Eretz Israel. To these must of course be added the Apocrypha and the beginnings of Christianity. It transpires, therefore, that Eretz Israel created not a little . . . It is not right to deny Eretz Israel its just deserts.

Equally mistaken is the argument that the Zionists wish to return us to Asia and convert us into Asiatics in the cultural sense, not the geographical sense. This claim is new to me. The opposite is true, because the Zionists have high hopes for the Europeanization of Eretz Israel. There are even naïve Zionists who believe that our mission is to carry European culture to Asia just as we once carried Arab culture to Europe.

A third argument (presented by Vladek) is also wrong, namely that for the Zionists a few hundred thousand Jews in Eretz Israel are more important than the millions in the Diaspora. This charge orginates from a mistaken interpretation, which I should like to clarify. The Zionists possess a national vision exactly like the Bundists and the Yiddishists. They wish for the continued existence of the Jewish people in the future too, again like the Bundists and the Yiddishists. The three currents agree that religion has grown weak and can no longer safeguard the existence of the people as it did in the past. Hence they seek other means that will occupy the role once filled by religion. According to the Bundists, the goal will be attained by means of the "cultural autonomy" program that they propose. The Yiddishists offer "Yiddishism." The Zionists put forward the "homeland" project. The Zionists do not believe that the Jews can achieve cultural autonomy in the Diaspora, and neither do they believe in the power of Yiddishism. They fear that the Jews in the countries of the Diaspora will sooner or later assimilate and disappear. They strive to avert this process through the Jews having a homeland of their own.

The ideology outlined here does not state that all the Jews in the world must be gathered into the Jewish homeland – an impossible endeavor. Eretz Israel cannot realize this except by a miracle, and there is no other country capable of doing it. The homeland, small as it may be, can serve as a center for the Jewish people dispersed all over the world. It is a fact that Eretz Israel was never, except in antiquity, anything other than a center for the people. Jews were spread throughout the Roman empire even when Eretz Israel was still theirs. The Zionists hope that by means of this center it will be possible to assure the continued existence of the people in the Diaspora also.

One may agree or disagree with them, but they cannot be accused of giving more consideration to the few hundred thousand Jews in Eretz Israel than to the millions in the Diaspora. The importance of the hundreds of thousands in Eretz Israel lies in the fact that they are likely to vouchsafe the continued existence of the entire people.

Vladek makes another accusation, namely that they, together with the communists, are terrorizing Jewish life . . . What is to be done – the facts do not match the charges, certainly not in America. Matters may be so in Poland, but it may also be that the information reaching us from there is subjective.

The reader has no doubt discerned that so far I have not mentioned the communes in Eretz Israel and their meaning for socialism; the reason is, that I do not regard myself as an expert on socialism. For me, socialism is more than a "science," it is a lofty universal ideal, the existence of which pre-dates Karl Marx. It is my hope that sooner or later it will be realized, but I do not know how and in what way this will come about. One thing I do know is that never have such experiments at socialism been made as at present. The experiments are being conducted in two laboratories: one in mighty Russia and one in poor, weak Eretz Israel. The ways adopted in the two laboratories are different. It is hard to foretell which laboratory will produce the hoped-for results, and perhaps both will fail. In any event, it seems to me that every socialist should be pleased with the experiments and should look forward to the results. Those who are not pleased

with the method applied in Russia, which it is one of orders and dictatorship, should certainly treat the experiments being conducted in Eretz
Israel more warmly.

I have not touched on many subjects because the article has grown long
. . . As for Cahan's articles, they are too cautious for my taste, and he is
too little of a Zionist. It turns out that what for me is too little, for others
is too much. The chief thing is that he remained loyal to himself and
expressed his truth; this is what was to be expected of him.

New York, 23 January 1926
5. Abraham Litvak
The Debate on the Articles on Palestine

My article will be the fifth in the debate and the third expressing the
position of the opponents, so I shall try not to repeat things stated by
others . . . I would, of course, prefer to debate with Zionists than with the
supporters of Zionism among our comrades, who protest morning, noon
and night that they are not Zionists. They accept the conclusions of
Zionism, although they refrain from accepting the principles of Zionism.
Sometimes they do the opposite: they accept the principle and reject the
conclusions. Yea and nay are applied by them in confusion. It is hard to
know where you stand with them. It is especially hard for me with
Comrade Cahan, for whom everything is based on emotion, and it is well
known that emotions change . . . In New York we have not heard him say
that we should participate in the Histadrut fund-raising campaign, but in
Chicago he made the request "to help the delegation of workers from
Palestine at present in America so that they may act on behalf of the interests of the workers' institutions, the trade unions, and the cooperatives
there." It transpires, therefore, that one should join in activities for the
Histadrut campaign.

The debate is difficult because it is not based on logic but on feelings
. . . Dr Ginsburg's starting point, for example, is that the Jewish people
is in love with the Land of Israel, and love, as we all know, is blind . . .
Ginsburg believes in the power of love, so he assumes that Zionism can
be realized . . . He just forgets that many peoples have fought for their
independence with the best of their powers, their love and their devotion,
but they did not achieve the longed-for independence because the inimical objective conditions were stronger than all these. True, the feelings
of a people, the outcome of historical development, are a factor to be

considered, but they are not the only factor, nor are they the most forceful . . .

Dr Ginsburg will argue that this is perhaps so for other peoples but not for the Jewish people, and in the relations between them and Eretz Israel no rule has been laid down and nothing is impossible. Jewish history does not support this approach. Since the beginnings of the exile the Jews have loved Eretz Israel no less than they do now, so why did this love not cause them to rebuild the land? To this you may answer that those were other times and different circumstances: which means that love alone does not solve everything, and times and circumstances are important . . . Our friend Ginsburg knows no less than I that in the Second Temple period large sections of the people lived outside the Land of Israel in Babylonia, Persia, Egypt, Syria and Rome. Their love for Eretz Israel was stronger then than it is now. The leaders of the people tried then to retain as many people as possible in Eretz Israel, and for that reason they declared the land of the gentiles unclean. None of this helped, because the economic conditions, which caused a decline, were more powerful than the fear of living under foreign rule.

The people love Eretz Israel, but this is not the same as their love for Palestine. Eretz Israel is located in the domain of religious sanctity. It is something that belongs more to the next world than to this. Turning it into a state like all other states removes it from the sacred and places it in the profane. Palestine is something else, belonging to the sphere of politics, business, livelihood, and therefore the Jew measures it on an earthly scale. Is it worthwhile or not? Palestine is for the body, while Eretz Israel is for the soul. The love of Eretz Israel is most fierce among the pious, yet still they are opposed to Zionism.

When the great migration from Russia began after the pogroms of 1881–2, was there not then a love of 3000 years for Eretz Israel? Did not the Hovevei Zion then fire up this love sufficiently? The dream was still fresh, and the land seemed accessible and within reach, yet despite this the great majority emigrated to America and not to Palestine. The old love remained in the heart, while the feet were directed by concrete conditions. None of this matters to Dr Ginsburg, who states that for a livelihood Jews would emigrate to Mexico, to Argentina, to Brazil – anywhere on earth; but pioneers who with their fingernails are plowing the poor, desolate dry soil – this is to be found only in Eretz Israel. He ignores the fact that a settlement can be built only in a place where the masses migrate, or can migrate, while with the pioneers, who are diverging from the highroad of the people, it is not possible to build anything. This would apply even more if those masses did not send money to Palestine, for then the pioneers, with all their idealism, would not endure. Only in Zionist rhetoric is it possible to cultivate the land with the fingernails alone.

When Dr Ginsburg mocks the livelihood of Jews in the countries of the Diaspora he identifies with the Zionist attitude to the Jews in exile, namely to 99 percent of the entire Jewish people. As for Argentina, Ginsburg disregards facts recognized by all. Jewish settlement in Argentina began ten years after the settlement in Palestine . . . Despite all the problems, today about 30,000 people live in Jewish villages (slightly more than in the *moshavot* in Palestine . . .), which are economically independent and are not in need of help. All journalists who have been there in recent years report unanimously that a healthy Jewish population lives there, attached to their land and thirsty for culture. No miracles are told about the Jewish villages in Argentina, but the greatest miracle, perhaps, is the very fact of their natural existence without miracles. It seems that Dr Ginsburg's love of Eretz Israel is blind if he cannot see these facts.

In any event, Dr Ginsburg, by his thinking, is a Zionist, although he himself still does not know it, and when he realizes it he will be alarmed . . . But Comrade Cahan is not a Zionist, but still sentiment plays an important part in him and he repeatedly states that the Jews sympathize with the Zionist ideal. They do not have to be encouraged in this. Comrade Cahan knows that throngs of Jews support the *rebbe* of Gur, the *rebbe* of Sedigora, and the *rebbe* of Lubavitch. The sympathy of the hassidim in Poland for Gur is no less than the sympathy of the Zionists for Palestine. And for Gur too there is enthusiasm and excitement. If so, should we begin to adore the rebbe of Gur? Perhaps the United Jewish Unions should organize a fund-raising campaign for him? . . . Sentiments do not live forever; old ones sometimes die and new ones are born. Concurrently, in the people, there are sentiments of yesterday and sentiments of tomorrow; sentiments that feed both reaction and progress. We do not bow our heads before any sentiment just because it exists in the people. We intervene in the conflict between sentiments. We strive to strengthen the sentiments that work for our benefit.

The sentiment for socialism in America is still young and weak, but this is our sentiment, one that heralds the future, and we must develop it and strengthen it. Zionist sentiments harm socialism. The Jewish masses in America are not sufficiently involved in the struggle for tomorrow. They are interested in pragmatic concerns alone – a slice of bread and butter. Our task is to educate them and point out to them the necessity for the struggle for tomorrow, the necessity for idealism and enthusiasm. In these circumstances, if the attention of these masses is deflected to Eretz Israel, if they are given the chance to fulfill their duty to idealism through a donation for the *halutzim* in Palestine, this harms socialism; if the Jewish masses are constantly told, as they are by Po'aley Tziyon, that the Jewish problem can be solved solely in the framework of the Jewish state. Even if Comrade Cahan in his speech in Chicago strained to find signs of anti-Semitism in America, and used this to point with emotion at Palestine – where there are many one-eyed Arabs while the Jews have two eyes – this reinforces Zionism at the expense of the force of our struggle in America. When Po'aley Tziyon assures one and all that in Poland the Zionists are those standing at the forefront of the struggle for liberation and equal rights for the Jews (which, by the way, they believe it is impossible to achieve in the Diaspora countries), and in parallel Comrade Cahan does not cease telling of the warmth the Jewish bourgeoisie is showing to the workers in Palestine – do they not weaken class consciousness and feelings? Do they not thereby strengthen the feeling of solidarity of all Jewry? The situation might be otherwise if the energy and enthusiasm were directed to the benefit of the socialist movement in America, rather than acting for the pioneers. If instead of planting in a Jewish youth the desire and the dream of being a pioneer we were to plant the desire and dream of being a fighter for the workers, a revolutionary, then socialism could be built out of this. The sentiments that nurture Zionism and the sentiments that nurture socialism are separated by an abyss. Each can develop only at the expense of the other. Therefore the Zionists work hard to stifle our sentiments. We must do the same to theirs.

Dr Ginsburg tries to shift the debate to a different track entirely when he argues that Palestine will not solve the problem of the Jews, but it will solve the problem of Judaism. There a center of Jewish culture will arise on which the Jews of the Diaspora will draw and through which they will sustain their Jewish identity. This cultural center will develop and flourish even after the Jews in the Diaspora disappear. This whole concept of Ginsburg is Ahad Ha'amist. How is it possible to differentiate between Judaism and living Jews? Judaism hanging in the air cannot be. If the great majority of the Jews remain in the countries of the Diaspora, Palestine will not become a center of Judaism for them. Eretz Israel ceased to be such a center the moment the masses of the Jews left it. Our forefathers said that whither Jews are exiled, thither they take the Divine Presence. There is no Judaism without the Jewish people ... The creative "Jewish spirit" wandered with the masses of the Jews from Eretz Israel to Alexandria in Egypt, to Babylonia, to Spain, to Poland, and now to

America. That is how it was in the past, and in the future too it cannot be different. In general, it is hard for me to comprehend the idea that it is possible to save Judaism in America with a little Hebrew in Palestine . . .

It is ridiculous to assume that the sons will soon forget that they are Jews and only Zionism is what will save us . . . Do you understand the absurdity? The son will remain in New York or Philadelphia, he will not know Yiddish, he will have no residue of Jewish culture, he will be cut off from a Jewish environment. All this will have happened because the father himself educated him in this way as he believed that the less Jewish his son was, the more successful a career would he have. And then, suddenly, he sees the yawning chasm as a result of the education he has given his son, and he becomes panic-stricken. Suddenly he sees that his son is no longer a Jew. In his distress he tries to save his son's Jewish identity by means of the Star of David and by making contributions. No, my dear friend, it doesn't work that way! If you cannot give your sons a modern, vital, Jewish education, don't bother your heads with a mummified corpse. The mummies of Egypt are important because once they were living people, but who needs such walking mummies?

The ITA correspondent, Lekrav, reports, through the Warsaw journal *Volks Zeitung*, a conversation he held with Comrade Cahan, who told him, among other things, that Palestine fulfills for the Jewish intelligentsia the same role that the Western Wall fulfills for religious Jews. I do not know if Comrade Cahan actually said this, but the words express exceptionally well the nature of the love for Palestine that has lately been acquired by some of our comrades. This is a romantic monument to their Judaism. If they are searching for a handhold for the continued existence of Jewish identity, they should seek it among the tens of thousands of school-children at Jewish schools in Russia, Poland and Lithuania. There the living plants are located. Cannot these arouse romantic feelings? Why should it be that precisely those who have so much sentiment for dreaming of Palestine have so little faith in the continued existence of Yiddish language and culture in the Diaspora? Recently they have been shouting out that they are nationalists, but this is a zoological nationalism. They look only at the troubles of the Jews, not at Jewish creativity . . .

Some may argue this way: What do you want – Comrade Cahan only described what he saw. What should he have done – deny the facts? The point is that everyone chooses his own facts. It depends on the kind of glasses you are wearing. Remember that there are two countries that are concerned with propaganda, and in them a foreigner may see only what he is shown. These are Soviet Russia and Palestine. In Russia it is done crudely, . . . in Palestine in a more accomplished manner. It seems to you that you are by yourself, and by chance you meet a certain man, or come across him. In fact, you are being led by a fine cord, and everything is planned. All means are kosher for stealing into the visitor's heart, especially when the visitor is an important person and there is a chance that his sympathy may be translated into real coin . . . in Palestine enthusiasm is at once converted into hard currency. The new settlement prospers in this way no less than the halukah Jews, and Tze'irey Tziyon as well as Po'aley Tziyon no less than the General Zionists.

In one of Comrade Cahan's articles I read that in Palestine the Sabbath is observed even by free-thinking socialists . . . In fact the situation is by no means so smooth. In Tel Aviv, for example, it is forbidden to travel on the Sabbath . . . it is forbidden to speak over the telephone . . . to smoke in the street. The Sabbath in Tel Aviv is observed down to its last detail. The clericalists predominate in Palestine, and the workers suffer by this no little, and it is also felt in the schools. All this is not by chance, because if the religious hue is seriously neglected the rabbis will create havoc and the religious Jews in the Diaspora will stop giving money. As to the true condition of Yiddish, there is nothing left to say. In Poland the language enjoys a status ten times better than in Palestine.

And again, concerning the workers in Palestine. We are assured that they are moved by socialist ardor, but no one notices that in fact they are moved by Zionist, not socialist, ardor. The communes, the Histadrut and all the workers with all their institutions survive only by virtue of the support given by the countries of Diaspora. The moment this ceases no sign of them will remain. Po'aley Tziyon in Palestine operates hand-in-hand with the Zionist bourgeoisie, with the Weizmanns and the Sokolovs, because these grant them privileges and financial support. The fact that the Histadrut receives privileges and money from the Zionist movement gives it a monopoly in handing out jobs and in running welfare institutions for the workers. Only thanks to this monopoly can the Histadrut supersede the religious workers on the one hand and the communists on the other – all owing to the assistance given by Weizmann. The present Zionist leadership – the worst grovellers before the British Empire – support the Histadrut because it, together with Right Po'aley Tziyon, is among the supporters of the Zionist leadershp at the Zionist congresses . . . The communes and the socialists in Palestine maintain permanent peaceful relations with the Zionist bourgeoisie.

It was written that the Jewish colonists in Palestine are great idealists . . . When talking of an important movement it is important to note what this idealism refers to. Once again, here we come to the question of the objectively possible and impossible. It is impossible to be content with sentiment. If indeed Palestine does not solve the problem of the Jews, and neither does it become a significant Jewish center that absorbs Jewish immigration – and here Cahan agrees with us – then what good does all this idealism do us? Just the reverse: it is a negative manifestation because so much self-sacrifice is being wasted and lost.

Some say, alright, let's leave it be. It's a dream, and a nice dream also has value. This is true, but only in poetry. In politics the dream that can be realized has value. Any other dream is only an obstacle in politics, and you pay dearly for it. On a hopeless dream, strengths are being wasted that might be devoted to real goals, and when you awaken from it, all that it has brought is despair.

Comrade Cahan describes at length, and in fine style, the pioneers filled with ardor. Why does he not tell of those pioneers who were disappointed, who despaired, and are seeking any way of getting out of Palestine? Is he short of these?

It is argued that Comrade Cahan is only expressing his feelings, and he is permitted to do so. Indeed he is. There is no ban on feelings, but nowadays there is a devaluation on the stock market in feelings. Comrade Cahan had hardly got back from his journey than Max Pine was already hurrying to organize the fund-raising campaign for the Histadrut on behalf of the United Hebrew Trades. The ink of Comrade Cahan's articles was barely dry but a special delegation arrived from Palestine to collect money. The entire bourgeois press is charging Comrade Cahan that he does not translate his feelings into political coin, into declarations, into any measure that can also make a contribution in the financial sphere.

Comrade Cahan certainly has a right to express his feelings, but no less than this, we have a right to express our positions and to oppose the special campaign. Some say that we do not have the right! At present work is taking place to raise $15 million for the JDC, of which Palestine is to get a third: does this count for nothing? Concurrently, the Zionist movement is at work raising $5 million. The workers of Palestine will almost certainly get a hefty share out of both of these. In this setting appear the United Hebrew Trades, organizing yet another campaign, amounting to a quarter of a million dollars . . . All this is going on at a time when in Poland terrible unemployment prevails and people are dying of starvation. It is entirely clear that it is now impossible to run a special fund-raising campaign for the Jews of Poland. An attempt is being made to organize aid and fund-raising for specific places. This is being done by national orgnizations and the *Arbeiter Ring* . . . The contributors will be workers and the Jewish masses. Quite obviously, the campaign for Palestine will harm this effort.

The United Hebrew Trades have no time at all to think about unemployment in Poland. They are busy with their special campaign. It would all be understandable if the Zionists were doing this. Even Right Po'aley Tziyon believes that Palestine is going to solve the problem of the Jews of Poland also, so that meanwhile the Jews of Poland can die of starvation. But should the United Hebrew Trades behave that way, speaking in the name of the Jewish trade unions? Does Comrade Cahan agree with this? Does he want this? Here it is not a question of feelings but of deeds. Comrade Cahan's feelings are his private affair, but his deeds are the concern of the Jewish workers' movement, the concern of socialism.

New York, 30 January 1926
6. **Hillel Rogoff**
The Debate on the Articles on Palestine

On one point I agree with Comrade Litvak, namely, that it is easier to debate with an absolute opponent. For me too it would be far easier to understand the positions of the various Zivions and the Litvaks if they were totally opposed to Jewish nationalism and Jewish identity, and supported assimilation. If indeed that were the case the debate could be conducted on the pure level of logic, cold figures and dry facts alone. But in reality the Bundists who fight against Palestine hold semi-nationalist positions. They are sentimentalists! They too are subjected to "accursed" emotions, instinctive feelings and sympathies. They have been caught in the act, despite all their declarations of adoration of the god of pure logic.

Where is the heart of the Jewish problem to be found? It is focused on one major area: the Jews wish to preserve their Jewish identity. Why do we concern ourselves with Palestine, with the idea of Jewish autonomy, with Jewish schools? Only because we do not want to forego our Jewish identity. We are divided only on the issue of the best way to safeguard the continued existence of the Jewish people. Can this goal be achieved by means of schools, through the development of a special and separate Jewish culture in the countries of the Diaspora, or by means of a Jewish homeland in Palestine? Who then is the greater dreamer, who has the more remote, vain images – is it the Bundist, who hopes to preserve the Yiddish language and to create a Yiddish culture in Europe and America, or is it he who supports Palestine because he believes that it is possible to build a national life there?

The Bundist coming from Poland, where the Jews have been forced into a spiritual ghetto, may believe that the first possibility is easier. He believes, unconsciously, that this situation will continue in Poland, in which in the future too the Jews will not be allowed to set foot or be accepted in the national schools. He believes that the state of economic discrimination against them will persist, and therefore he will always live a Jewish life in complete isolation from economic society. By contrast, the American Jew, who draws on the American reality, reaches a different conclusion. He sees that in the countries where the Jews are not oppressed they lose their identity. We believe that the moment the conditions in eastern Europe change, matters will develop there in the same manner as in America. We believe that there are greater chances for the continued preservation of Jewish identity in a Jewish homeland in Palestine.

I wonder if comrades Zivion and Litvak have ever considered the following question: How is it possible that our comrades who immigrated in their youth to America, where they contributed to the building of the Jewish workers' movement, and in parallel were involved in the political and professional activity of the workers' movement as a whole – how come that these people treat Palestine sympathetically? This is not the case with our comrades who immigrated here later, and even today remain half, or a third, Polish or Russian socialists. How come that the founders of the movement here have never had reservations about Palestine, while our young friends, who get their spiritual sustenance from across the ocean, and to whom Polish Bundism is dearer than American socialism, how come they grow angry whenever a good word is said about Palestine? Nevertheless, something must have happened in the conditions prevailing now in the world that has led to a shift in positions with regard to Palestine.

Let me explain to you our point of view, that of the American socialists. Our attitude to the question of Palestine is less emotional than yours, it is calmer, and it has less bias than yours. With us there was never that deep-rooted hatred for Palestine, the legacy of years of struggle against Zionism. We have never fallen victim to the "propaganda" that wafted out of your wars there. Our position is as follows.

Zionism was foreign to us until after the war. The movement simply did not interest us, so much so that we did not even hold debates with them. Thus we never entered into conflict with them. They did not concern us, and we did not concern them. All this applies to the years when Zionism seemed to be a fantasy, and beyond sentiment it had nothing at all in it. In those years the Zionists hoped to have Eretz Israel freed from Turkish rule through the Tsar or other political means of that sort. At that time we were indifferent to Zionism because the condition of the Jews was more or less normal. The Jews felt at home here. The persecuted and suffering Jews across the ocean were thronging to America. Our gates were wide open before them. The massive and unending flow of Jewish immigration created a vibrant and wide-ranging Jewish life here. Every difficult problem found an easy answer here. To the question of what to do about the persecuted Jews in Russia the answer was "send them to America." To the question of what was to happen with the continued existence of Jewish identity in America the answer was that there was nothing to worry about, considering effervescent and developing Jewish life. Nor did we have to fight it because, as I mentioned, it did not disturb us in our work. Zionism did not gain any real foothold among the masses of the workers. The membership of Po'aley Tziyon was small. From time to time they issued written material criticizing us, but the effect of their criticism was negligible, and it was not worth a response. Who cared?

Then the war broke out, and everything changed, in Palestine, in Europe and in America. Palestine ceased to be a dream and became a reality. Palestine was given to the Jews. A wave of anti-Semitism gathered in America. The troubles of the Jews in eastern Europe increased incomparably, and then, precisely, the gates of America closed before them. The entire prewar situation was reversed. These were the circumstances that caused us to re-examine our attitude to Palestine. Now we found in Palestine a pragmatic and effective movement. We began to study it. The deeper we delved and became acquainted with what was taking place in Palestine, the greater became our sympathy for the enterprise there.

You too, the Bundists from Poland, would have changed your emotions and your position were it not for your ancient and entrenched hatred of the Zionists. This hatred arose as a result of the bitter struggles you conducted for years against them in the past. Those struggles had nothing to do with Palestine. You did not fight the Zionists because of their Palestine, but because of concrete issues concerning Poland or Russia, Your battle was not over the territory of Palestine but over the territory of Poland. Your present hatred toward them is historical, not current. It is a legacy of the tradition from the last generation. You wish to impart this hatred to us simply because of the fact that we belong to that same family of socialists. We are not interested in this gift, and forego it.

In what is my Palestinism expressed?

The states where Jews are at present to be found may be divided into two groups: in one group their rights are restricted, while in the other there are no such restrictions. In the first group of states the Jewish spirit is strong, but the material life of the Jews is sick. In the second group of states the opposite is the case: material life is good, but Jewish identity, the Jewish spirit, is sickly. I see in Palestine the possibility that the Jews will develop there both a robust material life and a robust spiritual life. There it will be possible to uphold Jewish identity without having to pay for it with social and economic restrictions and discrimination.

It is you, comrades Zivion and Litvak, who are carried away by your daydreams, while we stand firmly on the ground of reality. It is you who go about filled with hopeless dreams and with your heads in the clouds. We do not want to delude ourselves that it is possible to maintain Jewish life in the Diaspora. In Poland, you have Jewish schools because you are not accepted in Polish schools. In Lithuania, you have secondary schools because Lithuanian education is on a lower level. You pay for this luxury with blood and tears. It is a crippled Jewry. In America, there is a regression in Jewish identity. All the artificial means that are applied to preserve Jewish consciousness will not work. In all the Jewish schools together we only have a few thousand Jewish children, while at the general schools there are about half a million Jewish children. For every young Jew at work in Yiddish in literature, art, science or any other sphere, thousands of young Jews are at the same time working for American culture, in English, and in the spirit of American culture. Over there in eastern Europe we are in retreat in the domain of material life; here we are in spiritual retreat – the retreat of Jewish identity. Only a Jewish homeland can save us. If you do not assimilate you must be a supporter of the Palestinian movement.

You rail against the investments in Palestine. You claim that Palestine costs a fortune of money. You fear that this support will harm the enlistment of aid for the Jews in other countries, in particular for the Jews of Poland, where the situation is grave. I will offer a few responses to that: (1) Aid for Palestine is aid for the Jews of Poland. The sums invested in communes, cooperatives, trade unions, and even in the Keren Hayesod – it all goes to preparing the land for the absorption of Jewish immigrants. Were it not for the funds collected for Palestine five or three years ago, those thousands of families would not be able to migrate there, at a time when they are barred entry into other countries in the world. (2) Who is so wise as to be able to say, absolutely, that help of one kind is preferable to help of another? Which man will make so bold as to measure the degree of relevance of the various activities in the domain of enlisting support? All we know is that millions of Jews are in need of help. Some may think that the greatest and most immediate help should be sent to those wandering the highways. Others hold that it is more worthwhile to support the Jews of the townships in Russia, or the project of settling them in agriculture. Still others will prove to you that most important of all is to support the institutions in Poland. The question is, who is right? We cannot, nor should we, determine this question. Let everyone help those wretched people about whom he retains the strongest feelings and to whom his heart goes out especially. (3) The calculation made by Comrade Litvak is wrong. For all the fund-raising campaigns for Palestine, it receives less than Russia and Poland. Account has to be taken not only of the campaigns, but also of the total sums remitted by all the Jews to the destinations mentioned, which include support sent to relatives and friends, the support sent by *Landsmannschaften* to the various townships, to institutions and to movements. The flow of money from America to Poland and Russia is large.

Essentially Comrade Zivion's criticism of Palestine is based on arguments to do with economics and industry. He would be willing to forgive those working on behalf of Palestine if he were convinced that their labor would bring about real results. Zivion proves, by means of the figures and scientific calculations he presents, that Palestine is not worth anything, and however much money is invested, nothing will come of it. The best answer to this criticism is the facts themselves. Why bother our heads with the numbers of Jews who will live there a hundred years from now? What matters is if there is room there today. What matters is whether the Jews can migrate there, and with the help of money prepare a place for thousands. It is not a question of millions at the moment, but of the second hundred thousand: for a hundred thousand room can be found, even according to the Swiss calculation. Let us accomplish this, and concerning the millions, we'll worry when the time comes . . .

We believe that the development of the socialist movement here depends on economic conditions. When the time is ripe for the appearance of a large socialist movement in America, it will in no way be harmed by the quarter that the Jewish tailor gives for Palestine. If he donates half a dollar he will be a better socialist than he is today, when he donates nothing. Our socialist worker is a human being as well as a Jew. Just as you cannot expect him to abandon his personal and family interests, you cannot expect him to abandon his Jewish interests. Certainly the danger exists that in some worker or other, national feelings will grow so strong that that he will forget his obligations as a socialist – just as there is a danger that he will desert everything in favor of his personal and family interests. There is no remedy for this. I hope, Comrade Litvak, that you are not numbered among those socialists who believe that a worker may not read any literature except socialist literature, that he may talk only about socialism, and that he may not laugh at a joke unless it carries a socialist moral.

The work in Palestine that we wish to support, and about which Comrade Cahan is so enthusiastic, is socialist work. The debate between us is not about Zionism in general, but about certain spheres of activity in Palestine: about the communes, about the cooperatives, and about the trade unions. For you, the projects of the Palestinian workers' movement are also excluded, because they receive support from the accursed Zionist bourgeoisie. You say that Po'aley Tziyon in Palestine collaborates with the Weizmanns and the Sokolovs because the latter grant them privileges and money, and that the communes and the entire socialist movement there survive only through collaboration with the Zionist bourgeoisie. It is not at all clear to me how accurate this argument is. In the last elections to the representatives' congress, held several weeks ago, I believe that the workers did not collaborate with the bourgeoisie but nominated candidates of their own, and ran a tough election campaign against the candidates of the bourgeoisie. But let us assume that you are right in this particular instance: in such a case our duty to help them is even greater. If the workers have to compromise with the bourgeoisie because of lack of means, let us free them of this necessity, and then they will not have to make compromises.

I will not argue with Comrade Zivion over the issue of the extent of our help to the communes and the trade unions. He is a qualified engineer, and a few years ago he himself visited Palestine. It is possible that he checked and studied everything there in the bowels of the earth and in the interior of mountains. I wish to stress that we should concern ourselves less with the future and deal more with the present . . .

Comrade Litvak's strongest argument is the socialist argument. For him activity for Palestine will harm socialism . . . Veteran members will undoubtedly recall that a similar argument was voiced by the Litvaks of 1900 against the founding of the *Arbeiter Ring*, claiming that it would deflect the masses and weaken the socialist movement. Revolutionaries once used similar reasoning against the establishment of trade unions . . .

Several of Comrade Litvak's arguments belong to phraseology, and

they are not to be taken seriously. Examples are (1) His claim that if sentiment is after all being applied as something legitimate, then why does
Comrade Cahan not sympathize with the sentiments felt by *hassidim* for
their *rebbe*? (2) The Zionists bewitched Comrade Cahan and cast a spell
on his eyes when he was in Palestine. In his articles, Comrade Cahan did
not write about the enthusiasm and ardor of just any Jews, but about the
enthusiasm and ardor of socialist Jewish workers in Palestine. He also
explained that even if we assume that the work of the pioneers on the
communes does not bear any fruit at all, even so we should do them honor.
Who is the socialist who is ready to dismiss all this out of hand? Would
Comrade Litvak dare to ridicule the first of the utopian socialists, who
several decades ago tried to establish communes in America? All those
initiatives ended in failure. Nevertheless, we consider those initiators
heroes, whose experiences are dear and sacred for socialists.

Litvak also argues that Cahan was deceived. What right has he to make
such a claim? How does he know? Was he there? Did someone from there
report to him about it? Does he have any proof of it? Comrade Cahan is
not the only one to visit the communes: other socialists have been there
too, Jewish socialists and others, from different countries and different
currents. All returned with the same impression. The German communist, Ernst Thaler, the British socialist leader MacDonald – all spoke of
what is being done there with greater enthusiasm than Cahan's.
Therefore, a serious publicist may not make use of such nonsensical arguments as these.

New York, 6 February 1926
7. Judge Jacob Panken
The Debate on the Articles on Palestine

I do indeed appear in the debate not according to the original list drawn
up when *Forward* announced the opening of the discussion. However, I
am very pleased to have been given the opportunity to express my
opinion. The truth must be told. The telegrams and articles sent by
Comrade Cahan from Palestine and subsequently, which also led to this
heated and prolonged debate, aroused feelings in me different from those
in the writers who have so far participated in the debate. Zionist sympa-
thizers found reinforcement for their views in Cahan's telegrams and
articles . . . The supporters of Zionism interpret his articles to show that
Cahan himself is a supporter of Zionism. Litvak, blinded by his hostility

to Zionism, likewise interprets the articles in this way. He is entirely wrong, just as the supporters of Zionism are wrong in their interpretation. But I shall deal with this later. I have read Cahan's articles very closely, and nowhere in them did I find that he supports Zionism. I can understand why the supporters of Zionism grasp at every word of sympathy that appears there and infer from it that Cahan is a Zionist. They do this because his views are of great importance and they wish to make political capital for their movement from his positions. But it is not at all clear why anti-Zionists such as Zivion and Litvak go hand-in-hand with the Zionists in the interpretation given to Cahan's articles.

Either side in the debate finds different meanings in Cahan's articles. Neither is correct in its assessment of him. It is impossible that a man can be all things at once: for some he has become a Zionist, for others he has become a semi-Zionist; but in my view he has nothing of the Zionist in him. Dr Ginsburg shows his blindness when he argues for Cahan's being a Zionist. Cahan wrote that Zionism is a dream, perhaps a fine dream, but nevertheless a dream, which can never be realized. If so, how can it be claimed that he is a Zionist? . . .

Socialists know that to exist, every society requires an economic basis. There is no need to contend here with historical facts, which show that the culture and civilization of nations develop according to the level of their economic development. Culture and civilization go hand-in-hand with economic opportunities. My friend, Rogoff, undertook to speak as a socialist, and to defend the socialist philosophy against Litvak. He even was so bold as to speak in the name of the American socialists. As for me, I do not know who "American socialists" are . . . but from his article it is clear that he himself is a "Zionist socialist" or perhaps a "hypnotized socialist" . . . From the perspective of socialist philosophy, I wonder how it is possible that in the course of just a few years a wild dream could become reality . . . Obviously, the fact cannot be denied that the war caused major changes in the world, but the claim is entirely wrong that the conditions of the Jews became worse. The Jews in eastern Europe, namely Poland, Lithuania, Latvia, and Russia, now have, in terms of the law, fully equal rights. The Jews in these countries no longer live under the scourge of discriminatory political laws. At present they are suffering, with everyone, owing to the economic crisis. They suffer from anti-Semitism, but they suffered from it before the war too. Yet despite all the foregoing Rogoff still argues that the situation has grown worse. Therefore we, the "American socialists," have consciously altered our positions towards Zionism, and consider it a solution to the Jewish problem. At a certain place in his article Rogoff states that Palestine was given to the Jews. Was it indeed? To the best of my knowledge Palestine was given as a mandate to Britain. If he meant that the Balfour Declaration granted Palestine to the Jews, he goes too far in the interpretation he gives to the intentions of the Declaration. He forgets that most of Palestine belongs to the Arabs, and the number of the latter compared with the Jews is six to one. Rogoff's logic is a little confused . . .

When a nation has some economic security, some leisure time and an opportunity for cultural development, such a nation will in time develop a spiritual life too. It is superfluous to provide proofs showing that a nation living in primitive conditions, and under a despotic government, cannot attain the same cultural level as modern nations living in freedom and democracy. There are Zionists and friends of Zionists who argue that Palestine will become the center of the spiritual life of the Jewish people: it will become a cultural center. Has Palestine been selected to be a spiritual and cultural center because of the troubles that the Jews will endure there? Because from Rogoff's arguments it transpires that in a place where the Jews suffer and their material life is misshapen, there the finest spiritual creation flourishes and the people grow strong . . .

Last summer I was in Poland and Lithuania. In both countries I met Jews who had been in Palestine and had returned. I recall that one of them had had a small business, which he sold in order to emigrate and settle in Palestine. He did not succeed in making a living there so he returned. There is no doubt that he went to Palestine because of the harsh economic and social conditions. He was in the position of the drowning man who clutches even at a straw. But the straw did not save him, and when he returned he had nothing, and was without any means of existence. The central question is this: is Palestine capable of absorbing such a number of immigrants that it will be able to ease the situation of the Jews in eastern Europe generally and in Poland particularly? We are told that every year about 40,000 people immigrate to Palestine. In reality, only about 125,000 Jews live there. There is a good reason for the fact that the Jewish population in Palestine is not growing. There is seemingly a good reason why 40,000 Jews do not migrate there each year, and there are many who leave the country.

Socialists know, and statistics confirm, that immigration and emigration of the masses depends on economic conditions. Workers migrate to a place where there is demand for a workforce, and they leave places where the situation is otherwise. In 1907, many workers left America because of the economic situation. I accept Cahan's opinion concerning the economic opportunities of Palestine, and this explains why so few Jews immigrate there and also leave. As Dr Ginsburg says, Jews can be great lovers, and love can also be blind. But no people has ever been blinded by its love. For many Jews, Palestine can be an ideal and a dream, but throughout the centuries their behavior has been determined not by ideals and dreams but by the economic laws that shaped their lives.

The entire foundation of Zionism, as far as I can see, and the Zionists agree with this, is sentimental and emotional. Zionism appeals to the emotions. The tradition and history of the people are attached to Palestine; there is an emotional influence. But a people has never yet been built on emotions. Peoples build and fortify themselves only in places where economic conditons allow it. What then are the economic possibilities in Palestine? All admit that this is not a fertile land. Even Dr Ginsburg, for all his dazzling love, admits that the country is desolate and parched. Palestine has no natural sources of wealth and its economic opportunities are restricted. Clearly, people's deeds and sacrifices powerfully affect the emotions and human imagination, especially when these are accomplished by others. When young university graduates give up the chance of an easy life and prefer a harsh tortuous existence in order to realize a dream; when young people are ready to endure want and hunger, and are willing to toil from the crack of dawn to the setting of the sun – then clearly they are driven by ideals. This certainly makes an impression on the imaginations of people, and more so on sentimental people than on people moved by logic. It is completely clear that we are dealing with emotions alone when people wish to tell us that the fact that young Jewish men and women settlers on the soil of Palestine is what will solve the Jewish problem.

In Palestine at present there is less than 1 percent of the total Jewish people. About 60 percent of the total live in eastern Europe. In the best case, about 6 or 7 percent of the entire people could settle in Palestine. How then can it be argued that Zionism will solve the Jewish problem and will relieve the people of their suffering?

Personally, I have nothing against young men and women college and university graduates sacrificing so much, but I cannot see in this any idealism that can fire me. The Indian holy man who remains motionless in a certain place for decades also has a certain ideal, but this carries no appeal for me . . .

If conditions existed in Palestine permitting the absorption of a large number of Jews, and also the betterment of their lives, then support for such a movement would be called for. But when it is argued that only a small number of people can settle there, and that the workers can earn only a slice a dry bread by their labor, and even this with great hardship and endurance, then this entire matter seems like trying to catch hold of a rainbow.

I respect pioneers. I saw a settlement of theirs in Lithuania, which was a sort of farm training school. The youngsters have to stay there for about two years to learn agriculture before migrating to Palestine. I saw how they live there: barefoot, in filth, without the conveniences that every human being needs, no shower, no real bed, no clothes. I asked them why they live that way, and they told me that they do it in order to become accustomed to the hard life in Palestine. They turn suffering into an ideal, and poverty into a great affair . . . For me, to inculcate such ideals into the youth is inadmissible. The question is, is all this worthwhile and desirable?

Let us not forget that the concern of most Zionists is for their Zionism rather than for the Jews. Dr Ginsburg states that for the Zionists those 200,000 future Jews in Palestine are more important than the 16 million Jews in the rest of the world. Presumably Dr Ginsburg knows what he is talking about. If indeed this is the situation, then from this we must derive our attitude to this movment, which gives precedence to the cause of 200,000 or even a million Jews over the kind of future in store for the 16 million Jews in the world. If there is a Jewish problem, it should be solved for the Jews all over the world, not only for the few who are already in Palestine or are going to be there.

The problem of the Jews has to be solved in the places where they live. If the Jews in Poland are in need of building assistance, then this has to be given in Poland itself. If the Jews of Russia require help to settle the land, then the help has to be sent to Russia. If the Jews in Romania can settle and transfer a Jewish family to agriculture for an outlay of $500, then this money has to be found for them, and given to them in Romania. If an attempt is made to solve the Jewish problem by a rationalist or a sentimental approach then cold reason states that it is preferable to settle Jews on fertile land in Romania or Russia than to send them to settle on the dry and desolate earth of Palestine. If we act according to cold logic, and not according to emotions, then we shall have to consider the fact that in Romania it costs $500 to settle a Jewish family in agriculture, while in Palestine it costs $7,000. However, Zionism is not built on logic but on feelings that lead in the wrong direction.

New York, 14 February 1926
8.   Sara Broyland
The Debate on the Articles on Palestine

If Comrade Cahan himself, after all he has seen, examined and studied
in Palestine, declares that he has not become a Zionist, there is nothing
left for us to say on this matter. But for all that: Comrade Cahan was exhilarated and excited by the idealism, the amazing energy and the ardor of
the workers, and also by the attitude the Zionist movement displays to
them. Very well: we socialists are obliged to continue to stand firm on the
grounds of logic. We cannot act on the basis of our feelings or of anyone
else's. We must not set aside even a fraction of our attention for empty
rhetoric.

We must admit that Comrade Cahan's articles create the impression
that he has in fact become a Zionist, although this is rather like Zionist
sentiment that has no rational basis, and therefore no attention at all
should be paid to it.

What I have stated in the foregoing is approximately the arguments
that Zivion posited in the debate. As for the personal issues that have
entered into the discussion, I am sure that Comrade Cahan can deal with
them himself. Likewise, he will certainly add, if he has anything to add,
to the twenty-odd articles in which he expressed, eloquently, honestly
and objectively, his impressions. But the question is not whether
Comrade Cahan has or has not become a Zionist. This was not the reason
why *Forward* initiated the debate. What we are concerned with is the
nature of our attitude to what is taking place in Palestine and to the work
of the Zionist movement – this on the basis of the facts that Comrade
Cahan set forth in his articles.

The descriptions set out before us clarify unequivocally that we may
not stand idly by and show indifference to the heroic work being accomplished by our brothers and sisters in Palestine. If we do not extend to
them our fullest sympathy and the best of our assistance it will be a crime
not only against them but against the entire working class and the Jewish
people. Similarly, our supportive attitude and our goodwill towards the
work of the Zionist movement in Palestine will not harm our class struggle
one jot. The opposite might be true . . . Comrade Zivion is a few decades
late in some of his arguments. In the days of Hovevey Tziyon the naïve
Jews who believed in the Zionist "dreams" were numerous. Now, in view
of prevailing conditions and the practical work of the Zionist movement,
it is by no means a crime to believe in these "dreams." Comrade Zivion

would have been right if the situation of the Jews today were like what it was 50 or 60 years ago, and if the Zionists came to the Jewish masses or the American Jews saying,"Jews! Leave your places of residence and your livelihood in the Diaspora and emigrate to Eretz Israel, where we shall establish a Jewish state and shall live as a free people in a free state flowing with milk and honey." In such a case there would have been room for Zivion's outcry: "Jews! Do not go! Remain in your places! You are being deceived!" But what is to be done when the reality today is completely different? Not only are the Zionist leaders not appealing for migration to Eretz Israel, the opposite is the case. They are doing their utmost to halt the flow of migration bursting in there from many European countries where the living conditions of the Jews have become hell. Even pioneers must wait their turn for emigration (I call to mind the protest demonstration by the pioneers during the Zionist congress in Vienna). Zivion's claims are quite out of place at the moment, in a situation where the Zionist movement is restricting its work to raising funds, by means of which it will e possible to support settlements and the existing communes in Palestine. This money likewise is meant to assist, as credit, immigrants who went there of their own accord and at their own risk, carrying very little money. The funds are also intended to support educational institutions, kindergartens, hospitals, etc.

Zivion admists that when a Jew decides to go to Palestine himself, not just to preach to someone else to go, he does not allow Zionist propaganda, which appeals to the emotions, to influence him. Similarly he does not rely on what he is told by fanciful people, but he thoroughly checks how worthwhile it is, and tries painstakingly to find out if he will be able to sustain himself in the new country. It transpires not only that no one misleads him, but that even if someone tried to do so he would not succeed. By what right, then, does Zivion declare that Zionist propaganda is deceitful and harmful? Elsewhere in his article Zivion himself admits that the Zionists have in fact accomplished many useful things and he is certain that they will continue to create a great deal more in the future. What then is the problem? Their work is too costly. In Cuba, in Mexico, or in Argentina it would be cheaper; in other words, he's dickering with them. As far as he is concerned, the business might be worthwhile if the Zionists could absorb some two or three million Jews in Palestine, and also give the Jewish people a Jewish state or at least a Jewish national home for their money. If this were assured, he would naturally agree that every Jewish worker or socialist should give five or six dollars a year. But since the outlook is that Palestine will be able to absorb only a few hundred thousand, and a Jewish state or Jewish national home is not a certainty, all your work, Zivion argues, does not seem right to me, and I am obliged to warn our Jews not to give their support to a thing that has nothing much to it or any future.

Let us ask Comrade Zivion what about those few hundred thousand that can be managed in Palestine: for them Palestine indeed can become a home. In Palestine not even the Arab can tell the Jew that he is alien there. Likewise, what about the settlements and communes that exist there? And what about the other projects that are now in existence there? Should they be allowed to disappear like snow on a warm day? Is this the purpose of Comrade Zivion's hostile propaganda? It is well known that sympathetic feelings and ideas are more vulnderable to scorn and ridicule than to serious argumentation. Comrade Zivion, who is a renowned journalist, uses these devices to hurt the Zionist movement . . . After he utters his diatribe against the Zionist movement he sets on the pioneers by the same methods . . . Comrade Zivion would like to see the communes living to a high and modern standard, but because they are poor he does not like them, so he has decided to come out against them, and against the only organization that supports them. The purpose of all this is to denigrate the little they have and bring about their extinction . . .

Regarding the criticism of "conquest of labor," I leave this to the people of Palestine to deal with. They will not remain silent in the face of this censure, and will reply to it better than I can, being far away and not familiar with the existing conditions there. Here I will say only this: the Zionist movement, no matter from what angle you view it, is a popular movement. As such, it arrays within itself elements that are progressive and reactionary, ultra-orthodox people and free-thinkers, as well as atheists, bourgeois, and socialists . . . If Comrade Zivion points a finger at the "conquest of labor" negatively, then I can point to the policy of the Arab workers' organization which is to fight against their exploitation both by the Jews and by Arabs. This organization also issues a socialist paper in Arabic. The aim of this group is to help to further the development of the Arab workers. It is obvious that sooner or later the Jewish and Arab workers will become organized in a single organization. It will be a different tune then. Secondly, Jewish settlements, businesses and enterprises in Palestine have been set up recently, while the Arabs have lived there for centuries according to their own ways and customs. Therefore, even if they are not allowed to work for the Jews for the time being, their economic situation will not grow worse. They will lose out economically only temporarily, but later on the Jews will provide them with economic and also cultural advantages. Until the joint Jewish-Arab organization is established it is true that they will not make gains, but nor will they lose anything. But for the Jewish workers the question of "Hebrew labor" is one of life and death. Neither Arab nor Christian employers take on Jewish workers. In this situation, if Jewish employers also engage Arab workers, what will be left for the Jewish worker? To emigrate from the country is impossible because there is no money for the cost of the journey and there is nowhere to go.

The question of Hebrew and Yiddish in Palestine is more complicated, so it is harder for me to deal with than with the subject of "conquest of labor." Personally, I love Yiddish greatly. Zivion, and all Yiddishists, will argue that Yiddish has greater merit to be our national language because it is spoken a hundred times more than all the other languages put together; similarly, Yiddish literature at present is far more beautiful than that written in Hebrew, and it also reflects Jewish life better and more finely. All this is true. But still there is a problem. The fact is that the Jews whose mother tongue is the dominant language of the land where they live, for example, in England, France, Italy, and so on, will in no way agree to use Yiddish, while Hebrew is acceptable to Jews in all countries, even the most remote. True, Hebrew is not used by the masses but by the intelligentsia – yet the latter exerts the greatest infuence on the shaping of life. Moreover, it is recognized by all that as regards the use of language, assimilation among the Jews has been a powerful process, especially in recent times. Not long ago a debate was conducted on the pages of *Forward* on the state of Yiddish at the schools of the *Arbeiter Ring*. Many people conversant with this matter held, correctly, that with the closing of the gates of America before Jewish immigration the death sentence was passed on the Jewish language and culture. Yiddish in America fulfilled an impressive role and contributed so much because of the continuous stream of immigration. The moment this was stopped Yiddish culture could be expected to disappear within two generations. Furthermore, some have stated that any attempt to halt this process by artifical means is harmful and reactionary.

The story is entirely different with Hebrew. Even when it was dead, even when the most committed writers of Hebrew did not speak the language, nor think it necessary to revive it, even then many Jews, in various places on earth, used the holy tongue. In this way the identity of the Jewish people was preserved. When the poet Yehuda Leib Gordon, with a sense of outrage and envy, watched the decline of Hebrew literature, and on the other hand the development of the Yiddish language (at that time jargon), he wrote his famous poem *Lemi ani amel* (For whom do I toil?). It transpires that his anguish was unnecessary. Hebrew has become a living language like all others, while a huge question mark hangs over the future of our beloved Yiddish. This is a great loss, but is it the only loss in Jewish life?

Comrade Zivion states that there is only one type of Zionist who has a consistently logical approach, namely the Zionist to whom a few hundred thousand Hebrew-speaking Jews, possessing true Jewish spirit and culture, are dearer than the millions of incomplete Jews, already semi-assimilated, ignoramuses culturally and spiritually, in the countries of the Diaspora. Moreover, these Jews, in the view of the Zionists, not only for the most part convert, but some even become anti-Semites and provocateurs ... For Zivion, this attitude means that the Zionists want to preserve in Palestine, as a sort of museum exhibit, a few hundred thousand Jews. I will not dispute with Comrade Zivion as to how many Jews they will succeed in "preserving" in Palestine, several hundreds of thousands, or more. History and sociology are not exact sciences like mathematics ... so it is impossible to predict in these fields. This circumstance also applies to Comrade Zivion despite his being an accomplished journalist ... It has to be admitted that the Jews are going to Palestine not because of their Zionist dreams, and not by virtue of Zionist propaganda. What moves them is their wretched state in the countries of the Diaspora. They are impelled by the unbearable political and economic conditions in those countries. They migrate to Palestine because in almost all countries, especially America, the gates have been closed to them. They migrate because of the drive to live and survive. The Jews have a "terrible" quality (in the view of those who hate them and also of some of their friends): they refuse to die! However hard you try to persuade them that it is worth their while to die, or at least to convert, they refuse, and want to continue living – and, indeed, to maintain their Jewish identity. Now I come to the main point.

By what right does Comrade Zivion take the liberty of calling those he deems logical Zionists "preserving" Zionists? Comrade Zivion might have been right if just Agudat Yisrael or Mizrahi members belonged to the Zionist movement: those who proscribe any book concerned with worldly matters, who on witnessing a person carrying a gas canister on the Sabbath treat this as sinful, those who desire that the Jews study only *Gemara* and *Poskim*. But Comrade Zivion is entirely wrong since the Zionist movement is led by people of science, renowned journalists, writers, and their like. He is utterly mistaken because the Zionist movement, in addition to everything that has already been said about it, provides the Jewish settlement in Palestine with primary schools, secondary schools, and a university.

The Jewish people, if they wish to continue to exist as a healthy and normal nation like all other nations, must acquire the three following possessions: (1) one language and culture to be the heritage of all; (2) a farming class, and the larger the better; (3) a corner of their own in the world where no one can tell them that they are foreigners and only subtenants.

The only country satisfying these requirements is Palestine. True, the land is small and has many drawbacks, but what can we do? . . . The subject of love has already been mentioned. We do not love everything that is lovely, but what we do love is lovely. Comrade Zivion complains that Palestine is pricey for the Jews. But every cent given by America for the settlements, the communes and the other institutions in Palestine has been worth it. The investments will bear fruit, and the Jews of America have made a good "deal" here. Cultural deeds cannot be viewed only through financial spectacles . . .

Comrade Zivion holds that Zionism is a national movement, and that nationalism is an expression of reaction. Indeed it is not: this is completely false. Nationalism may be reactionary, but it may also be progressive. It depends on the nature of the specific national movement. If it tends toward defense of the liberty, the language and the culture of the people, then it is a progressive movement. Garibaldi's nationalism was progressive. Jewish nationalism is essentially progressive, and it could not be otherwise even if it wished.

I would like to explain why the Zionist workers allow themselves to treat Yiddish the way they do. This treatment is not a cause of pleasure, and in fact is painful, but conditions are such that they can do no other. Among languages, as among living creatures, there is a struggle to survive. In many senses, a language is like a living organism, which exists, grows, develops, fights, undergoes change, and finally dies. The national tongue of the Jewish people can only be the Hebrew language. If the soil for its vitality can only be in Palestine, where it must contend with Arabic and English, why must it be forced to fight yet another battle there against a language that is quite superfluous, because the masses speak Hebrew? Why spend precious energy on an unnecessary struggle when in any case it is clear that Hebrew will triumph . . . .

New York, 20 February 1926
9.   Jacob Lestchinsky
The Debate on the Articles on Palestine

> Palestine is a tiny country. It land is scanty, dry, and poor. Agriculture can
> in the best case support only a few small towns. Take the religious tourism
> away from Jerusalem, and it too will decline to the status of a small town
> . . .

Dozens of Zionist journals have copied and published lengthy passages
from Comrade Cahan's rapturous articles on Palestine, and not one of
them has paid any mind to the words cited above. I fear that even readers
who peruse the articles closely and diligently have not absorbed them.
From the quotation given above it is quite clear that Comrade Cahan has
not accepted the Ten Commandments of Zionism, and this is so despite
the fact that the Zionists loudly declare that Cahan is now one of their
own. Here lies the danger of the articles he published. The passages in
which Cahan realistically presents the truths of Palestine, such as
Zionism's flights of fancy regarding Palestine and the impossibility of
realizing its ideology; his dismissal of the overblown accomplishments
which exist only in Zionists' imagination; his astute analysis of the actual
circumstances, in consequence of which he shows that the enterprise in
Palestine has no foundation, and hence no future – all these accounts are
dwarfed and lost within his articles that are so full of fire and enthusiasm
about what he saw there.

I must assume that perhaps I too would have been carried away had I
toured Eretz Israel. Remember that Comrade Cahan traveled to Palestine
by way of Europe, where Jewish life lies in rack and ruin, and there is no
domain there from which to take heart. We – those who carried on our
backs and suffered the agonies of the Jewish socialist movement and
Jewish culture in Europe – we still derive some comfort from the fact that
a handful remain to keep the flame alight, but there is nothing there at all
that might stir the visitor from America. In this setting, when one reaches
Eretz Israel, and sees the huge concentration there of idealistic strength,
a core of willingness for dedication that is but rarely encountered, an altar
at which thousands of priests minister with faith and devotion – in this
setting any believer in possession of a soul must be exhilarated and enrap-
tured. Anyone who still dreams and carries some feeling in his heart must
be enlivened and moved by what is being done. This is exactly what
happened to Comrade Cahan. But when one steps a little way aside, when
one distances oneself from the enchanted place, one can reach realistic

conclusions and understand how dear the people will have to pay the moment they are cured of their blindness. The instant the spell is broken the people will stand before the ruins of their false hopes. Therefore, an effort must be made to regain sight as soon as possible so as to consider rationally the practical achievements of this idealism and the actual opportunities. Let us examine what is being done in Eretz Israel, and what implications it may have for the Jewish people.

The work done in Palestine may be divided into two parts: prior to the World War, under Ottoman rule, and after the war, under British rule.

It is a mistake to think what has been done in Palestine in recent years is the outcome of the altered political conditions. No changes have taken place that will reduce the cost of settlement, will promote the development of industry, or will act as an incentive to commerce. The political regime is better and more orderly, but off a better political order it is still not possible to live. The British government has done nothing for the development of the economy, particularly concerning strengthening Jewish influence on it. High taxation on agricultural produce and manufactures remains in place. High customs dues on imports of machinery and raw materials do not further the development of local industry. Low duties on imports of goods from Britain and its colonies likewise do nothing to advance the development of local industry. Anyone probing deeper into the economic condition of Palestine may think it perhaps better to remain a backward agricultural state like Turkey, which had no industry of its own, than to become a colony of a highly developed industrial state, which cannot allow its colonies to compete with it.

It seems to me that what gave rise to the wave of idealist pioneers, the building of the few new *moshavot* and of Tel Aviv, was not the Balfour Declaration, the new political circumstances in Eretz Israel, or the big nationalist movement within the Jewish people: it all occurred as a result of the great destruction that has befallen European Jewry. These are nothing other than acts of desperation on the part of the masses of Jews dying of hunger who have nowhere to go. The young Jew who has no chance of existing in Poland, and therefore goes to the *kevutzot*; the hassid who has lost his livelihood and therefore has become an idealist farmer; the merchant who has gone bankrupt and who migrates and builds a house in Tel Aviv; the craftsman who for six months has had no work, and in fact has been in this condition for years now, and therefore joined Po'aley Tziyon and is an adherent of the pioneering effort in Eretz Israel – all these stem from the same source, the despair, the ruin, the hunger and the hopelessness of the Jews in the countries of Eastern Europe.

We Marxists do not exclude the idealism of individuals even if it derives from social conditions. I bow down before the hundreds and thousands of young Jews who are sacrificing themselves on the fields of Eretz Israel. But at the same time this does not blind me from seeing the future disasters that are bound to come whether we like it or not. This idealism, stemming from the depths of a historic destruction the like of which has never before been seen, would be able to move worlds were not Eretz Israel "a tiny country with sparse lands that are poor and dry, whose agriculture can, in the best case, support only a few small towns." Here lies the tragedy. What do we see? In the last five years hardly 50,000 Jews who are not poor have migrated to Eretz Israel. About thirty million dollars have been taken into the country as private capital, and a similar sum as public capital. It is not the subject of money that is important: any sum is good and valuable to the extent that it brings the target closer and creates conditions for the absorption of masses of poor Jews. All this is worthwhile insofar as a healthy infrastructure is created, capable of bearing fruit; it is worthwhile when the tree that is planted, regardless of cost, can really grow. But unfortunately all the building being erected there is constructed on sand; . . . there is no benefit from it for the masses of Jews . . . From Comrade Cahan's articles it is also perfectly clear that the building is hanging in thin air . . .

Clearly, both Zionists and socialist Zionists were very pleased when the speculators swarmed in and built Tel Aviv. Now they are left in a difficult situation. A city of thirty-odd thousand inhabitants should have its own advanced industry and a market where it can sell its goods, or else it has to be based on a large agricultural hinterland which it can serve. Tel Aviv has no industry because it does not have, and will not have, any market. Nor is it based on an agricultural hinterland that consumes goods. If people are waiting for the growth of such a hinterland, they will have to postpone the construction of Tel Aviv for several years. Why does Eretz Israel not have industry, and why can it not have industry? Because it has no raw materials. Comrade Max Pine makes his task easy when he claims that raw materials can also be imported, offering as an example the fact that America also imports raw materials from India. Comrade Pine only forgets that the United States, which has only 6 percent of the world's population, controls 60 percent of the world's copper, 42 percent of the coal, 70 percent of the oil, 70 percent of the iron, 22 percent of the cereals . . . When you control such a range of raw materials you can allow yourself to purchase a few items in other countries, to manufacture finished goods out of them, and even to compete with the country from

which you bought the raw materials. There are a few more such examples
. . . But Palestine has no coal, iron, or other raw materials . . . "Its land is
limited, poor and dry" – thus Comrade Cahan characterizes Palestine.
Those three words, "limited, poor and dry," say it all. I shall deal with
"limited" below. Here I wish to state clearly that, to our misfortune,
Palestine is very poor. However talented the Jews may be at moving
worlds the tragedy lies in the fact that they cannot build the worlds that
they are able to move.

At the last Zionist congress Dr Ruppin, a man who knows Palestine
perhaps best of all, portrayed the great difficulties that industry will face,
should it develop, in Palestine . . . All the foregoing undermines the likelihood and the hope that Palestine will be able to serve as a mediator
between west and east. There is no hope that it can develop huge ware-
houses in which to store European goods intended for sale in the eastern
countries: namely, that Palestine will fulfill a sort of service function for
the industrialized nations. Why is this so? Because the industrialized
nations can manage on their own . . . If the issues of industry and
commerce are dropped, there is still the issue of working the land. In this
regard I refer you to the words of Comrade Cahan's articles quoted above
. . . In Ruppin's book *The Building of Eretz Israel*, written in German, it
is stated that "when it is considered that prior to the World War 100
million francs (about \$20 million) were invested in agricultural settle-
ments, and without taking into account that there has been a rise in prices
of land, it may be stated that the value of the property in these settlements
does not exceed 60 million francs (about \$12 million). Hence, the entire
settlement enterprise looks like an effort that has failed economically"
(pp. 53–4). Later Ruppin tries to explain that it is wrong to make calculations and to compare cost with values, because the view must go further,
to the broader economic aspect, namely the viewpoint of the building of
the Jewish people. I understand him, but I must say in parallel that
precisely from the viewpoint of the broader settlement Palestine is bankrupt. We have before us the only instance in history of settlements in
which after 35 years of labor (until the war), during which not only 100
million francs were invested, but also the endeavors of an entire generation with many victims, the property remaining is worth less than the
investment. Clearly, it is not the 100 million francs are important, but the
expense serves as proof of the conditions prevailing over agriculture in
Eretz Israel. Moreover, what have the Jewish people received for that
expenditure of 100 million francs and the sacrifices of an entire generation of settlers? Have lands been prepared on which new masses of Jews

can be absorbed? . . . The settlers have also become contractors who engage Arab labor, while they themselves do not work and their time is spent on business . . . In the report of Po'aley Tziyon of 1921 they write about the settlers as being ill-tempered people, who do not work in their fields, who depend on money from abroad and markets abroad, no less than the storekeepers whom we know from Lithuania and Poland (*Work in Palestine*, p. 44). It may be thought that this was several years ago when the Jewish settlers mostly took on Arab labor, but perhaps it is not so now. Unfortunately, the situation at present is no better. The entire press in Eretz Israel is full of items about the fact that in Tel Aviv alone there are today 4000 Jews without work, while on the *moshavot* much Arab labor is employed . . . The paper, *Davar*, prints stories almost daily of Jewish workers who have been fired and replaced by Arab workers. At the moment I am not dealing with the problem of how the principle of Hebrew labor accords with the principles of socialism; I merely wish to state that despite the fact that enormous efforts – financial and other – were invested in the old *moshavot*, this has not turned the settlers into true farmers living off work and not off exploitation. The investments have not created a young generation that will be attached to nature and the land, and will not run off to business or the free professions. Nor have the *moshavot* become centers of Hebrew labor or Jewish strength.

Anyone who determines his stance on the Jewish settlement in Eretz Israel honestly and without bias must learn from the experience of the old *moshavot*, whose establishment has been going on for 45 years – more than that of the new settlements in existence just a few years. In my view, it is no longer possible not to say anything about the communes. In any event, Comrade Cahan is dubious as to the chances of their survival. But let us adopt the viewpoints of the supporters of the communes and agree with their statement that private settlement has failed entirely; that this is because the fathers became exploiters and not people of labor, while their children did not become attached to working the land. Nor did the veteran private settlement prepare workplaces for the Jewish workers; therefore the communes had to be founded. Let us accept these arguments! The question is, how much public money and public effort can be mobilized in order to establish communes? Private capital can in no way be considered, bankrupt Jewish storekeepers and Jewish speculators can in no way be considered for the communes; so only pioneers of the first rank can be considered. How many young people of this sort can be taken in in a year? A thousand, two thousand! The greatest dreamer cannot imagine that it is possible to settle more than two thousand such people in the course of a year. Out of two thousand settlers a few thousand more providers of services can make a living – and that's all! Here is the true iniquity inherent in the demands of the adherents of the communes, if they are serious about what they say and write.

What then is the picture that emerges? The development of urbanization is hanging in thin air. A cry is being sounded now in all the Zionist papers demanding a halt to immigration. Private settlement has gone bankrupt and does not bring the goal any closer – because it does not create a class of Jewish farmers, because it is not connected to the soil, but the opposite: it is developing along the usual capitalist path in serving private interests. All this taking place despite the fact that much public money has been sunk into it. And the communes? In the best case they will make for the immigration of a few thousand Jews annually. This is the picture that emerges regarding the land of the new immigration and which so enthralls the new adherents of Zionism. If only I were wrong; but unfortunately signs already exist attesting that in the coming year there will be limited Jewish immigration to Palestine. Let there only be no emigration from it . . .

Everyone now is rightly excited about the enormous sacrifice of the pioneers in Eretz Israel. But I would advise them to open the newspapers of the first years after the establishment of Rishon Letziyon, Zichron Ya'akov, Petah Tikvah, and other *moshavot*, when the sacrifices were perhaps even greater and the idealism was no less, nor the dedication. We can read of the consequences of that idealism and those sacrifices in what the Zionists themselves publish regarding the old *moshavot*. No one can assure us that the present sacrifices and the present idealism will yield better fruit and that they will have a better future. In addition to idealism there have to be actual supporting conditions, and these do not exist in Palestine. A well-known rule is that the deeper one is in the ground the more one dreams. In this sense Palestine is a real bargain for the Jews, it is truly a dream, an ideal that is becoming the historical tragedy of the Jewish people.

I have been attempting throughout to address the subject from the viewpoint of the ability of Palestine to create wide opportunities for large Jewish settlement, for large-scale immigration. For the Zionist to be able to come to the Jewish people and demand of them the necessary and great sacrifices, Eretz Israel has to be one of two things: either it should be capable of absorbing many Jews and of providing a proper and comprehensive solution to the needs of Jewish immigration; or if it can absorb only a small number of Jews it should be able to change them to the point

where we can say that in Eretz Israel a new Jewish society is being created
that is unlike Jewish Diaspora society, which has no basis of existence.
The experience gained over 45 years of settlement there shows that
Palestine offers neither of these two possibilities. The farmer from Petah
Tikvah who exploits the Arab worker and deals in speculation and foreign
currency is not exactly the noble type on whose account we must abandon
the interests of the Jewish masses in the Diaspora and apply all the attention of the Jewish people to the interests of that settler.

With the communes we must wait. No one can foretell their future.
There is much genuine idealism in them, an abundance of enthusiasm and
self- sacrifice. But how many times in human history have we seen that
in the end the idealism of individuals or of small groups comes to naught,
or terminates in an even uglier reality. Idealism can be frutiful only when
it is linked to the interests and desires of the masses; interests of the kind
that spring out of real everyday life.

Unfortunately, it is by now evident that Eretz Israel will not turn into
a land of immigration for many Jews. It transpires that it is easier to move
worlds than to build them. Every fantasy is harmful. As it is, the Jews of
America devote too little attention to the problems of Jewish migration,
and now, in this setting, they have become convinced that the Jews of
Poland have a land, not far from them, which is taking in tens of thousands of Jews. This indeed occurred, but only for one year; and not tens
of thousands were absorbed but less than twenty thousand . . . The gates
of Eretz Israel are in fact being closed now to Polish Jews, but before the
gates are finally closed by Lord Plummer, who intends to close them, the
cry of the thousands of Jewish unemployed in Eretz Israel already serves
as a clear warning to the Jews of Poland not to immigrate to Eretz Israel.

Comrades come and say they harbor sentiments for Eretz Israel.
Insofar as this is a private matter, I wish them well. But insofar as this is
our concern on the public level a different attitude is required. Every
Jewish socialist party without exception, in Poland or in America, must
fight against those movements in the Jewish people that spread false hopes
among the masses and deflect the attention of the masses away from their
true interests; movements that create confusion in the mind with hopes
that cannot be realized. In this sense grave sins lie on the conscience of
Zionism. Hence there can be no admission, nor is it possible to say, that
it is not wrong to support Zionist enterprises when you are not a Zionist
and do not believe in Zionism. The deeper one is buried in the ground
the higher the dream flies heavenwards; therefore our struggle must be
against illusions and fantasies, against vain aspirations and futile plans of

being bigger, stronger, deeper, and broader. In Jewish life too little is invested in practical daily labor for the interests of the masses, so we cannot afford the luxury of supporting the Zionist wagon, in which we do not believe.

New York, 27 February 1926
10. Alexander Kahn
The Debate on the Articles on Palestine

When discussing the subject raised by Comrade Cahan in his articles, there is no place to discuss Zionism. These are two things that must be kept separate. I am aware that this is not easy, because as soon as Palestine is mentioned memories arise of party struggles that are hard to forget. But times change, and new times bring new perceptions and require new paths. It is always necessary to try to learn, but it is also necessary to be able to forget certain matters. It is perhaps not nice to mention now that many of us once used to say that we were not Jews but Yiddish-speaking socialists. This is forgotten because we have eliminated it from our actions and our attitudes. It is essential to forget other things too, among them some of the things about Zionism that we hated. Comrade Zivion himself admits that for the moment there is still no socialist code that forbids socialists from being Zionists, and this is merely a question of logic. I too assume that all agree that neither is there a socialist code by which it is possible to deliver a verdict that Zionism is unrealizable. If people do not agree with me on this point I will be obliged to mention socialists of international standing who are also Zionists.

As I stated above, this has nothing to do with the question under review. Just as we may be Zionists at the same time as being socialists, so are we permitted to support the work being accomplished in Palestine and for Palestine without being Zionists. If this position is not acceptable in our circles, this is because we are all members of the Jewish people, so we are in search of the Messiah whether we believe in him or not. Fervent Jewish socialists treat socialism just as fervent religious Jews treat belief in the Messiah, and just as fervent Zionists treat Zionism. Religious Jews believe that all the sorrows of the Jews will vanish the instant the Messiah appears. Fervent Jewish socialists believe that the sorrows of the Jews will vanish with the realization of socialism. Likewise, fervent Zionists believe that the realization of Zionism will bring about the end of the suffering of the Jews. Each professes to supply the panacea that the people need.

There is nothing new in the fact that the one does not understand the other and is hostile to his opponent. What is new is the fact that the misunderstandings and the bitterness are not greater. This is so because our generation is suffering an abundance of trial and tribulation. I do not believe that Zionism can solve the Jewish problem or even the major part of it, just as I do not believe in the Messiah. But at the same time I do not believe in being idle and doing nothing in face of the catastrophe, or that the Jews must wait for the realization of socialism to contend with their problems.

For this reason I put forward a different question from Comrade Zivion's: I ask "Is it logical for a socialist to believe in Zionism?" and "Will any profit accrue to the Jewish people through working for the sake of Palestine?" Comrade Zivion's question is right for people who like to split hairs, while my question deals with the problems and needs of the Jewish people, who cannot afford the luxury of spending their time on pedantries of that sort. My question refers to work in Palestine, not to Zionism. This may seem like a contradiction in terms, but contradictions are not rare in history. The Bolsheviks, for example, began at the end of communism, and everyone now sees the process of nationalization of agriculture. The Zionists began with a process the goal of which was to found a Jewish state, and as matters emerge, they are succeeding, for now, in turning Palestine into a center for Jewish immigration. If indeed this entire process ultimately concludes with the establishment of a Jewish state, my sympathies will be with the opponents of Zionism, but I certainly shall not grieve.

I admit that in the course of the debate serious arguments have been put forward against political Zionism. I also admit that there are arguments against Zionism that I cannot meet. Therefore, I am not a Zionist. But it is not clear to me why, in the current debate, Zionism is attacked, when not one of the debaters is a Zionist. Palestine today is absorbing over twenty thousand Jewish immigrants a year. Since America closed its gates to Jewish immigration, Palestine has become the major country for it. The Jews who immigrate do not live in comfort there, but they are more content than those who migrated to other countries. True, they get assistance, but do not the Jews of Russia and Poland get assistance? No one migrates from America to Palestine. Everyone who goes there is maintained only by the Zionist movement. In Palestine the Jews are not supported by their relatives. If the Jews of Russia and Poland were not supported by their relatives, how would they survive at all?

How did the first Jewish immigrants live in America? Comrade Zivion came here when the paths had already been forged and various matters had been settled. The Jews already had daily newspapers and periodicals. But at the beginning of the immigration the Jews worked here harder than the *halutzim*. They had their own "Arab" problem. The Irish immigrants were stronger and more brazen than the Arabs. Bearded Jews did not dare to be seen on Monroe Street or Cherry Street. Jewish beards were pulled, and even Jewish blood was spilt. Despite all, the Jews got by. You argue that America is a rich land while Palestine is a small, poor land, that the best thing that Comrade Cahan found there was the cool evening breeze. You also go on to claim that if the idea of establishing the national home is eliminated, then Palestine will be like a squeezed lemon. If it is to be regarded as a destination for Jewish migration, then countries such as Mexico, Brazil, Cuba, and Argentina are better; these are Zivion's arguments.

Let us deal with them. In Cuba several thousand Jews have settled in recent years, and all of them without exception live off the assistance they receive. In Mexico the situation is similar. The Jews there are unable to accomplish anything. The weak die there and the strong run away. As for Brazil and Argentina, does Comrade Zivion know how much it costs to send a Jew there from Poland? How many Jewish immigrants might have been sent there with the money available to the Zionists?

Various experts have dealt with the question of how many Jews Palestine can absorb. It is commonly held that there is no room there for more than a million Jews. If so, it may be asked if there is any place on earth that can absorb a million Jews, even living there in such strained conditions as in Palestine. There is no such place. But even assuming that such a place does exist, there is still the question of if it will be possible to muster up massive and united Jewish support for that place, as has been done for Palestine.

Comrade Zivion argues that if Comrade Cahan knew that Mexico, for example, can absorb more Jews than Palestine, he would support Mexico, while a Zionist will always, unconditionally, be an adherent of Palestine; therefore it is impossible to separate Palestine and Zionism, hence one must consider only the question of how far Zionist ideology can be realized there. It seems to me that here Comrade Zivion has gone off course. What interest do we have in Ussishkin's sayings? From Zivion's words it may be inferred that if a Jewish state could be established in Palestine he would not oppose it, but since he does not believe that this is possible, what use have we for the entire business? Why does Zivion demand more than the Zionists want? The Zionists are ready to accept the chance that has been created; why is Zivion not willing to risk it? It is out of fear that it might work? Comrade Zivion himself admits that the results of the experiment in Palestine will be proven only many years after our demise. If so, he will not lose anything, but meanwhile many Jews could find their home in Palestine.

Why cannot the subject be addressed from the viewpoint of turning Palestine into a country of immigration? If Comrade Zivion wishes to debate Zionism, let him select a Zionist he can debate with. But if the discussion focuses on the subject of Palestine as a country of immigration, then many of his arguments are irrelevant. For example, he argues that the communes are not socialist, and the pioneers are chauvinists because they are fighting for Hebrew. Comrade Zivion would most probably agree that if a land such as America, say, could be found, he would support such a land at least as a country of immigration, if not as a homeland for the Jews. Was the life of the first immigrants in America more ideal than that of the *halutzim*? . . . The red-light district was right in the heart of the Jewish neighborhood. The immigrants did not base their lives on Hebrew, nor on Yiddish either. Here there were no communes or unions. I do not ask what position Comrade Zivion would have adopted then regarding the future of Jewish life in America, but every thinking person must admit that the life of the workers and of the Jewish masses in general was not notable for its lofty content. By contrast, and in comparison with life in America, the beginnings made in Palestine are far healthier and better. Why then is Comrade Zivion so concerned about the future of cultural life in Palestine? Does he expect, in the course of four or five years' intensive immigration, geniuses to have been born who will perform miracles and wonders?

Again, according to Zivion the Jews did not evince great deeds and marvels when they dwelt on the soil of Palestine, and only in exile were the mighty works born. Does Zivion know of other peoples, of the same era, who created more? In his opinion, were the Jews, compared with other contemporary peoples, barbarians? Zivion argues that even rabbis are imported to Palestine from Poland; in this way Zivion wishes to point out the paltry image of Palestine. Against this it can be proven that until now Jews journeyed to Palestine to die there, while today they go there to live.

Let us assume that the pioneers in Palestine had a worse start under the leadership of Ben-Gurion than the first Jewish immigrants had in America. Let us even assume that their cultural future is in peril. The question still remains if we can, in the given situation, concentrate on anxiety for the cultural future, and at the same time neglect the masses of Jews about to be strangulated in Russia and Poland. Zivion speaks of Mexico, Brazil and Argentina: can the Jews expect a better cultural future in these countries than in Palestine?

Zivion distinguishes Eretz Israel from Palestine. I wish to go somewhat further, and make a distinction between Zionism and Palestine. I am not obliged to believe in the dreams of Zionism, but when the Zionists are engaged in practical work and are concerned to make a home for thousands of Jews they wish to save from hunger and disease, I can help them. Zivion admits that he would not argue with the Zionists if they did not pretend to be the bearers of redemption to the Jewish people; but he fears that they are deceiving the people, and this cannot be passed over in silence. It is worth considering this "deceit." First, the statement is incorrect. Not all Zionists claim that they are bringing redemption to the people, and Zivion himself admits this: for him, this posture is attributed to foolish Zionists. The fact has to be recognized that such "deceptions" are carried out by foolish Bundists and also by socialists. So one should not assail the Zionists on account of flaws existing in other movements, including our own.

The hatred of Zionism that lives on in some socialists is the legacy of the past, when every movement held a monopoly on the Messiah. The world has changed since then. The European socialist movement has gone far, and is trying to create socialist society. But with us, in Jewish society, people still sit in the synagogue and dispute over who will bring the Messiah. The socialist world sees no conflict between itself and Zionism, and the Zionists attend socialist congresses. No one is forced to become a Zionist. Everyone has the right to oppose Zionism. But when some socialists attempt to found this opposition on socialist principles, it is necessary to say to those socialists, as Zivion says to the Zionists, "You are deceiving the people."

Comrade Vladek admits that the Zionist movement has done much for the revival and fostering of the national idea. He admits that the Zionists' work in this domain, among the Jewish intelligentsia and the Jewish middle class, is like the work of the Bund among the Jewish working masses. Such an avowal cannot be dismissed out of hand. Such an avowal is particularly important for the Jews of America. These are ceasing to be employed workers. They are in a state of rapid transition to the middle class. This class is a producing class, and the European socialist parties are seeking to draw close to it so as to absorb its members into their midst. This middle class, and also the intelligentsia, are an important part of the

British Labour Party, and of all the European socialist parties. The Zionist movement has ignited the flame of ardor and idealism in the American Jewish middle class. This class does indeed contain negative people within it, but the great majority are idealistic and with liberal leanings. Many of them have socialist leanings. If so, what is the significance of attacks on these people and their ideals? What outcome is to be expected from them?

It is argued against us that wherever there is an encounter between socialism and Zionism the latter overpowers the former. This claim might be of some import were it true, but this has not yet been proven. There are no supporting facts. The workers' movement in Palestine is stronger even than the American Jewish socialist movement and the Bund in Poland. Many of the American Jewish workers who support Palestine are good socialists.

Vladek further contends that the Zionists are extremist fanatics, like the communists. To a certain extent this is true. If the Zionists had been given a monopoly on solving all the problems of the Jewish people, an extremely difficult situation might have arisen. However, if they wish to exert influence on the means assigned to resolving only part of the problem of the people, then a positive position has to be adopted toward the work being accomplished in Palestine.

In times like these it is impossible to go up to a Jew and tell him, "Don't look at your wife, because if you look at your wife you'll begin, God forbid, to look at her sister. The minute you look at her sister, you'll start staring at other strange women and then God knows how this might end up." It is absurd to go up to an American Jew and tell him that he must not show sympathy to Zionism because this will divert him from the right path. We must be appreciative of the work of the Zionist movement, and at the same time fight against its fanaticism. If this is our position, there is a chance that they will be appreciative of our criticism, and then we too will be able to make a positive contribution. By contrast, if we immediately launch an attack, and against everything, we will achieve nothing and only do ourselves damage.

Comrade Cahan's articles showed that in Palestine new Jewish life is steadily being created. Such a fact even a good journalist cannot invent; he can only take note of it and describe it. Throughout the years of the Zionists' dreams they have never succeeded in interesting the Jewish masses, but now they are doing real things and building Palestine. Their endeavor is already producing positive results, and it contains the promise of even better results in the future.

New York, 8 March 1926
11. David Einhorn
The Debate On the Articles on Palestine

Zionism is a beautiful idea. On the shores of the Mediterranean Sea, between Asia and Europe, between ancient culture and modern culture, there lies a small land enfolded in myth, sacred to all peoples. Every stone and place there are mute witnesses to historical events and dramas. The stage is set by the endless blue sky and the flourishing valleys, waiting as if for the legendary Shulamite to appear and walk through them. There too are fields, just to be settled, silent sandy deserts for wandering prophets. In short, this is a place to be enchanted by, to fall in love with.

In parallel, there moves around the world an eternal people with a centuries-long drama-filled history. A people that has produced seekers of the good for human society, heralds of freedom for the world, prophets, many Shulamites . . . In short, a people of noble lineage.

Between this people and that land a true love story has been going on for 2000 years. This is a kind of love full of sacrifices, the like of which has never before been witnessed. Which hard heart will not melt, who will dare to arise and prevent the two lovers from joining? Who knows – perhaps the renewed union will beget another new religion, not one, but two, three, four, and five – or perhaps a new Messiah will be born from it? Who is there who will not wish to be connected to such a union, even if it is necessary to invest much money in it, of the order of tens and hundreds of thousands of dollars? As it is, we invest much money in other places. Everything could be so pleasant and lovely. No one can hold anything against Zionism, even if it is but a dream, a utopia, or a fanstasy that cannot come true. Good God! In our world there are so many dreams that we know cannot come true, and still they manage to excite us and we find joy in their beauty. We pay five or even ten dollars for a theater ticket, a show with a fictional plot. Whom does this show harm? Zionism too, as a beautiful fantasy, might have been worthy of a review in the style of the theater critics. Whom would it hurt? But precisely here you stop short! The dreams evaporate in an instant, the blue skies cloud over, the valleys turn out to be desolate, the fields, in reality, are just a pile of jagged rocks, and the seemingly holy Shulamite appears with a painted face covered with powder: suddenly you find yourself in the presence of Zionism. It is like a beautiful Catholic ritual, immediately after which comes the priest's sermon, urging wars, an inquisition, and ranting against strikes while hurling abuse at the godless socialists.

So who is harmed by the young girls clad in white, with flowers in their hands? Who is hurt by the pictures portraying a young woman holding her child in her arms? . . . None of this would be harmful if behind the romance there did not stand a real party with political aims intended to serve only a small group, working to the disadvantage of millions. It would not matter to anyone, if only Zionism remained in the realm of a beautiful utopia. It is a different story when behind the utopia lurks an actual political party, which sticks its nose into every political pot, aiming to skim off the cream for itself, in sanctimonious disguise, while for the millions in the Diaspora it leaves only the watery part, the dregs of the broth. It is a party striving to win power, by means of the utopia, in places where there is no interest in Zionism. It is a party which in millions of Jews, again by means of the dream, destroys the ability to function in actual reality. It is a party which spreads uncertainty among the masses in the Diaspora, and thus it weakens their vitality, needed to conduct their fight for existence. It is a party that tears down the centers and the strongholds of Jewish existence in the Diaspora solely in order to fortify Palestine. To such a party we, the socialists, say, "Stop!" So far Zionism has been a beautiful dream, but from now on it assumes the form of an ugly political party . . . willing to accept the loss of thousands in the Diaspora merely for the the survival of ten Jews in Eretz Israel. Justs as we rip off, mercilessly, the fine religious mask from our opponents, so do we rip off, mercilessly, the romantic mask from Zionism. Let us detail the damage caused to millions of Jews by the Zionist utopia in the last 30 years.

In the last 30 or 40 years Jewish life in Russia has undergone a great revolution, full of hope and catastrophe . . . The loss stemmed from the fact that the Jewish people was obliged to pass through enormous economic and spiritual changes in a short time – changes that other peoples experience in the course of two centuries . . . In such times, all forces in the people should have been united to conduct the struggle within the new reality . . . All means, economic and spiritual, should have been placed at the disposal of the people.

Zionism has to be considered against this background. Never was there a movement such as the Zionist movement that caused so great a disaster for the Jewish masses. Zionism constitutes a kind of escape, a kind of desertion from harsh reality. The intelligentsia of the middle and petty bourgeousie were so alarmed and frightened that instead of contending with the reality face-to-face, they went off like cowards and hid in the historical past. Instead of fighting to build in the places where they lived, they "escaped" to Eretz Israel. The result was that they caused even greater fears among the masses instead of diminishing them . . . Instead of acting positively they sent up a shout: "Escape! Save yourselves!" And sure enough, the flight to Palestine began. This was an escape of the kind that Mendele Mocher Seforim writes about. The Jews sold everything, down to the shirts on their backs, destroyed their lives, and fled to Eretz Israel. In Eretz Israel hunger became rife, the people had nothing to live off there, so, disillusioned, they started escaping from there to America. In Poland we are seeing now an almost exact replica of what happened in Russia. There too the Zionists are shouting, "Jews! Escape!" The same situation has arisen in Eretz Israel, and now there are thousands of people without work there, but there is hardly anywhere to escape to. Never was there a situation like this in the past . . .

I have a question for Comrade Cahan, who was so moved by his encounter with an old acquaintance at one of the *moshavot* in Palestine. That acquaintance fled to Palestine at the same time as Comrade Cahan migrated to America. I want to ask Cahan how the Jewish masses in America would look if Cahan, together with his other comrades who established and built the powerful Jewish trade unions, freed the masses from the sweatshops, created the *Arbeiter Ring* and *Forward*, and helped millions of immigrants to organize and build themselves up – how would all this have been done if Comrade Cahan and his comrades had fled, together with that old acquaintance, to Palestine, and had been dreaming there for the past 30 years? In such a case, in America no trade unions or *Arbeiter Ring* would have been founded, and millions of Jews would have continued to suffer agonies in the sweatshops. Let me go further and ask Comrade Cahan: how would life in America look to him if he and his friends had been joined by about a thousand more members of the intelligentsia, who would have helped them in their great work of building? Who knows how the Jews of America would have appeared today! Just count up the number of Zionists who assisted in this mighty endeavor and you will see that you will not find a single one. Now they have the impertinence, the chutzpa, to take advantage of everything that has been built. They want to exploit the enterprise that they not only did not build but the construction of which they actually hindered. Here lies the crime of Zionism.

Let me ask you, Comrade Cahan: place on one side of the scales your and your comrades' human socialist endeavor of the last 30 years, the work you have done with your ten fingers without help from any quarter; and on the other side the activity of those who 30 years ago deserted to Palestine. Do you not see, Comrade Cahan, what weighs heavier? As you toured the desolate valleys of Palestine, did not your way of life appear before your eyes like a towering skyscraper, as against the nothingness of Zionist deeds! . . .

Let us remember the spiritual and material forces that the Zionists took from the millions in the Diaspora and carried with them to Palestine; millions of confused Jews groaning under a burden of punishments. All this, yet still not counting the doubts and despair that they sowed among those masses. "Oho!" they shouted, "Here in the Diaspora there is nothing to be done, because the situation here is hopeless. What are you dreaming of in the Diaspora?" they queried. "The fight here is for the sake of others, not for your sake. Therefore, there is no reason to build in the Diaspora since everything built will be razed the following day." Despite their preaching, the Zionists knew well that three-quarters of the people would be forced to remain in the countries of the Diaspora. The Zionists knowingly harmed the lives, the happiness and the future of those 75 percent of the people for the sake of the dream of settling 25 percent of the people in Palestine. So in fact they were the arch foe of millions of Jews who were to remain in the Diaspora. When a small part of these managed to break free of this despair, and assumed the struggle for the future of the Jews in the Diaspora, the Zionists went out to fight them, and to strike at their work. Have our comrades already fogotten how much slime, how much slander and demagoguery the Zionists hurled against the Bund? . . . Have our comrades already forgotten the Zionists' attacks against us? The mud they flung at our innocent and blameless comrade Medem, whom they accused of wanting "to oil the wheels of the revolution with the blood of Jews"? And who was it who launched all these accusations? Weizmann, who is greasing the wheels of his machine with the troubles and the tears of Jews. This is the same Weizmann who invented a gas that caused many Jewish soldiers on the Western Front to suffocate to death. These are the same Zionists who with the blood of the Jewish legionaries smoothed the colonial policy of imperialist Britain. These are th same Zionists who for their purposes exploited the victory won by the working class in Tsarist Russia . . . What were the Zionists doing during the war, when hundreds of thousands of Jews were sent away, and wandered in misery all over Russia, desperately in need of help? They were living in London, selling the Jewish outcry against Russia, Britain's ally, in return for the worthless Balfour Declaration, which caused only catastrophe for the Jews of Palestine . . . When Poland was granted independence, and it might have been possible to organize the masses of Jews there, what did the Zionists do? In the elections they collaborated with the Polish anti-Semites, with the National Democratic party, whose influence they helped to spread through the Jewish vote – as they did just recently when they achieved the empty "understanding," equally devoid of influence on real Jewish life as the Balfour Declaration. They deluded them with the idea of a Jewish state, and bluffed them with false hopes . . .

If there still are organized masses in Poland who have no doubts about their way and are waging a heroic struggle for the future, these are the Jewish working masses of the Bund. By contrast, among the Zionist masses, doubts, fears, hopelessness reign . . . Now, when the Jews of America are becoming organized and are again ready to extend help to the Jewish masses in the old countries, who stands in opposition, and fights this by creating a special campaign? The Zionists. As far as they are concerned, the Jews of Russia and Poland can die, just so that the few "only sons" in Palestine, who have been living for 30 years now at public expense, the *kest kinder* of the Jewish people, can live well there . . .

The Zionists interfere in the politics of the Jewish masses in the Diaspora not because of their concern for the interests of these masses, but because of their concern for Zionism. Whenever a conflict arises between the interests of Palestine and the interests of the Jews in the Diaspora, they betray the latter. Zionist politics in Poland bears a Jesuit character. The well-being of the Jewish masses in Poland does not interest them in the least, because for them Palestine is all. They are ready to sell the interests of the Jews of Poland to the anti-Semites in return for a good word about Palestine.

Not long ago, Sokolov visited the bloodthirsty hound of Romania. The visit apparently was necessitated by the interests of his backdoor Zionist policy. When he returned from his visit he stated in a press interview that the Jews in Romania are not living badly. Recently, the Zionist Dr Reich, father of the "understanding" with the Polish regime, gave an interview to the *Neuer Freier Presse* in which he greatly lauded that notorious anti-Semite, the Polish Minister of Culture, Wladislaw Grabski, the inventor of the *numerus clausus*. The minister threw hundreds of Jewish students out of the Polish universities . . . It seems that this paean by Reich was a function of the needs of Zionist diplomacy. If Dr Reich is the representative and expression of Zionist policy, this shows that the Zionist leadership supports his political line, and not the policy of the fair-minded Greenboim, who still possesses some consciousness of the Jews' needs in the Diaspora.

I have nothing to add about the Zionist utopia itself, as Comrade Cahan himself, among his other criticisms, criticized that too . . .

The Zionists always like to talk about the 800,000 Arabs and the 150,000 Jews who live in Palestine. This calculation is false. Palestine is not an island, but constitutes a part of the overall Arab area. To count only 800,000 Arabs, omitting the 40 million Arabs in the region, is like counting only the Jews of Manhattan as the New York Jews, leaving out the Jews in the Bronx, Harlem, and Brooklyn. There are actually no borders between Palestine, Syria, Mesopotamia, and Egypt, and with the Arabs' national consciousness steadily growing – and this is an open secret – the 150,000 Jews are up against 40 million Arabs; and these have the backing of 100 million Muslims, for whom Palestine is as just as holy as it is for the Jews. Jabotinsky and his legions will not be able to do anything about this fact.

Nor is there anything to add about economic development and building of industry. As long as Britain rules, it will not allow industry to develop in Palestine and it will endeavor to retain Eretz Israel as a market for its own industry. That this is indeed the case may be gathered from the protest initiated by the Zionists against British customs policy, which is strangling not only industry but also Jewish craftsmen, namely the tailor and the shoemaker . . . Recently unemployment has grown greatly there, and this has led, among the Zionists themsleves, to doubts about the future of the enterprise. In Tel Aviv alone there are more than two thousand people out of work . . .

Furthermore, I wish to say one thing to our comrades, Liessin and Pine, the supporters of Zionism. Do you believe that the path of Europe leads to socialism and a better future? Do you believe that Europe must step onto the road to peace, to freedom and to the creation of the United States of Europe? If you answer in the negative, I will tell you that if indeed Europe is sinking, and marching to perdition, war, and hatred, then you are bound to stop believing in the power of Europe in Asia, namely that Britain's future is retreat. The decline of Europe means the liberation and rise of Asia, and this will put an end to Zionism. It is absolutely clear that without the support of British cannons the Jewish settlement will be wiped out in three days. If you do not believe in all this, you must believe in the rosy future of Europe. In such a case, the number of Jews who will emigrate from Europe to Palestine will match the number of those now emigrating to America. Finally, a few words about Zionism in America. American comrades who sympathize with Zionism state that they cannot determine their position according to the reactionary and anti-socialist policy of the Zionist movement in Poland. By their argument, the situation in Poland is different, because in America the Zionists do not engage in politics, as in Poland, but in charity. Our American comrades are making two mistakes: the first is their lack of concern for what is taking place in Europe. The Monroe Doctrine [American isolationism regarding events in Europe – Y.G.] has long been discarded. In fact, there never was a time of such great proximity between Europe and America. When the war [World War I – Y.G.] broke out in Europe, America lost several hundred thousand of its young men in it. When a crisis erupts in Europe, the workers in America feel it. If an epidemic rages across Europe, thousands of people in America die from it. If fascism prevails in Europe, this promotes the growth of the Ku Klux Klan in America. f communism rules in Russia, this causes splits in the American trade unions. The same rule applies to Zionism. Our American comrades are completely wrong in thinking that American Zionism does not engage at all in politics. It is precisely in America that Zionism is a danger. Precisely in America, where a political struggle is being fought that is not based on ideological platforms but on "issues" surrounded by ordinary moods and sentiments, precisely in the country where in elections "issues" play a greater part than political platforms, where moods can change the directions of voting, precisely in such a country the socialists must beware of charity organizations. Among the Jews Zionism too is a mood, which even Tammany Hall can bet on. For example, let's say that in the next city elections Tammany Hall puts up its own candidate against our candidate, and the former wins over the Zionists, or some senator expresses support for Eretz Israel, . . . then the Jewish masses will go and vote for him contrary to their own interests. Hillquit and Vladek, for all their tolerance, will not be able to join the blue-and-white flag to the red banner. Even if they do so, it will not have the same effect as a gentile with pull in Washington doing it . . . The upshot will be that Tammany Hall or the Republicans or the Democrats will beat us with our own charity. The Zionists are always ready to sell their support at a good price, and we will pay for our sympathy for Palestine with voters' ballots. The masses do not think much, and the moment they see the blue-and-white pennant in Tammany Hall they will suddenly remember the *halutzim*, the communalist settlements, Tel Aviv, the holy idealists – and then in spite of all their radicalism they will go after Tammany Hall . . . Comrades can learn from what happened in Poland how political demagoguery is disguised as Zionism. When the Polish government sent 9000 books to the university in Jerusalem the entire Zionist press in Poland became extremely wrought up for about two weeks, as if this had saved the Jews; but it remained silent on the *numerus clausus* and on the hundreds of Jewish students thrown out of the Polish universities. Not long ago the Polish Consul-General arrived from Jerusalem, and conducted a fiery propaganda campaign for Zionism, and the Zionists acclaimed him. What Polish reactionaries can do American politicians can do, and better. If you want to find poison, pay heed to what your enemy advises you to drink. I wish to ask our Palestine-sympathizing comrades: "Comrade! Do you believe so much in the realization of Zionism that for its sake you are willing to forego even a single representative in the Town Hall or in Congress? Answer me yes or no! Do you believe so much in this utopia that on this account you are willing to weaken the socialist endeavor in America? Answer yes or no!" . . . If we treat Zionism with favor, then we must say "amen" to the Kolo in Poland and Britain's colonial policy in Asia . . .

New York, 13 March 1926
12.   Dr Chaim Spivak
The Debate on the Articles on Palestine

I do not wish to debate Cahan's articles on Palestine, but not because I have nothing to say about them. The opposite is the case. All my life I have been engaged in debates and I have found that there is some point to them only when a clear position can be adopted: beautiful or ugly, helpful or harmful, good or bad, wise or foolish. But all matters connected with social subjects, such as national and economic questions, issues of ethics, morals, politics, or literature – all these still do not count as exact sciences, and, therefore, anything to do with them may be subject to dispute . . . Cahan's articles arouse dispute, and the divided opinions should be published in the press. It is difficult for me to add anything to what has already been published.

My love for the Jewish homeland is not a product of the mind, but comes from the heart, and there can be no debating with the heart. Even if Eretz Israel were four times smaller than it is, ten times more distant than it is, possessed disadvantages a hundred times more than the "antis" enumerate – even then I would remain the same eternal devoted Zionist . . . All those who rely solely on "wisdom, understanding, and knowledge," on "and thou shalt study," and on "and thou shalt teach diligently," but not on "and thou shalt love" – all those are incapable of comprehending the spiritual and immediate needs of the Jewish people.

The Jew begins his prayer with "And thou shalt love" . . . If the Jew were to cast off the feelings of his heart and "And thou shalt love," and to rely only on "the mind," then long ago not a single Jew would have been left on earth. And truly, what is the logic of continuing to preserve Jewish identity? In terms of logic, of the mind, it would be better to become a non-Jew.

It is amazing how much the Jewish "heart" has proved, for thousands of years, that all the yearnings and longings, dismissed by people possessed of "logic," ultimately led to "wisdom, understanding, and knowledge." Ultimately it always became evident that the heart achieves mental things. Take, for instance, the Zionist movement: it began at a time when the gates of almost every country were open to the Jews. The mind caused the migration of the Jews to America. People who were moved by feelings of the heart went on foot to Eretz Israel, while we, the men of mind, came here. It is very nice and good for us here. And then came the world war, and the gates of all countries closed. The gate of Eretz Israel stands open. The heart "prophesied" what was going to happen in the course of time. The heart gave the true prophecy.

Prophecy is a mental thing that derives from the heart . . .

The development of love for Eretz Israel in modern times constitutes a romantic chapter in the history of the Jewish people. Slim volumes as well as weighty tomes have been penned about it, and more will yet be written. On this theme dramas and operas will be composed. Here I shall briefly note the main stages of the development of the different groups. The Zionist movement began among the intelligentsia of the middle class. This was the start. Then the middle class was swept up in the current. Now comes the turn of the workers. In his articles Cahan has done a most important service. It may be stated that through Cahan's articles the workers in America have learned, for the first time, the truth about Palestine. When they learned this, something happened to them that happened to other Jewish strata before them: their Jewish heart welled over. In the history of the Zionist movement, Cahan's name will be inscribed in letters of gold.

New York, 22 March 1926
13. S. Rabinowitz
The Debate on the Articles on Palestine

I will not be startled if, as a result of Ben-Zvi's article, a large group of

New York Jews begin selling their property and migrating to Palestine. For it is an easy matter for Ben-Zvi to whip out of his satchel a new map, mark signs on it, put forward programs, figures, statistics, plans for concessions, and all the things he offers the *Forward* readers. Now, imagine: you all know that figures do not lie. Ben-Zvi is a realistic politician and you won't find the word "dream" in his article. Nor will it evince the usual Jewish groans. He does not shed even a single tear for the fate of the Jewish Diaspora, as the half- or quarter-Zionists do. The claim that "love is blind" does not appear in his writing either. He is in no way blind. With him, everything is measured and weighed out in a businesslike manner. Before you is the truth and now give me the money. The only unclear thing in his article is his critical comment about Comrade Cahan's articles: "Comrade Cahan saw a great deal of us, far more than what others managed to encompass in two months. He also learned something. I and my comrades got the impression that he changed his opinions on Zionism" . . . Note the phrase "saw a great deal" and also "learned something"; now this "something" does not refer to Zionism but to socialism:

> He began to be convinced that apart from the path of political dictatorship and the political struggle there is another path for the realization of socialism, and this is the path of constructive cooperation . . .

Considering that Comrade Cahan has always opposed political dictatorship, and that he does not set much store by "constructive cooperation" in Palestine, it seems that he learned very little. This is, in fact, the only unclear statement in the article; now let us turn to the numerical reasoning set forth in Ben-Zvi's article.

Zivion accuses the extremist Zionists of chauvinism. He berates them for placing a ban on Yiddish in Palestine and for suppressing the language in various ways. Ben-Zvi counters with this with numerical arguments:

> Four years ago the government conducted a census among us, and according to this, 95 percent of the Jews reported that their mother tongue was Hebrew, 2.3 percent Yiddish, and the rest reported about 60 languages. It appears thus that only 2.3 percent of the Jewish population requires Yiddish as a national language. Can Zivion thus accuse 97.5 percent of the Jewish population that they "brutally oppress . . . ."

Ben-Zvi's claim is strange in terms of both its numbers and its logic. If indeed there is in Palestine a negligible number of Yiddish speakers, of the order of 2.3 percent, this does not accord with what is told by Comrade Cahan, who in Ben-Zvi's words "saw a great deal," that the main language spoken in the market of Tel Aviv, the chief city of the Cossacks of Hebrew, is Yiddish. There, of course, the Cossacks of Hebrew cannot do much. Pogroms they can carry out only at meetings. And again, if the number of Yiddish speakers is really so tiny, why are so many Cossacks needed to ensure that Yiddish, God forbid, is not spoken?

Ben-Zvi promises:

> The attitude to Yiddish on the part of the responsible circles in the labor movement is highly civilized, it is an attitude full of attention and respect.

Maybe. At the same time it transpires that the "responsible circles in the labor movement" in Palestine interpret the phrase "civilized attitude," and also "attention and respect," in such a way that the words do not stop them from organizing pogroms against Yiddish-speaking Jews. We learn this from *Forward*'s correspondent, Comrade Galut. He reports on the pogrom organized by the Cossacks of Hebrew at the meeting of orthodox Jews in Tel Aviv who wished to conduct the gathering in Yiddish. If this is not enough, it's worth reading the following item published in *Forward*:

> Tel Aviv, February 15 (JTA) Yesterday evening there were serious clashes here when the first meeting was held concerning the Yiddish language. The meeting was arranged by a branch of Po'aley Tziyon (Yiddishist Groups) in Tel Aviv. Members of the "Language Defenders' Battalion" burst in by force, disrupted the meeting and demanded that it be stopped. As a result clashes erupted, and the police were obliged to intervene.

These are the facts.

Now imagine that in Palestine there really are just 2.3 percent Yiddish-speaking Jews; so what would you call the foregoing "civilized behavior" of the "responsible circles of the labor movement" toward Yiddish? Chauvinist? This would be too gentle a term. To attack and murder a handful of Jews just because of their wish to speak Yiddish – only savages could do a thing like that!

Later in his article Ben-Zvi himself tells the whole truth about the attitude to Yiddish:

> At our meetings we take into account the need of the immigrants to speak Yiddish during the first two years.

So what happens when the immigrants continue speaking Yiddish after the first two years? It transpires that then they are exceeding what is permitted, and such excess must be punished. The Palestinian logic is apparently special, because immediately afterwards Ben-Zvi writes:

> I know that this situation does not satisfy Zivion(!), but if so he must admit that the problem does not lie in the fact that we suppress Yiddish, but that he wishes to force the majority who think otherwise to use the language, whose prestige he desires ...

And Ben-Zvi ends in a pathetic manner:

> We of course shall fight in every possible way against such a tendency.

Zivion proves be to blame for everything. He wants to force the majority to speak Yiddish. He wants to become a dictator – a sort of new Mussolini!

I have dilated somewhat on the subject in order to show once more how every nationalist movement carries within itself the disease of ugly chauvinism. Not even radical Zionists of Comrade Ben-Zvi's type can shake off this malady.

Ben-Zvi gets into a similar situation on the issue of the Arabs. He assures Zivion that there is no ban against the Arabs. In his words,

> The old internationalists, those who settled the old *moshavot*, employ between 70 and 80 percent Arab workers; so far, the Jewish worker has not penetrated these *moshavot* sufficiently.

This statement is about right, but the question is if Po'aley Tziyon are satisfied with this situation. Obviously not. They are conducting a struggle to have the Arab workers fired so that their place can be taken by Jewish workers. The farmers on the *moshavot* take on Arab labor because it is cheaper. So why doesn't the Histadrut organize them? The point is that it is not a question of organizing the workers but of the "conquest of labor," namely pushing the Arab workers out and having all areas of work grabbed by the Jews. This is an extreme chauvinist principle, and it sends shudders through the Jewish workers in the Diaspora countries, because the gentiles could try out this principle against the Jewish workers in those countries.

We now come to the major issue of Palestine. On this subject Ben-Zvi has succeeded, and I must give him credit for this, in creating the biggest sensation of all. He declared, no less, that the figures set forth by Zivion regarding the size of Palestine are wrong, and in fact it is twice larger. In this he relies on another expert in geography, Max Pine, who also holds that Zivion knows nothing about geography and that Palestine is three times larger than Zivion's figure. As I said, this really is sensational: first, the statement that Zivion knows nothing about the geography of Palestine, or in any case, even if he is acquainted with the subject, the figures he gives are wrong, which is even worse. Secondly, they place a question mark over Zangwill's authority too, because according to press reports, at a mass rally in London held on 13 February he said, among other things, the following:

Palestine is the size of Wales, which has adequate deposits of coal and iron, and still it has only 2 million inhabitants. If so, how can Palestine satisfy the needs of 16 million inhabitants? Zionism deals with the Jewish problem superficially, and in no way resolves it politically.

Such are Zangwill's words.

Now, imagine the impression made by the figures produced by Ben-Zvi, which are these: the area of Eretz Israel is not 10,000 square miles, but 21,000 square miles! If this is the case, then Zangwill too is an igno-ramus, or a liar! Thirdly, and this is the most important, in his data, Ben-Zvi cast doubts on the *Encyclopaedia Britannica*, and on the map of Palestine, for according to the latter even Zivion exaggerated by the addi-tion of a few thousand square miles to the area of Palestine. Ben-Zvi refers his readers to the book *Eretz Israel* written by himself and D. Ben-Gurion, but go and learn contemporary geography from a textbook by D. Ben-Gurion and Y. Ben-Zvi!

The only reasonable explanation for the differences is that no one erred, not Zivion, and not Zangwill, but the mistake arose from a single word. Ben-Zvi apparently meant to write 21,000 square kilometers, not miles. Even so, it is still excessive, but this figure approximates the truth more adequately.

After Ben-Zvi gave the figure of 21 [thousand square] miles, referring to the size of Palestine, he spread out before the reader the plan to attach Transjordan and other territories for the purpose of settling Jews. Let us not be misled because the areas in question are "at present under the rule of the British Mandate but with an Arab governor." Ben-Zvi's plan is marvelous, but in that case why not attach Mesopotamia too? And maybe the whole of the Arabian Peninsula? In this way it would be possible to create a big Palestine. But this is still not all. There is yet another plan, which, if it materializes, will make the Jews rich. This plan relates to the exploitation of the Dead Sea! Don't laugh.

> Some people believe that in the Dead Sea are to be found potash, phosphorus, and other minerals, which may be widely exploited for industry. In the near future a concession is to be obtained for the exploitation of the Dead Sea.

Who knows, when the concession is acquired and exploration begins, they might find fish there too. Does not the tale of the Dead Sea concession remind you of one of the Sabbath sketches by our own Kovner, in which the heroine Yenta of Lavenda shouts at Mendel, "Gevald, Mendel, buy (or get a concession for) the sea, and this will bring us riches!"

Comrade Rogoff in his article uses the term "we" in the phrase "we American socialists," namely, he has appointed himself "spokesman" of a very large group. It is worthwhile that "we" should know exactly who "we Amercians" are, and whom Comrade Rogoff deems a socialist who has passed through the American crucible. Does he determine this according to the years of residence in America? According to the level of knowledge of English? Is it according to the much desired citizenship? There are comrades who have been living in America for more years than Comrade Rogoff, yet still they do not agree with his views, just as there are comrades who speak excellent English and they too do not agree with his views. Rogoff's basic position may be characterized according to the following passage from his article on Palestine:

> The states where Jews are to be found at present may be divided into two groups: countries that restrict their rights, and countries that do not restrict their rights. In the first group of countries, Jewish identity is strong, but their "body," namely their physical existence, is sickly. In the second group of countries their material life is good, but the Jewish identity is "sick" and weak. I see in Palestine the possibility that the Jews will develop there a robust material life as well as spiritual life. There the Jew will be able to upold his Jewish identity fully, without having to pay for it with limitations on his human rights and restrictions on his economic opportunities.

No proof is necessary for faith. But it may be asked why the Rogoffs, the "we Americans," waited until after the war to discover that Palestine as the homeland for the Jews was to be the remedy that would heal the Jewish body and spirit? Were Jews not present in the countries he alludes to before the war too? If so, why is it that, "to us (to the Rogoffs, to the 'we Americans'), Zionism was foreign until after the war, and the entire movement did not interest us"?

And if Zionism was so entirely foreign to "us," how come that "we began to examine our old position on Palestine"? Earlier it is stated that "we" had no position on Zionism until the war, and the whole subject did not interest "us." What happened that the war "changed the entire situation"? The gates of immigration to America were closed? By Rogoff's logic, this would cause a reduction in the number of Jews whose Jewish identity was weakening. When the gates were open this likewise created problems because too many Jews joined the second group – that which suffered from a lowering of Jewish identity. And what actually does the term "the spirit is sickly" mean? Does it mean that the Jews living in countries where they are not discriminated against live there without ideals? What class is he referring to? If it is the Jewish working class, Comrade Rogoff knows well that it does have ideals. Has he never learned that "the working masses will necessarily reach socialism as a result of economic conditions"? In America too there are certain economic conditions. If Rogoff is referring to Jews in general, then in Palestine too there are merchants exactly as in the Diaspora. And what is the meaning of the term "sick in body"? The Jews live in the worst conditions in the Diaspora. Their economic situation is better than that of those living in Palestine. Perhaps by the term "the spirit is sickly" Comrade Rogoff is referring to the reality in countries where the Jews are not restricted in their rights and their Judaism is steadily declining – they are casting off their Judaism: if so, perhaps it would be better to begin propaganda for the maintenance of kashrut by the Jews, separation of meat and milk, and so on? Do you not think that this would develop true Jewish essence quicker than the homeland in Palestine that has been "handed to the Jews"?

Rogoff also wrote that the best thing that you, I and all of us together can do "for the sake of the movement that is dear to us is to work for it today. If the present produces results, then the future will certainly bring results too." Is that so? . . . This rule, Comrade Rogoff, does not work. The scientific socialist, and you, Comrade Rogoff, are certainly one of them, usually does not work for the sake of today, but he weighs up which future results will be achieved by the work of the present. It often happens that the work of today appears excellent, but it will not contribute to the future, so he abandons it. And the reverse: sometimes work at present does not seem good, but he does it if it emerges that it will contribute to the future . . . The Marxist thinks about the rosy future that will flourish out of the dark present. Will Zionist propaganda injure socialist work? Undoubtedly. Not only because the attention of the masses will be deflected from their own class interests. Nationalist propaganda causes greater damage. Nationalism and socialism cannot coexist. If the war taught us anything, it is the fact that extremist nationalism constitutes the best weapon in the hands of the capitalist class to sow bloody wars among nations. In practice this means war between the workers of one country and the workers of another country. It is argued against us that nationalism is part of human nature. Perhaps. So what? Does this oblige us to conduct propaganda on its behalf? . . .

I have hardly any criticism against the positions of Comrade Alex Kahn, because he himself states that he is not a Zionist, and is opposed to it:

> I cannot say that no powerful arguments have been raised against political Zionism. I accept that there are anti-Zionist arguments that cannot be refuted. Therefore I too am not a Zionist . . .

And later he writes:

> Why is it impossible to treat the subject from the viewpoint of turning Palestine into a country that absorbs immigration? When Comrade Zivion wishes to debate Zionism, it would be better for him to choose a Zionist for this . . .

If so, there is nothing to debate about. I do not believe that if Comrade Zivion is convinced that the Jews can live in Palestine he will be so cruel as to oppose this, and to prefer the Jews to die of starvation in the Diaspora countries. Against this background, listen to what Kahn has to say further on:

> The hatred for political Zionism that still exists in some socialists is the legacy of those times when every group had a monopoly on its own Messiah . . . The socialist world does not see any conflict between itself and political Zionism.

And so on to the end of the article. As you see, Comrade Kahn has forgotten that just before, he declared himself not to be a Zionist, and he has gone over to the defense of political Zionism. This is that same political Zionism against which there are many arguments which he, Alex

Kahn, cannot refute. But do not be surprised: Comrade Alex Kahn is just not as narrow-minded as the Zivions and the Litvaks. He does not believe in a particular Messiah who can bring salvation. He really is not a Zionist, but he is not at all sure that Zionism is a failure. Zionism most probably has many good sides. Why does one actually have to be a Zionist in order to defend Zionism? Kahn again:

> Fervent Jewish socialists perceived socialism just like pious Jews perceived the Messiah . . . Fervent Jewish socialists believe that all the troubles of the Jews will end with the realization of socialism . . .

He himself is simply not a fervent Jewish socialist. But while everything has to have some limit, Alex Kahn's "lack of fervor" is boundless. Kindly read what he wrote:

> Comrade Vladek admits that the Zionist movement has done much to awaken and preserve nationalism in the middle class and the intelligentsia, and its endeavors among these is like the endeavors of the Bund among the working masses . . .

Is this what Vladek says? Please read on:

> Such an endeavor cannot be dismissed out of hand. This is especially important for the Jews of America, who are gradually ceasing to be factory workers. Most of them are in a process of rapid passage to the so-called middle class. This is a productive class, and the European socialist parties are seeking approximation to this class in order to attach it to their ranks . . . Most of this class are idealistic and possess liberal attitudes, and many of them even hold socialist positions.

What transpires from this, for him, is that even if we are not Zionists, we at least should have a sympathetic attitude to Zionism.

In this short passage a new science and a new doctrine are set forth before you. We learn, for example, that all the Jews in America are moving into the middle class. The significance of this is the end of unions such as the Amalgamated, the International, the furriers, etc., etc. There is no need to worry about workers in the future, there are enough goyim for that. If so, what need is there here of the socialist Jewish *Farband*? It really will not be needed. Next we learn that the middle class is a productive class. It is not clear to me what this means. I deduce that the intention is that it is an efficient class, and not parasitic. Likewise we learn that most

of the class are idealistic, and above all, to us socialists information is
revealed that not one of us knew, namely that "the European socialist
parties are seeking approximation to this class in order to attach it to their
ranks."

Comrade Alex Kahn, please! You don't have to be a fervent socialist.
You don't have to believe in a socialist Messiah. But why are you tearing
to shreds our old socialist *Shulhan arukh*? And for what? For political
Zionism, in which, so you say, you do not believe!

New York, 18 April 1926
14. Morris Hillquit
Hillquit's Position on Zionism

A few words on how Mr Hillquit came to write the statement printed
below, following these explanatory sentences. The subject of Palestine
arose in a conversation held a few weeks ago between him and *Forward*'s
editor. In the talk the eminent socialist leader voiced extremely interesting
and important views on the Zionist movement. Mr Cahan urged Mr
Hillquit to commit his words to paper in order to bring his opinions to
the knowledge of the newspaper's readership, and to benefit them. Mr
Hillquit kindly acceded to the request. His statement is as follows:

"From the outset I wish to note that there is no organic hostility, or
even impossibility of coordination, between socialism and Zionism.
Zionism is a national movement, while socialism is inherently international. But sane internationalism does not negate the recognition of
legitimate national ambitions.

Socialism is international in the sense that in its goals, and in their
attainment, it encompasses the world. It likewise strives to eliminate the
hatreds and enmities among peoples. It does not consider the possibility
of removing nationalism. The opposite is true. It requires for all peoples,
small and large, the right to developed to the fullest extent their national
qualities and culture, and to be free of all interference and suppression
from without.

The direct cause leading to the founding of the first Socialist
International in 1863 was a general demonstration by the working class as
an expression of sympathy and support for the struggle of the Poles for
their independence. From that time on, the socialist movement has
remained constant in the support it gives to oppressed national movements that have striven for political integrity and the right to

self-determination. Is it possible to consider the Jews, without a home and dispersed, as a "nation" in the same sense, say, as the Poles after the partition of Poland? Or is a re-established Jewish state, or a center of specific Jewish culture, something possible, or desirable? The decision on this question rests with each individual; it is a function of feelings of the heart, not a matter of principle.

I, personally, am not a Zionist. I also have doubts about the present possibility of re-establishing a Jewish state in Palestine. Nor am I convinced that the Jews, as a nation standing on their own, will be able to make any outstanding or significant contribution to world culture.

Yet I am not an anti-Zionist either. While I cannot accept the practical Zionist platform in any formulation, I have come to recognize the fact that the value of social movements is not always measured by their actual achievements, or even by the possibility of realizing their goals. A movement may be utopian from the viewpoint of practical politics, but may still exert a powerful spiritual influence indirectly, but in the most profound form, to affect the course of human progress.

Zionism arouses in me a sentimental attraction, and this is because in essence it is an expression of the awakening of the self-respect of the Jewish people. I prefer to see the Jew who demands equality for himself alongside other races and nations of the world than to see him deny his origins, thereby indirectly accepting his national inferiority.

Clearly, a sharp line has to be drawn between legitimate demands for national equality and the absurd attitude that claims racial or national superiority. Zionism, like all other national movements, must safeguard itself against the danger of nationalistic decline. If it ever should develop in that direction it will lose any right to the sympathy of a socialist."

Part Three

Summing Up the Debate

New York, 6 May 1926
Abe Cahan
Summing up the Debate on the Articles on Palestine

The debate has been going on for too long, and I fear that interest in it has waned. The debate erupted on account of my articles, so I feel a duty to respond to all who have put forward objections and reservations. In my replies I shall limit myself only to those who came out against by views, and these were few. The essence of the opponents' words was directed not so much against the content of my articles and telegrams as against Zionism. The fact that I am not a Zionist was emphasized by all participants in the debate.

I am not a Zionist, but I have never defined myself as an opponent of the Palestinian movement. Furthermore, I have always shown sympathy toward the idealists in Palestine, even though I did not believe at all in their ideology or in their program. My visit to Palestine increased my sympathy significantly. I returned from my visit and I am still not a Zionist, just as before. On the other hand, my feelings have changed, positively, toward the socialist segment of the Zionist movement. Had I known about and understood the communes and the Histadrut, with all its ramifications and enterprises, I would have treated it previously with far more friendly warmth.

At the time of writing, there are in the United States four delegates from Palestine. These are the representatives of those communes and the Histadrut; they are Ben-Zvi, Remez, Hartzfeld, and Baratz. The United Hebrew Trades are helping them to set up a fund-raising campaign for their institutions, and already here I wish to state that they deserve the best possible assistance. By the way I feel, and as a result of my visit to Palestine, I would wish greatly to roll up my sleeves and be harnessed to cause of the campaign. We are obliged to do everything for the sake of our local *Farband*. Similarly, we must do everything for the hungry who are in our old countries. At the same time, we also have an obligation to help the idealists in Palestine.

The four representatives mentioned are personable men. They also fulfill an important function in the lives of the workers and settlers in Palestine. They enjoy the complete trust and respect that they deserve. These people work day and night for the interest of the workers of town and country there. Their labor is socialist labor. In their movement things are to be found that I do not understand at all, as I expressed in my articles and telegrams, and also as I told them at meetings and on other occasions in Palestine. But is everything comprehensible in all aspects with regard to ourselves, the American or European socialists? The idealism they represent belongs to the realm of noble idealism. I am very pleased to have had the opportunity of visiting their communes and trade unions, and I was able to set right faulty concepts I harbored about them previously. I now turn to the articles that came out against me in the order of their publication in *Forward*. Before sitting down to write my replies I read them through a second time.

The first article was published by Comrade Zivion. From it, it is clear that he is well familiar with the material I wrote from Palestine and about Palestine. Several times he mentions the fact that I am not a Zionist, and that I have great doubts about the present possibilities of turning Palestine into a great Jewish land, but that I sympathize with the Palestinian movement, especially the communes.

My attitude to Palestine is not one-sided; by contrast, Comrade Zivion's attitude is wholly hostile. I point out the enormous disadvantages and the problems, but with sympathy; while in his writing on Palestine there is nothing but negation and hostility. He does not appear as a judge but as an American prosecutor . . . Comrade Zivion published a full-length book on Palestine. There, as in his articles in *Forward*, first-class information is set forth. He presents various arguments in a well-written, forceful manner, with humor, but in every sentence he writes about Palestine there is nothing but hatred, sometimes not a small amount of venom. This tendency of writing obstructs the reader from entering into the body of the strong and logical arguments that he presents. The same may be said about Comrade Litvak, author of the third critical article, but I shall deal with that in its place. Comrade Zivion states that for him Eretz Israel is a subject belonging to the domain of "romance," a subject of his "youthful imagination," which, when he learned in *heder*, planted love for it in him. But he in no way shows this love – rather the opposite. By his account, I prove how slight the chances of success are for the communes and for industry in Palestine, and that my sympathy belongs to the sphere of emotion only. The same is to be found in him, except that his emotions are the reverse, so he sees everything in a negative light. I am sympathetic, but as Comrade Zivion himself says, this does not hinder me from seeing both sides of the coin. His spectacles, by contrast, are tinted with hatred alone, therefore he secs only the negative aspects.

Comrade Zivion's strongest arguments refer to the question of whether there is an economic basis in Palestine sound enough for it to become an all-embracing homeland of the Jews. As he himself mentions several times, I made it clear in my reports that in this area the Zionist exposi- tions may be defined as a dream. In my published accounts of the rapid growth of Tel Aviv, as well as the boom in real estate, I stated clearly that I do not regard these as a real foundation. This part of my article won a compliment from Comrade Zivion, and he sums up as follows:

> The next thing is the most important: when we speak of Palestine, if is it good or bad, we must never forget that we are discussing a defined idea and movement. It is a movement that does not see Palestine as a country for the Jews but as the country for the Jews. For Comrade Cahan the problem exists of whether Palestine is a good or a bad country, whether it can or cannot absorb Jewish immigrants. By contrast, for Zionism this problem does not exist. For Zionism Palestine is *the* Jewish land, and the future Jewish national home unconditionally.

It seems to me that these lines lead us to the nature of my sympathy for Palestine, and also the entirety of my understanding of the subject.

I would very much want Palestine to become the all-embracing Jewish home, but unfortunately I have to doubt the possibility of this, although I cannot claim that I totally disbelieve it, as we shall see later. But even if there are many or few Jews there, I love the Jewish villages, the cities, the small towns. All these, as a Jewish center, are dear to me. For me, the most important thing is this: all those things are dear to hundreds of thousands, even millions, of Jews. They treat Palestine in a special way and with special feelings: Look, there in Palestine, where once was the homeland of our people, a Jewish center is gradually being built, with a city like Tel Aviv, where the Jews feel at home and rule themselves. There they are completely free of feeling like a stepchild; they feel that it is their heritage wherever they are in the world.

Here I must refer to a passage in Comrade Litvak's article. He says that in an interview with a Warsaw journalist whom I met in Palestine I said the following:

For cultivated Jews, Palestine holds the same place as the Western Wall holds for pious Jews.

Comrade Litvak is not sure to what extent I did or did not say this. I wish here to confirm the report by the journalist. Yes, I expressed myself exactly in that way. When I saw the Western Wall it aroused in me feelings of joy that had nothing to do with religious emotions. In my talk with the Warsaw journalist I spoke of the Western Wall as a religious monument of religious Jews. In the hearts of our grandfathers there was a religious faith inseparable from national feelings: it could not be detached from them. Therefore, I said that the contemporary Jewish intelligentsia sympathetic to Zionism regards the Jewish settlements and towns in Palestine as a thing of national sanctity, exactly as the religious Jews regard the Western Wall as a thing of religious sanctity. During my sojourn in Europe, before traveling to Palestine, I was deeply impressed by these spiritual drives. I had a chance to talk to Jews from various countries of Europe, and I noted that everywhere the name Palestine stimulated warm reactions. As far as I could tell, and in contrast to Zionist propaganda, the question of the growth of the national home in Palestine is not so decisive for the average Jew. A mother loves her son as he grows into a tall and healthy youth, yet even if he does not grow, but remains small and skinny, she goes on loving him nevertheless. In recent years the Jews have suffered such harsh conditions and persecution that when one comes and tells them that there in Eretz Israel there is a city called Tel Aviv where a Jew feels at home, not like an unwanted son, when they realize that all this is taking place in Palestine, where once they had a state of their own – this realization arouses feelings of joy and serenity in them. Such a feeling is also the heritage of Edouard Bernstein, Léon Blum, and Morris Hillquit.

Comrade Zivion wrote:

> Comrade Cahan, with great sympathy and warm feelings, painted the life full of ideals led by the Jewish workers (in Palestine), and the pioneers in their communes. Yet all this is in the realm of poetry: where is the prose? Do the pioneers manage to maintain themselves on their communes? Not at all; daily life (the prose) is very sad. Comrade Cahan relates how poor they are and how primitive is the life they lead.

My answer to this is that the poem (the poetry) actually resides in the "poor prose." Their economic life is poor, they work hard and do not have enough to eat, but for all that they feel, at lease a good part of them, happy. At home, when I was still a boy, I sometimes heard the expression "full to overflowing with Torah." Mostly the words were spoken wryly, but I still remember the impression I got when once that phrase was said, in all seriousness, in reference to a Jew of the hassidic *minyan* of Vilna: of him they said, "He really is full to overflowing with Torah." The *talmid hakham* in question appeared in my eyes like a saint. My heart leapt when in my mind's eye I saw the picture of him with nothing to eat, but he sat day and night learning *Gemara*. The scholar was so engrossed in his studies, so happy, that he did not feel that he was hungry at all. A similar sort of feeling was evoked in me by the comrades, so full of enthusiasm and spiritual uplift, who live on the communes in Palestine. "They are full to overflowing with their ideals," I said to myself, recalling the story of the hassidic *minyan* from my boyhood days.

In one of my articles I described my visit to the Ein Harod commune. I related how we were served milk for supper, and how I found out that the members themselves did not get milk, because this was a luxury that the settlement could not afford. Milk is given only to children there. For us, being guests, they made an exception. Had we been aware of the situation, obviously we would not have drunk the milk. So there it is: those conditions, together with circumstances of devotion and spiritual elevation which I observed – these created in me the warm feelings with which I left Palestine. Did I pay attention to only one side of the coin? I shall deal with this question in my consideration of Comrade Litvak's article.

Comrade Zivion writes the following concerning his visit to Palestine:

> The only question in the matter of "what's mine is yours" that can arise is if someone eats a slice of bread or a spoonful of soup more than his comrade. In no other issue can the problem of "what's mine is yours" arise, because there were no possessions that could give rise to dispute. They all wrapped themselves in the most miserable coverings imaginable, and all the needs of existence on the commune ended in this.

Comrade Zivion makes his point as an argument to show that the communes cannot serve as laboratories and as paradigms for future life in socialist society. This is because he envisages socialism "only as a rich form of life, and possessing high culture and the most wide-ranging possibilities."

In this, of course, I see eye-to-eye with Comrade Zivion. But the same argument that seves him in one matter brings about his downfall in another. First, the poor way of life on the communes, the fact that at issue is an extra slice of bread or spoonful of soup: does not this touch the heart? Secondly, it would be wrong to think that the extra slice of bread or spoonful of soup are the only major questions dominating communalist life . . . The major questions over which they sit and discuss and deliberate, far into the night, belong to the sphere of abstract ideas, ideals, interests. Or actual, practical problems, which are also debated in the richest socialist societies. An example is the children's education.

Comrade Zivion reminds readers that in my articles I stated that I do not believe in the future of the communes in Palestine. This is correct, but as long as they exist they evoke our sympathy. As long as these communes of those self-sacrificing and devoted people endure, and are "full to overflowing with Torah," they deserve our complete heartfelt support. As to how long they will endure, in my humble opinion, as long as unfavorable conditions persist in Palestine this will be to the benefit of the continued existence of the communes.

I hope that I fully clarified this point in my reports. I believe that as a Jewish homeland gradually flowers in Palestine, with industry and Jewish cities, there will no longer be an existential basis for the communes. On account of exactly this reality, our communes could not exist in America. The attractive force of city life will draw the members from the communes to Tel Aviv, Haifa or other new Jewish cities. All this concerns the future, but for the present, industrialization is proceeding too slowly, and the boom in Tel Aviv real estate (the artificial nature of which I described in my articles) has burst. We must not despair. The work being done for the building of Palestine is positive work; but I shall deal with this later. Here it is important to note the significance in the present situation of the communes, and also of the other radical settlements. For the time being the pull of the city is not a powerful force, and does not yet constitute a threat for the communes to the point of members leaving and streaming to the city. This situation has not yet been reached. It transpires, therefore, that while Comrade Zivion tries to prove that there is no future for industry in Palestine, he in fact is proving that those same 15–18 communes in Palestine will continue to exist there for a long time to come. In this light, is it not most heartrending and moving to see how these devoted idealists, who barely have a slice of bread and a spoonful of soup to sustain their bodies, still persevere in their dedication? Can we deny them, and not extend help to them in their most vital needs? Must they present us with a "banker's check" as a guarantee that out of their communes socialist life will spring up that is "rich and possesses a high cultural level"? Is it not natural, as long as they exist, and lead the way of life filled with the idealism that we dream of, to show comradely compassion and sympathy, like that which they aroused in Max Pine and in the present writer, or in many other comrades here?

Orthodox Jews support the ascetics who sit and learn in the study-houses of Eretz Israel. They do so out of religious feelings, but in parallel there operates in them the feeling of common cause, in the sense of "how can we let those there go hungry?" A similar feeling, twofold, compels those who support the campaign for Palestine organized by the United Hebrew Trades.

I dispute many things regarding our comrades in Palestine, just as Comrade Zivion does. But are we obliged to be in agreement on all things? Are the pioneers obliged to show us certification that they have passed the examination in every single subject? Is it all that important, or even desirable, that we treat them unbendingly according to theory? Are we so certain that we observe theoretical socialism so rigorously that we may not digress from it one jot?

We must stand by certain minimal principles from which there can be no retreat. Our comrades in Palestine indeed do stand by those principles. They are socialists just as we are. They are our comrades and they are marvelous in idealism and in sacrificing themselves to their work and their lives. Let us not let them go hungry! We cannot sustain them entirely, but to the extent that we can, let us do so.

New York, 7 May 1926
Summing up the Debate on the Articles on Palestine (continued)

After I set out the great difficulties that beset the building of Palestine, I commented more than once in my reports, and I also stated clearly, that it is impossible to discard the possibility that industry will indeed develop. I drew attention to the extraordinary energy inherent in the Jewish people, and to the wonderful things that the enterprising spirit of this people has achieved. Therefore, I said, it may be expected that in Palestine the unexpected will be accomplished. Hence, with the assistance extended to them by the Jews of Europe and America, it is possible that despite all, large-scale commercial activity may develop. Responding to these statements of mine, Comrade Zivion argues that what I wrote is like "the old Jewish saying 'God will help' but in a different form." He is quite sure that nothing is capable of developing there. In this manner he makes himself a kind of prophet, while I hold that to engage in prophecy nowadays is a dicey business.

Take, for example, our socialist theory. In general, this is an accepted ideology. The stormy years of the war, and also the awful years that followed it, set us a hard test. In all matters of principle, our ideology withstood the ordeal admirably. Socialism became an accepted thing, and our movement in the capitalist European countries is today larger than it was before the war, and it also plays a bigger part than it did previously. All this is generalization, and in reference to the essence of our outlook, but it would not be a wise thing to say in reference to certain diverse aspects of our ideology. In various domains – quite significant ones – our forecasts have not materialized. On the other hand, processes that we did not envisage at all have come about.

I do not rely on God's deliverance. I do not believe in miracles. My entire position rests on the fact that I do not discard a particular possibility. I argued that with the mighty energy contained in the Jewish people, with their creative ability, their talents and their connections, the possibility exists that in Palestine a large commercial center will arise in the future that will be a junction for trade between Europe and the east. On this basis it will also be possible to build various industrial branches on a broad scale.

Palestine, Syria, Mesopotamia, and other nearby countries are populated by a people two or three millennia behind present-day European civilization. Industrial and commercial opportunities exist in these countries. With time, our Jews in Palestine will be able to exploit these opportunities, and also to develop them. No one can indicate the sphere in which this will take place. Nor can I give a guarantee that this scenario will in fact materialize. It is possible only to say in general that energetic people, talented people, with vision and European means – such people can do much. As stated, there is no guarantee that this indeed will be realized, but there is no doubt that such a possibility exists. I am not prophesying and stating that this will definitely occur, but equally I do not accept that one can dismiss such a possibility in advance.

Comrade Zivion argues that as socialists we are obliged first to take account of the existing economic data, and only then to take account of the forces and qualifications of the people who will have to operate in the given economic circumstances. Usually I accept this position. Karl Marx's economic doctrine is a work of genius and it provides a marvelous explanation of the anatomy and physiology of the capitalist system. It is also extraordinary in the dissertation by Karl Marx on the evolution of human history. But even in resepct of something correct one should not go too far. In the first quarter century of the socialist movement's existence, when Karl Marx's doctrine was still fresh and the practical facet of the socialist movement was still small and new, the ideological aspect predominated and it filled the hearts of the believers so much that it caused a schism over its practical significance. At that stage it was possible to forget that in human life, interests and forces are at work in addition to the economic factors, and these too play no small part. The economic doctrine is correct, but it is not the most important thing. A human being is not made up only of "economics." Everywhere we look we see how people can tear down their economic interests for the sake of things in the realm of feeling, not to mention such matters as love and jealousy . . . Similarly we have come to realize that occasionally the strength and personality of the individual play a greater part than economic interests. Our worldview did not deny all this, but nor did it ever underline the factors mentioned; it did not explain them in detail and courageously. The opposite is the case. Our doctrine gave too much room to the economic element, which it expounded with precision and in fine detail – so much so that we became used to seeing the economic element not only as a central force, but as the unique and exclusive factor that shapes the life of human society.

Man is a fragile and many-sided creature. Obviously, the economic problem is one of the chief concerns, sometimes the sole, dominating issue. But economics is not the only factor, and to understand human history correctly one must not disregard the other factors. What I am saying here is accepted today by every socialist movement, and as a matter of course by the British movement. The movement there stands totally on the basis of the view I have set forth here. The same may be said regarding the movements in the other countries. It is interesting that even in Germany, where the economic concept prevailed for many long years, even there a great change has occurred in the direction I have just outlined. The book of life, the most important of all books, is the book that has not yet been written, and the socialist movement has learned a great deal from it. As a result of this study, the movement has become wider, deeper and stronger. It has become less fanatical and more pragmatic, and it possesses great fighting ability . . . It was important for me to clarify here that the subject of economic possibilities has to be considered, but this subject must not be regarded as the most important thing.

Comrade Zivion goes on to voice reservations about my remark on the energy and the talents of the Jews. In his view, we exaggerate these matters. Then he goes further and argues that the talents evinced by the Jews in the course of generations found expression not in Eretz Israel but in other countries. As an example he even presents Hebrew literature, which the Zionists are attempting to develop with all their might: even this was produced in other countries. He points out that Palestine still has not produced an intellectual or a noteable writer, and that the various Bialiks and the great rabbis went to Palestine from Lithuania, Poland, Ukraine or Galicia.

When talent, drive, ability, and so on are at issue, one must consider the numbers of the different peoples. Today there are about 15 million Jews dispersed all over the world. Other civilized peoples number 40, 50, 60 millions, and sometimes even more . . . We are a small people. Most of the people live in uncivilized conditions. Hence, if despite all this the number of Jews with talent and genius is large, this is a wonderful thing. Perhaps it is a conincidence that Einstein is a Jew, but the fact is that renowned Jews are to be found in many and varied domains. Furthermore, it is a fact that the number of famous Jews is proportionately greater than that of other peoples. This truth cannot be dismissed out of hand. We are alright. Just about 40 years have passed since the custom became rooted in the Jews of Poland and Russia of sending their children to conservatories to study music, and the result is that almost all violinists and pianists, with a few exceptions, are Jews. Imagine how many gifted Jews there would be today if the Jews had begun to train 50 years ago. Who knows how many Einsteins we have lost. I would like to present a long list of examples regarding Jewish drive, but there is no need, because there is no argument regarding the drive and the gifts of the Jews.

Comrade Zivion argues that Jews became full of drive and talents because they absorbed European culture, not that of the Arabs or the Turks. True. But what does this mean? We are talking about European Jews who are migrating and settling in Palestine. They take there the virtues that they developed under the influence of European culture. With such virtues they can accomplish important things. Because of their settlement in Palestine, will they become detached from European culture? They will always remain tied to it, and will also carry it to Palestine, and through it, as bearers and transmitters of culture, they will have the opportunity of developing industry and commerce there.

My argument about the ratios that have to be considered also applies regarding the number of gifted Jews who have grown up in Palestine. Palestine is a small country. The size of the Jewish population there was tiny, while millions of Jews have lived elsewhere. So what is so remarkable in the fact that now more gifted Jews have arrived in the country than have developed within it? Take, for instance, Comrade Zivion's comment about the Hebrew writers. In Poland, Lithuania, Galicia, and Ukraine there are people who write good Hebrew. A Jewish population is to be found there numbering several millions, while in Palestine there lived only some tens of thousands. So is there anything surprising in the fact that those several millions managed to produce Bialik from their midst, while the several tens of thousands did not? The same applies to the rabbis. Comrade Zivion raises his finger and points to the fact that when the orthodox Jews in Palestine were in need of a great rabbi, they had to bring him from Lithuania. But how many rabbis live in the various Diaspora lands, and how many live in little Palestine? The ratio was 25 rabbis in Palestine as against 25,000. So what is so amazing about the fact that it is harder to choose out of 25 than out of 25,000? Such is the case with other matters too, good and bad alike. If, for example, it was asked, "Where is there a greater likelihood of finding a Jew with six fingers on one hand – in Palestine or in Europe?" obviously the answer would be that among the several million Jews there was a greater chance of finding an exception than among the handful of Jews in Palestine.

Now we come to the most important point in the range of arguments raised by our comrades from the Bund against the display of sympathy for Palestine. In their opinion, the interest shown in Palestine harms the socialist movement. Comrade Zivion refers to this, and writes:

> In the name of your imaginary Palestine you hinder all constructive Jewish work in the Diaspora countries. If you do not always hinder it directly, you always do so indirectly. All this is because with your imginary hopes for Palestine you weaken the hands of the Jews in the Diaspora.

And later he says:

> Zionism is a national movement that drags us backward. Zionism draws all its vitality from the Jewish past, and it drags us backward to moldy antiques, long forgotten. Zionism cannot live with socialism. Wherever an attempt is made to join them, Zionism swallows up socialism.

This entire description is glaringly exaggerated. Does Comrade Zivion really believe that our showing friendship to the communes in Palestine will disrupt our activities and our ties with the Socialist Party here? Really, this description is tinged with the fanciful. To follow this line further, it would be forbidden to show sympathy to relatives, and even to parents, lest this deflect us from our socialist activity. Indeed, there once were such extremists who spoke thus, and even demanded behavior of this kind. We are doing all in our power for our countries of origin, but when Comrade Zivion tells us that love for Palestine will hinder our constructive work in Warsaw or Bialystok, for example, it is a baseless claim. To be consistent with this line, Comrade Zivion should say to the Jewish socialists in New York:

> What right do you have to occupy yourselves with your hungry countrymen and with their constructive work? It deflects you from your socialist activity! Keep away from those affairs. Close your eyes and ignore the cry of misery, because this deflects you from socialism.

Logically, the same thing may be said to the Bundists, whose concern is for Jewish cultural work in Warsaw, Kovno or Riga: "Forego these pursuits! They are sapping your powers, which you must devote to constructivist work here in New York as members of the Socialist Party!" Statements of this kind are not heard from us. From our standpoint, advancing such demands means imprisoning the socialist spirit in a girdle of wild fanaticism. We have to teach the socialist the opposite lesson: not to be fanatical, not to be narrow-minded, not to be limited to one issue only, but to be a person moved by a range of human interests, to do everything that possibly can be done regardless of whether it is or is not connected with the Socialist Party. If we do not behave this way, it will do more harm than good for the Socialist Party.

Comrade Zivion writes about Zionists whose entire ambition is to preserve a few hundred thousand Jews in Palestine. Naturally I do not believe in that kind of Zionism, but at the same time I do not believe in "ossified socialism" either. I am against the tendency that wishes to freeze-preserve all socialists according to the interests of their socialist party, in such a way as to prevent them from the possibility of involvement in any other human activity. Comrade Rogoff put forward one of the most interesting arguments in the entire debate, the essence of which is the following: the Bundists should be the last to dare to bring the charge of chauvinism against those who sympathize with Palestine because it was those Bundists who were the first to carry Jewish nationalism into Jewish socialism. It is they who dedicated themselves to the development of Yiddish, and an outsider may, by inference, wonder how chauvinism expressed in the development of Yiddish is more proper than chauvinism expressed in the development of Hebrew.

No one disputes what Comrade Zivion wrote about our socialist duty to develop the Jewish masses, and also to work on their behalf in all economic and spiritual domains. I fully subscribe to this, as will every socialist. But what connection is there between this and the warm feelings that a simple man of flesh and blood like me has for the toiling and hungry idealists who live by my socialist ideal?

The second debater who had reservations about my positions which found expression in my reports was Comrade Vladek, but the differences of opinion between us are smaller than those between myself and Comrade Zivion. Comrade Vladek tends more to sympathize with the good things being done in Palestine, and he tends less to frighten and to warn against displays of sympathy to them. It is difficult to accuse him of one-sidedness, because he writes, for example,

> It is necessary to support everything whose aim is to strengthen the Jewish spirit in any way. Therefore I would support the Hebrew University in Jerusalem, and therefore when Bialik comes to America I shall show him respect, even though I am not a Hebraist, and even though he is coming on a Zionist mission . . . Furthermore, I believe that on the subject of the preservation of national pride among Jews, Zionism has contributed greatly. The same enterprise that the Bund carried out among the Jewish masses, namely making them aware of their Jewishness, Zionism has carried out with the middle class and the Jewish intelligentsia. I am indeed pleased when I see a lawyer or a possessor of a doctorate, already half-assimilated, taking an interest in Jewish problems and not afraid to display their Jewishness in public.

This is the right spirit, which speaks to me. This attitude may be characterized as tolerance and breadth of mind, and not conservative and ossified socialism. Later Vladek wrote:

> Here emotions are unimportant. One person may be more nationalistic and another less, but the chief thing is the answer to the question "Palestine also, or Palestine alone?" Comrade Cahan expressed himself here along the lines of "Palestine also," and nothing can be argued against such a stance. At the same time, discomfort would be justified if anyone in our movement tried to force us to say "Palestine alone."

I agree entirely with this position of Vladek. But further on, Vladek expresses an attitude with which I cannot agree:

Comrade Cahan described with very great excitement the pioneers and the communes. All comrades sympathetic to Zionism base themselves on this part of his reports more than on other areas of life in Palestine that he wrote about. I must confess that despite the fact that the reports impressed me because of Comrade Cahan's writing style, their inherent truth and the fire pent up in them, the story itself made no unusual or striking impression on me. Meeting an idealist is always a pleasant and uplifting experience. Obviously, I have the greatest respect for those women and men who have foregone the advantages of advanced civilization for the ideal of building a Jewish homeland. But among Jews this manifestation of idealism is not new. We always had, and we have now, more negative people and idealists than other nations have. The entire history of Jewish youth in the last forty-odd years is the history of idealism in its various expressions . . . The Biluim and the Jewish Narodniks, the earliest pioneers of Jewish migration to America, the Bund, the Jewish youth that created the United Hebrew Trades and the *Arbeiter Ring* in America, and also the youth that burned with the fire of the Russian Revolution . . .

Subsequently Vladek argues that the fact of exhilaration with an ideal does not make the ideal better or more attractive. All this is true, but if he wishes to state from all this that in Palestine there is nothing to be excited or exhilarated about, if he wishes to state that the idealism expressed in the settlements there is nothing new among the Jews, and therefore there is no need to get so excited about it, if this is his intention then I should like to ask: if there is a beautiful sunset, are you, on that account, not to enthuse over a lovely flower-filled meadow, or a fine seascape?

If there are also other idealists, are you not to be uplifted and exhilarated by the idealists who are in Palestine? We hold Vera Finger in the highest esteem: is this a reason for us not to have sympathy and esteem for those young men and women who labor to build Eretz Israel on socialist foundations?

Comrade Vladek offers a number of very successful analogies and arguments, which I identify with completely, for example, when he writes about the negative aspects of life in small republics; when you consider all the troubles and problems concomitant with politics. Of course, these are the negative sides that have to be considered when Palestine is under discussion. But nothing exists in life without troubles, difficulties, and problems . . .

Summing up the Debate on the Articles on Palestine (continued)

Comrade Litvak opens with a remark that he "would debate with greater willingness with a one-hundred percent overt Zionist than with our Zionist supporters, who ceaselessly assure us that they are not Zionists," and later he writes:

> It is especially difficult for me with regard to Comrade Cahan, because with him it is all a matter of mood, and moods change everyday. Today he believes less and tomorrow he believes more. Today there is no chance of realizing Zionism, and tomorrow it perhaps seems to him "possible" or "maybe." In New York we never heard him say that it is necessary to join the Histadrut fund-raising campaign, but in Chicago he turned to his audience and sought their blessing for the Histadrut delegation from Palestine which is at present in America, and assistance for the interests of the workers' institutions, the trade unions and the cooperatives there. So it seems that we do have to take part in the Histadrut campaign.

Comrade Litvak bases himself on what was published in reports. He himself was not present at meetings, the private discussions I held in New York, nor at the meeting where I spoke in Chicago. Comrade Litvak is wrong. When I returned from my journey and heard that the United Hebrew Trades were working to conduct the campaign for the Histadrut, I said the following to Comrade Pine, and also to other UHT delegates:

> The campaign is a good thing, and I shall help them as much as I can. At the same time, I think that you were wrong in hastening to begin it. I am very happy that my reports were able to promote the campaign, but you began to use them too soon. Personally, I believe it would have been better to have begun to use them only after my return. Then we could all have worked together. Naturally, a debate would have ensued, but I am certain we would have won it.

To this Comrade Pine replied that he agreed with me entirely, but the moment the campaign got started it was the duty of everyone sympathetic to the socialists in Palestine to do everything possible on its behalf.

In the course of my discussions with comrades I spoke out dozens of times in favor of the campaign. If I did not explicitly mention the campaign at the first meeting I held at the Manhattan Opera House in New York, there was nothing significant about this. The content of my speech at the Manhattan Opera House was entirely in favor of a project such as the campaign. My speech was marked by great sympathy for the communes and the Histadrut. My speech in Chicago bore exactly the same character, and there was not the slightest difference between this speech and the New York speech. Where does Comrade Litvak get the idea that in me there is an attitude of "today more no than yes, and tomorrow more yes than no"?

True, it is a question of mood, but this is one of those moods that do not change so quickly, like, for example, the mood concerning a brother or sister. If the word "mood" is not fitting for relations between brother and brother, then Comrade Litvak has not grounds for resorting to this word when he discusses my feelings toward members of the communes and the Histadrut in Palestine.

Comrade Litvak characterizes my attitude to Palestine as a matter of "emotions, of feelings, excitement and romance." The nature of his article throughout is such as to deem it a cardinal sin, and a great obstacle to the movement, for a person indeed to have feelings and to show interest in the romance of a fine movement. With me, it is the opposite. I, for example, believe that in our socialist movement we have for too long limited ourselves to dry theory and have paid too little attention to the fine idealistic dimension of socialism. I refer to that "romance," to those lofty feelings and marvelous sentiments, of which comrade Litvak speaks without any such appreciation. I believe that in our propaganda we need, apart from correct theory, to consider the human interest, one's sympathies and one's fervor.

Further on Comrade Litvak writes that the love the Jewish people has for Eretz Israel is a thing of religious sanctity, "while Palestine is a different matter. It is a matter of politics, of business and a livelihood. The Jew measures this by a ordinary and secular yardstick . . . Palestine is for the body, while Eretz Israel is for the soul. In whom is love for Eretz Israel so strong as it is in our orthodox Jews, as it is in the pious? And it is they precisely who oppose Zionism." I must admit that these words surprised me. Does Comrade Litvak really think that in all those who are sympathetic to Palestine, their sympathy is based on expectation of sterile, pragmatic solutions that Palestine is going to offer the Jewish people? Does he mean to argue that the Zionist bourgeoisie, not the socialists, have only "economic expectations," and not even a trace of "deep feelings" for Palestine? Adoption of such a posture is fanatical excess, a display of intolerance. It is permitted to be convinced of the rightness of one's ideals, but to disallow the possibility of being an idealist and believing in a different ideal – to me this smells of excessive partisanship.

Our socialism is correct, wide-ranging, and sacred. But we do not have any monopoly over enthusiasm and fervor. The Zionists are serious and idealistic in their way, just as we are in ours. Of course there are exceptions, namely people who joined the Zionist movement for personal motives or because of political frictions. But such exceptions are to be found among us also. I know a quite considerable number of Zionists, and many of them are filled with the excellence of their beliefs. For them Palestine is a heavenly, spiritual thing in the national sense, just as for devout Jews Eretz Israel is a heavenly, spiritual thing in the religious sense. My wish has always been to see more toleration in our movement, and inasmuch as my slight powers have permitted, I have always acted, as far as possible, to implant this attitude in our movement. I have written more than one article, delivered more than one speech, on this issue. We must teach the workers to be faithful to socialism, but at the same time we must also teach them to respect the noble feelings of people possessing different attitudes, on condition that they are true to their spiritual subject.

Comrade Litvak has devoted his entire life to working for our socialist ideal, and I know Zionists who greatly appreciate this, and hold him in the highest esteem. Comrade Litvak is one of those who especially emphasize the economic aspect of our ideology; yet for all that, I do not believe that any Zionist will say of him that his socialism is a body without a soul. Later in his article, Comrade Litvak refers to the fact that in the last 40 years "the principle of migration to America, and not to Palestine, has been at the fore." Is this something new for us? Can this be an argument against the idealistic work in Palestine? There is no dispute about the fact that America has a greater likelihood of attracting migration than small, poor Palestine. The question is different, in essence whether it is permitted to show sympathy for those few who migrated to Palestine, and tried, like true heroes and martyrs, to build it. I stress here the phrase "whether it is permitted," because according to Comrade Litvak's doctrine it is forbidden. In his view this is a danger to socialism. The same thing may be said of the 30,000 Jewish settlers in Argentina, whom Comrade Litvak presents as an argument against Palestine, where the number of Jewish settlers is smaller. If there were room in Palestine, if Palestine had the agricultural and material conditions that exist in Argentina, there would not be 30,000 there but tens of times more.

Comrade Litvak writes of the assistance remitted to Palestine from other countries, and states that without the help extended to them the pioneers could not survive. If for him this constitutes an argument against those who are sympathetic to Palestine, let me ask him this: what about the assistance we send to our comrades in Warsaw, Lodz, and Bialystok, or the aid sent for their schools and printing houses? To be consistent, one should use Comrade Litvak's argument against this work too. And if the settlements in Palestine are incapable of existing by themselves, it is forbidden to support them! And if the Jewish schools in Vilna, Warsaw or Bialystok cannot exist by themselves, it is forbidden to support them! Not at all: in both cases it is imperative to extend help. If they need it, it is our duty to hasten to their assistance. Wherever positive work is being carried out we are obliged to do all we can to help.

Later Comrade Litvak wrote the following:

> Comrade Cahan is not a Zionist, yet he is filled with feelings of great purpose. He repeatedly stresses that the Jewish masses sympathize with the Zionist ideal and they should not be spurned. But Comrade Cahan knows well that the Jewish masses support the *rebbe* of Gur, the *rebbe* of Sadigora, and the *rebbe* of Lubavitch. So perhaps we ought to start singing songs of praise to the *rebbe* of Gur? Perhaps the United Hebrew Trades should organize a fund-raising campaign for him?

With this attitude it is as if someone came and said, "All fiddlers sleep with their eyes closed, and all chimney-sweeps sleep with their eyes closed, therefore all fiddlers are chimney-sweeps." Comrade Litvak may use his argument in his propaganda on behalf of Yiddish with exactly the same degree of reason as he uses it regarding what I state about the popularity of Palestine. Many Jews speak Yiddish, therefore this language should be dear to us; many Jews believe in the *rebbe* of Gur so the *rebbe* should be dear to us . . . This kind of analogy is not acceptable to me. Popularity alone is not sufficient; it is important what the particular popularity attaches to. The American criminal Chapman, for example, is very popular. The popularity of Palestine among Jews – not necessarily Zionists, but any Jews – has a tragic dimension that has nothing to do with chauvinism. It is this tragic dimension that speaks to me. Anti-Semitism is spreading. In recent years it has assumed new proportions even here in America. As a result, Jewish youth, which formerly denied their Jewishness, are now coming back to their Jewish identity. At the universities, in offices and in other places, in all walks of life, young Jewish people are being made to feel that they are undesirable. When I spoke about this in my speech in Chicago, which Comrade Litvak mentions in his article, I said among other things:

The students at the universities have fraternities, but these do not accept Jewish students. Therefore, the Jewish students have been forced to set up fraternities of their own. This is a sad state of affairs. The Jews regard Palestine as a kind of Jewish "fraternity," and it is in this manner that it reverberates in the heart of Jews, and in this manner that it is popular. The Jewish fraternities at the universities strike a sympathetic chord in me because of the tragic dimension of their popularity among the Jews. I harbor a similar feeling for Palestine.

Whether or not Palestine becomes a real homeland for the Jews, the feeling will remain the same. The knowledge that Jews there are attempting to create even a little Jewish life, in a place where they will no longer be stepchildren, and also the knowledge that all this is taking place in the old homeland of the Jewish people – this is what makes Palestine popular. This popularity, with the tragic dimension contained in it, finds an echo in my heart. What connection is there between this and the popularity of the *rebbe* of Gur? Look – the *rebbe* of Yablonka is also a hassidic rabbi, but I feel great warmth toward him despite his hassidism, just as I feel great warmth toward the Palestinian communalists despite their chauvinism. If Comrade Litvak is wrong in protesting against the sympathy and respect I feel for this fine personality because the *rebbe* of Yablonka is a hassidic rabbi, he will be equally wrong in protesting against my sympathy for Palestine because the Zionist movement is hostile to our comrades in Warsaw or Bialystok.

Comrade Litvak writes about the feeling for Palestine: "Sentiments do not live forever. Old ones die and new ones are born periodically." But Comrade Zivion, who is on the same side of the divide as Comrade Litvak, argues against this – that the feeling for Zion will remain always. In these circumstances I tend to believe in the correctness of Comrade Zivion's position. This is one of the basic data that give Palestine a special hue and a special place in the hearts of Jews. Incidentally, this reminds me of an interesting notion in Comrade Zivion's article. He states that the Messiah lives as long as he does not appear. If he appeared, this would be the end of the religious fantasies of the Jews. He says the same about Zion: if it were proven that Zionism is realizable, this would be the end of the Zionist dream. I do not know what will happen in the future, but for the time being Palestine is popular and elicits warmth. Note also that what Comrade Zivion says about the Jewish Messiah also holds for various beliefs in other messiahs. Just think, for example, of what happened to the messiah of the Russian Revolution. (Non-socialists will ascribe this to our movement. Fortunately, it is not so. Communist tyranny had very little to do with socialism, exactly like the tyranny of Robespierre and his two collaborators. Apart from this, in the course of realization of the best and finest ideals, negative manifestations can appear. The aspiration itself is finer than the actual reality. But this is not to say that one should stop striving for noble things.)

Comrade Litvak too, like Comrade Zivion, fears lest sympathy for Palestine harm our movement. This is what he writes: "If the attention of the Jewish masses is diverted to Eretz Israel, if they are given the chance of doing their duty by idealism through donating a quarter to the pioneers in Palestine, this injures socialism." I know that in Poland the Zionists and the Bundists clash in the field of local politics and over various other public matters. These struggles are the source from which grows the hostility and bitterness of the Bundists toward Palestine. But we here do not have such problems. Here bitterness toward Zionism is foreign to us, and so therefore is hostility toward Palestine. Moreover, when a socialist shows sympathy toward a different subject, which deserves it, this in no way prevents him from serving his movement, but the opposite: it makes him more fit to serve it. It produces a socialist of wider and better horizons. The socialist who is tolerant of other ideals, who is not a fanatic, who is not a narrow-minded mad zealot, the socialist who takes an interest in human feelings, and not just in abstract scholastic theories – such a socialist, in my humble view, does more good for our movement than an "apostate socialist" (if I may use Comrade Zivion's expression here). This is what Litvak writes:

When even Comrade Cahan takes the trouble, in his speech in Chicago, to display signs of anti-Semitism in America, and in consequence he points with enthusiasm to Palestine, where many Arabs have only one eye (owing to the blazing sun and eye diseases), while the Jews have two eyes, does not this cause a strengthening of Zionism at the expense of our struggle in America?

So now one may not report in *Forward* on various instances and obstacles encountered by young Jews in their application to medical school. One has to keep silent, otherwise this will harm our socialist propaganda! One must similarly keep quiet and not present the fact that Jews in Palestine live in hygienic conditions and therefore they are healthier than the Arabs! Likewise I transgressed because I wrote that the Zionist organization treats the socialists in Palestine very well.

And again, Comrade Litvak writes further on:

Is class consciousness thereby not weakened? Is the feeling of unity of all Jewry thereby not endangered? So what do you think? If the drive and enthusiasm devoted to the pioneers were directed to the benefit of the socialist movement in America; if instead of planting in a Jewish youth the ambition of being a *halutz* or a *shomer*, if in him were planted the ambition and the dream of being a fighter for the workers, of being a revolutionary – would socialism gain from this, or would it not?

I am convinced that with postures such as these one harms the drive and enthusiasm of the socialist movement far more than with displays of sympathy for Palestine. I do not preach that our young people here should leave the trade unions or the Socialist Party, and migrate to Palestine to be pioneers there. Even if I did preach this to them, they would not listen to me. Secondly, in Comrade Litvak's words there sounds a note of fear and trepidation lest our socialist infant be hurt. From his words one might think that our socialist movement is so wretched, so puny . . . that when our socialist infant gives a spoonful of milk to the neighbor's kid, Comrade Litvak is terrified that heaven and earth will collapse about his ears. According to Comrade Litvak, the spoonful of milk has to be saved for our little ones alone.

Comrade Vladek in his article states that the amorous glances that Cahan casts in the direction of Miss Zion are not a disaster. By contrast, Comrade Litvak believes that they in fact are a disaster. Vladek apparently holds that one should not overdo jealousy, that it is better for love if one does not keep the loved one under lock and key all the time; but as against this, Comrade Litvak believes that every word exchanged between the groom and another girl is an infringement of what is permitted, and should be forbidden. Over and over again he stresses that sympathy shown to Palestine hurts the love that we ought to feel for our socialism. So bolt every door and every gate! Put up the shutters to stop the groom from peeping through the windows out into the street! He must look only at his bride all the time! This is not how I understand our movement. This narrow-minded sectarian approach has harmed our movement far more than it has benefited it.

I say again: Comrade Litvak, and also all the Bund, of which he is an outstanding member, have worked wonders for the Jewish worker. But if instead of the narrow sectarian approach Comrade Litvak's educational work had been noteworthy for greater breadth of outlook, greater tolerance, more open to all mankind, then the fruits of his labors would have grown exceedingly. When I was younger our socialism also had reservations over the idea that a Jewish people existed. We thought that we had to call ourselves not "Jewish socialists" but "Yiddish-speaking socialists." When the Bund became an organization of Jewish socialists we saw this as a danger to our ideal. They were the first to introduce *yiddishkeit* [Jewishness – Y.G.] into the movement, and they are to be complimented for it. But now, when the fences of fanaticism are being torn down, the Bundists shout out and make a call to be at the ready! This is reminiscent of what happened with the first English settlers in the American colonies. They had left England because of religious intolerance, but in America they themselves became intolerant.

Later there is a comment referring to whether during my sojourn in Palestine I did in fact see "both sides of the coin." Comrade Litvak says that I failed in this. He explains that the Histadrut leaders let me see what was worthwhile for them, but they kept hidden from me what was not. He is convinced that they treated me just as the Soviet government treats various delegations from other countries who have come to see what is taking place in their country. Namely, they welcome the visitor very nicely, but surround him with people who make sure that the guest sees only what the communists consider is to their benefit. To this I can say only one thing. I'm afraid that Comrade Litvak looked at my articles in the same way that he believes I saw Palestine. He apparently did not have a chance to read all my reports on Palestine, but only some. This is because in some of my reports I expressly stated how careful I had been not to be drawn into a situation where I saw only one side of the coin, which is exactly what he is talking about. I explained in minute detail how from the start I thought up ways and means of seeing the other side of the coin. Comrade Litvak is bound to admit that I am not "green" in such matters. As a veteran journalist I know very well how to reach the all-round truth, whether the local powers-that-be like it or not. I do not know how it is in Russia, but in Palestine there is no Cheka [secret police – Y.G.] to surround you on all sides and prevent you from seeing what you want. I met enough people who are sworn opponents of the Histadrut and of the settlements [apparently the communal settlements – Y.G.], and I spent much time with them. The local powers-that-be had no idea of this.

Comrade Litvak tries to explain why Dr Weizmann supports the Histadrut and the communes: it is all in order to facilitate his fund-raising for Palestine. Why is it so hard to accept that Weizmann feels genuine sympathy for the socialists in Palestine? Weizmann is an intelligent Russian Jew, an idealist who has devoted all his strength to Zionism as he understands it . . . For a man who has experienced the radicalist crucible it is entirely natural to feel sympathy toward young socialists. I am not closely acquainted with him, but I am convinced that he feels these sentiments with all his heart.

There are other articles, by Comrade Judge Panken, by Comrade Lestchinsky, by David Einhorn, and by Rabinowitz. Unfortunately I have no space or time left to reply to them. As it is my response has proved longer than I foresaw. Still, I believe that the three articles I have published here contain an answer to all the main points raised against my position on Palestine. Lestchinsky's lucid account, for example, is essentially an argument against the Zionist mvement, but not against me. I have dealt with the few points referring to me in my replies to comrades Zivion and Litvak.

Index

Abramson, M., 63n
agriculture
   Cahan, 84–5, 126–8
   Lestchinsky, 201–2
   Pine, 154
   Zivion, 40, 143
   see also kibbutzim; moshavim
Agudat Yisrael, 196
Ahad Ha'am, 40, 68, 177
Ahdut Ha'avodah, 91, 106, 119
Alexander II, Tsar, 1
Am Olam group, 16, 66
American Federation of Labor (AFL), 13–14, 34, 58n
American Socialist Party (SP), 4, 44–5, 63n, 66, 68
American-Jewish workers' movement, 2, 5, 13–14, 17, 59n
anti-Semitism, 1, 2, 114, 131, 247
   Poland, 8–13
   Soviet Union, 76
Arab Executive Committee, 108
Arab labor, 121–2, 140, 157, 202, 222
Arab problem
   Broyland, 194–5
   Bundists, 42
   Cahan, 30, 62n, 94–5, 108–11
   Einhorn, 216
   Zivion, 143
Arab workers' organization, 194
Arbeiter Ring, 59n, 69, 161, 181, 195, 243
Argentina
   Charney-Vladek, 164
   failure of Jewish settlements, 49
   Ginsburg, 175, 176
   Litvak, 246
   Zivion favors for settlement, 40, 138, 150, 193, 207
Armenians, 153
Austria, 154

Babylonia, 145, 156
Balfour, Arthur James, 1st Earl of, 108, 109
Balfour Declaration, 4, 42, 53, 108, 189

Baratz, Yosef, 62n, 116, 230
Belkind, Yisrael, 16
Ben-Gurion, David, 111, 208, 223
Ben-Zvi, Yitzhak, 62n, 81, 219–24, 230
Beney Moshe, 68
Bergelson, David, 15–16
Bergson, Henri, 145
Bernstein, Edouard, 33, 114, 233
Bialik, Hayyim Nahman, 75, 79, 113, 162, 240, 242
Biluim, 161, 243
Bismarck, Otto, 130–1, 134
Bloch-Blumenfeld, David, 79, 81
Blum, Léon, 33, 114, 233
Bolshevism, 103, 107
Brazil
   Charney-Vladek, 164
   failure of Jewish settlements, 49
   Ginsburg, 175
   Zivion favors for settlement, 40, 138, 150, 207
Brenner, Joseph Hayyim, 24
Britain, 95, 107–11, 130, 133, 144, 152, 216
   colonial policy, 40
   development of Palestinian economy, 199
   industrial policy, 155
Broyland, S., 64–5n, 192–7
   Arab problem, 194–5
   Palestine, 192, 197
   Yiddish culture and language, 64–5n, 195–6
   Zionism, 192–3, 194
Der Bund
   aid to Palestine, 33, 43–4
   Arab problem, 42
   Cahan, 31–2, 241, 250, 251
   Charney-Vladek, 66, 161, 162, 242, 243
   Diaspora, 37, 38, 51
   Eretz Israel, 39
   Ginsburg, 172–3
   Histadrut Appeal, 43
   idealism, 161, 243
   Jewish immigration, 41–2
   Liessin, 54–5
   Litvak, 68–9